AMC'S BEST DAY HIKES IN THE
SHENANDOAH VALLEY

Four-Season Guide to 50 of the Best T———
from Harpers Ferry to Jefferso———

Second Edition

JENNIFER ADACH & MICHAEL ——— RTIN

Appalachian Mountain Club Books
Boston, Massachusetts

AMC is a nonprofit organization, and sales of AMC Books fund our mission of protecting the Northeast outdoors. If you appreciate our efforts and would like to become a member or make a donation to AMC, visit outdoors.org, call 800-372-1758, or contact us at Appalachian Mountain Club, 10 City Square, Boston, MA 02129.

outdoors.org/books-maps

Distributed by National Book Network.

Front cover photograph of Devil's Marbleyard © Michael R. Martin
Back cover photographs (left to right) of Big Schloss © Karan Girdhani and of Buzzard Rock © Michael R. Martin
Title page photo of Cedar Run © Michael R. Martin
Interior photographs by Jennifer Adach and Michael R. Martin, except where noted
Maps by Ken Dumas © Appalachian Mountain Club
Book design by Abigail Coyle

Library of Congress Cataloging-in-Publication Data

Names: Adach, Jennifer, author. | Martin, Michael R., author. | Mudie, Timothy, editor. | Dumas, Kenneth, cartographer.
Title: AMC's best day hikes in the Shenandoah Valley : four-season guide to 50 of the best trails from Harpers Ferry to Jefferson National Forest / Jennifer Adach and Michael R. Martin.
Other Titles: Appalachian Mountain Club's best day hikes in the Shenandoah Valley | Appalachian Mountain Club book.
Description: Second Edition. | Boston, Massachusetts : Appalachian Mountain Club Books, 2020. | Series: Appalachian Mountain Club Books |
"Distributed by National Book Network"--T.p. verso. | Summary: "A four-season guide to some of the best day hiking trips in the Shenandoah Valley"-- Provided by publisher.
Identifiers: LCCN 2019040234 (print) | LCCN 2019040235 (ebook) | ISBN 9781628421071 (Paperback) | ISBN 9781628421088 (ePUB) | ISBN 9781628421095 (MOBI)
Subjects: LCSH: Day hiking--Virginia--Shenandoah River Valley (Va. and W. Va.)--Guidebooks. | Hiking--Virginia--Shenandoah River Valley (Va. and W. Va.)--Guidebooks. | Walking--Virginia--Shenandoah River Valley (Va. and W. Va.)--Guidebooks. | Backpacking--Virginia--Shenandoah River Valley (Va. and W. Va.)--Guidebooks. | Mountaineering--Virginia--Shenandoah River Valley (Va. and W. Va.)--Guidebooks. | Rock climbing--Virginia--Shenandoah River Valley (Va. and W. Va.)--Guidebooks. | Trails--Virginia--Shenandoah River Valley (Va. and W. Va.)--Guidebooks. | Outdoor recreation--Virginia--Shenandoah River Valley (Va. and W. Va.)--Guidebooks. | Shenandoah River Valley (Va. and W. Va.)--Description and travel. | Shenandoah River Valley (Va. and W. Va.)--Guidebooks.
Classification: LCC GV199.42.V82 A34 2020 (print) | LCC GV199.42.V82 (ebook) | DDC 796.5109755/9--dc23
LC record available at https://lccn.loc.gov/2019040234
LC ebook record available at https://lccn.loc.gov/2019040235

The paper used in this publication meets the minimum requirements of the American National Standard for Information Sciences-Permanence of Paper for Printed Library Materials, ANSI Z39.48-1984. ∞

Outdoor recreation activities by their very nature are potentially hazardous. This book is not a substitute for good personal judgment and training in outdoor skills. Due to changes in conditions, use of the information in this book is at the sole risk of the user. The author and the Appalachian Mountain Club assume no liability for accidents happening to, or injuries sustained by, readers who engage in the activities described in this book.

Interior pages and cover are printed on responsibly harvested paper stock certified by The Forest Stewardship Council®, an independent auditor of responsible forestry practices. Printed in the United States of America, using vegetable-based inks.

MIX
Paper from
responsible sources
FSC® C005010

5 4 3 2 1   20 21 22 23 25

In memory of
Ernest Adach

LOCATOR MAP

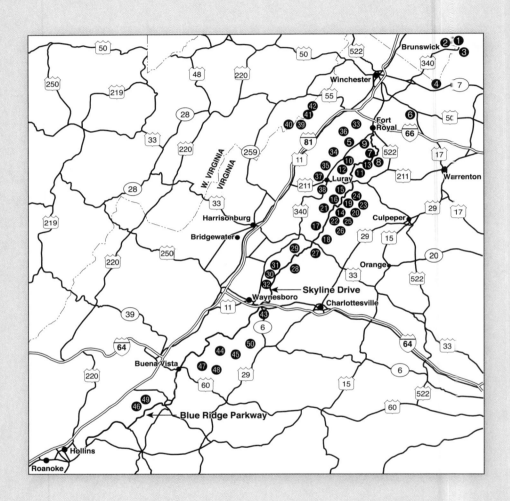

CONTENTS

ESSAYS

AT-A-GLANCE TRIP PLANNER

TRIP NUMBER	TRIP NAME	LOCATION	DIFFICULTY	DISTANCE
SECTION 1: HARPERS FERRY AND NORTH VIRGINIA PIEDMONT				
1	Virginius Island	Harpers Ferry National Historical Park	Easy	1.2 mi
2	Maryland Heights	Harpers Ferry National Historical Park	Strenuous	4.4 mi
3	Loudoun Heights	Harpers Ferry National Historical Park	Strenuous	7.8 mi
4	Raven Rocks	Bluemont, VA	Moderate	4.7 mi
5	Shenandoah River State Park	Bentonville, VA	Moderate	6.5 mi
6	Sky Meadows State Park	Delaplane, VA	Moderate	5.1 mi
SECTION 2: SHENANDOAH NATIONAL PARK, NORTH DISTRICT				
7	Compton Gap	Shenandoah National Park	Easy	2.2 mi
8	Big Devils Stairs	Shenandoah National Park	Moderate	4.7 mi
9	Dickey Ridge	Shenandoah National Park	Easy-Moderate	4.9 mi
10	Overall Run	Shenandoah National Park	Strenuous	9.5 mi
11	Little Devils Stairs	Shenandoah National Park	Strenuous	5.7 mi
12	Jeremy's Run and Knob Mountain	Shenandoah National Park	Strenuous	13.2 mi
13	Bluff-A.T.-Mount Marshall Trails	Shenandoah National Park	Strenuous	13.5 mi
SECTION 3: SHENANDOAH NATIONAL PARK, CENTRAL DISTRICT				
14	Limberlost	Shenandoah National Park	Easy	1.4 mi
15	Mary's Rock	Shenandoah National Park	Moderate	2.7 mi
16	Stony Man	Shenandoah National Park	Easy	1.5 mi
17	Lewis Falls	Shenandoah National Park	Moderate	3 m
18	South River Falls	Shenandoah National Park	Moderate	4.9 mi
19	Rose River Falls	Shenandoah National Park	Moderate	4.4 mi
20	Dark Hollow Falls	Shenandoah National Park	Easy	1.5 mi

Elevation Gain	Estimated Time	Trip Highlights	Fee	Good for Kids	Dogs Allowed	Waterfalls
17 ft	1-2 hrs	Easy walk to explore historic landmarks	$	✔	🐕	
1,378 ft	2-3 hrs	Historic landmarks; Civil War ruins	$		🐕	
2,278 ft	4-5 hrs	Jefferson Rock; view over Harpers Ferry	$		🐕	
1,744 ft	2-3 hrs	Rock hop to big views			🐕	
1,368 ft	3-4 hrs	River walk over easy terrain	$		🐕	
995 ft	2-3 hrs	Meadow rambles	$		🐕	
763 ft	1-2 hrs	Views; regional geology	$		🐕	
1,313 ft	2-4 hrs	Overlooks; hollows; rhododendron	$		🐕	
1,130 ft	2-3 hrs	Park history; family farm ruins	$			
3,094 ft	4-6 hrs	Spectacular 93-foot falls	$		🐕	〰
1,940 ft	3-5 hrs	Classic, wild VA climb	$		🐕	〰
3,154 ft	5-8 hrs	Wet, wild leg-stretcher	$		🐕	〰
2,089 ft	6-7 hrs	Big views for testing out long hiking days	$		🐕	
91 ft	1-2 hrs	ADA-accessible trail packs in blooms and geology	$	✔		
1,043 ft	1-2 hrs	360-degree views; rock scrambles	$		🐕	
407 ft	1-2 hrs	Park's second-tallest peak; loop hike	$			
997 ft	1-2 hrs	Waterfalls; Blackrock Cliffs	$		🐕	〰
1,914 ft	2-3 hrs	Wading in the falls	$		🐕	〰
1,189 ft	2-3 hrs	Two waterfalls; views; loop hike	$		🐕	〰
445 ft	1-2 hrs	Waterfalls	$	✔		〰

TRIP NUMBER	TRIP NAME	LOCATION	DIFFICULTY	DISTANCE
21	Hawksbill	Shenandoah National Park	Moderate	2.8 mi
22	Rapidan Camp	Shenandoah National Park	Moderate	7.5 mi
23	Old Rag	Shenandoah National Park	Strenuous	9 mi
24	Mount Robertson, Corbin Hollow	Shenandoah National Park	Strenuous	9 mi
25	Whiteoak and Cedar Run	Shenandoah National Park	Strenuous	8 mi
26	Bearfence	Shenandoah National Park	Moderate-Strenuous	1.2 mi

SECTION 4: SHENANDOAH NATIONAL PARK, SOUTH DISTRICT

27	Hightop Mountain	Shenandoah National Park	Easy	3.5 mi
28	Doyles River, Jones Run Falls	Shenandoah National Park	Moderate	8 mi
29	Big Run, Brown Mountain Loop	Shenandoah National Park	Moderate	9.3 mi
30	Trayfoot and Paine Run Loop	Shenandoah National Park	Strenuous	9.2 mi
31	Blackrock	Shenandoah National Park	Easy	1.2 mi
32	Riprap Hollow	Shenandoah National Park	Strenuous	9.5 mi

SECTION 5: MASSANUTTEN MOUNTAIN

33	Buzzard Rock	George Washington National Forest, VA	Strenuous	9 mi
34	Kennedy Peak	George Washington National Forest, VA	Moderate	5.2 mi
35	Duncan Knob	George Washington National Forest, VA	Moderate	3.5 mi
36	Signal Knob	George Washington National Forest, VA	Strenuous	10 mi
37	Strickler Knob	George Washington National Forest, VA	Strenuous	10 mi
38	Emerald Pond	George Washington National Forest, VA	Moderate	8.8 mi

SECTION 6: GREAT NORTH MOUNTAIN AND RAMSEYS DRAFT WILDERNESS

39	Big Schloss	Great North Mountain	Moderate	4.4 mi
40	Tibbet Knob	Great North Mountain	Easy	3.1 mi
41	Halfmoon Mountain	Great North Mountain	Strenuous	8.9 mi
42	White Rock Cliff/Opa Overlook	Great North Mountain	Moderate	9.3 mi

ELEVATION GAIN	ESTIMATED TIME	TRIP HIGHLIGHTS	FEE	GOOD FOR KIDS	DOGS ALLOWED	WATERFALLS
1,089 ft	1-2 hrs	Park's highest peak	$		🐕	
1,623 ft	3-5 hrs	Historic presidential retreat	$		🐕	〰
2,812 ft	4-7 hrs	Popular summit; lots of scrambling	$			
2,136 ft	4-6 hrs	Views and solitude	$		🐕	
2,720 ft	3-6 hrs	Classic VA hike to an unforgettable waterfall	$		🐕	〰
300 ft	1-2 hrs	Short hike with a challenging rock scramble	$			
999 ft	2-3 hrs	Steady hike; scenic summit	$	🚶	🐕	
2,257 ft	3-5 hrs	Attractive waterfall walk	$		🐕	〰
2,464 ft	4-7 hrs	Pools and cascades deep in the park	$		🐕	〰
2,500 ft	5-6 hrs	Ridge walk; big views	$		🐕	
300 ft	1-2 hrs	Gentle hike to 360-degree views	$		🐕	
2,365 ft	5-6 hrs	Swimming holes; waterfalls; big views	$		🐕	〰
3,433 ft	4-6 hrs	Knife-edge ridge			🐕	
1,192 ft	2-4 hrs	Views of Fort Valley and more			🐕	
1,163 ft	2-3 hrs	Scramble up to wide vistas			🐕	
2,919 ft	5-6 hrs	Wild; remote; big, big views			🐕	
2,215 ft	5-6 hrs	Rocky ridge walk			🐕	
1,562 ft	4-5 hrs	Swimming holes and valley views			🐕	
1,297 ft	3-4 hrs	Cliff-top views			🐕	
1,001 ft	2-4 hrs	Scramble to vistas			🐕	
2,469 ft	4-6 hrs	Big gains; eagle's-eye views of the valley			🐕	
1,460 ft	4-5 hrs	Dramatic views all the way to Shenandoah National Park			🐕	

SECTION 7: JEFFERSON NATIONAL FOREST AND THE BLUE RIDGE MOUNTAINS

Trip Number	Trip Name	Location	Difficulty	Distance
43	Humpback Rocks	Glenwood-Pedlar Ranger District, George Washington and Jefferson National Forests	Strenuous	2 mi
44	Spy Rock	Glenwood-Pedlar Ranger District, George Washington and Jefferson National Forests	Moderate	3.2 mi
45	Crabtree Falls	Glenwood-Pedlar Ranger District, George Washington and Jefferson National Forests	Strenuous	2.8 mi
46	Apple Orchard Falls	Glenwood-Pedlar Ranger District, George Washington and Jefferson National Forests	Moderate	5.7 mi
47	Cold Mountain	Glenwood-Pedlar Ranger District, George Washington and Jefferson National Forests	Moderate	5.1 mi
48	Mount Pleasant	Glenwood-Pedlar Ranger District, George Washington and Jefferson National Forests	Moderate	6.5 mi
49	Devil's Marbleyard	Glenwood-Pedlar Ranger District, George Washington and Jefferson National Forests	Moderate	3.2 mi
50	Three Ridges	Glenwood-Pedlar Ranger District, George Washington and Jefferson National Forests	Strenuous	13.2 mi

Elevation Gain	Estimated Time	Trip Highlights	Fee	Good for Kids	Dogs Allowed	Waterfalls
900 ft	2 hrs	Sharp climb to dramatic rock formation			🐕	
1,223 ft	1-2 hrs	Rhododendron in the spring; steady climb on a fire road			🐕	
1,642 ft	1-2 hrs	Blue Ridge vistas after a steep climb; one of Virginia's prettiest waterfalls	$		🐕	♒
2,438 ft	3-5 hrs	Popular hike to a 200-foot cascade			🐕	♒
1,586 ft	5-6 hrs	Alpine meadows with abundant spring wildflowers			🐕	
1,781 ft	3-5 hrs	Expansive views of the Blue Ridge Mountains			🐕	
1,073 ft	2-3 hrs	Giant marble boulders			🐕	
4,914 ft	6-7 hrs	An epic hike; great views and waterfalls			🐕	♒

ACKNOWLEDGMENTS

The outpouring of support from our friends and families for this book was over-whelming. People shared their time, gamely posed for pictures, and kept checking in to see what they could do to help. Words fail to express the full extent of our appreciation. Special thank-yous go to Marika Oliff for being a faithful hiking companion and impromptu photographer, and to Maria Eckrich, who took the time to help us get the right photo.

The list is endless and could be a book itself. A deep thanks to everyone who joined us on hikes and otherwise provided support throughout this journey. We could not have done it without you.

To our fellow backpackers at DC UL Backpacking: Thanks for indulging our creative routing as we explored new trails and reexplored faithful favorites for this book.

Thanks to the wonderful staff at the Appalachian Mountain Club, including Tim Mudie for shepherding this book. We are truly blessed to have the opportunity to write about one of our favorite activities.

To our families: Carol and Katie Adach, who continue to give unconditional support. And to Bob and Emile Martin, Michael's champions and buyers and distributors of many books. And also his parents. Thank you.

INTRODUCTION

Home to presidents, cradle of Colonial America, Civil War battleground, and crucible for the United States' recovery from the Great Depression, Virginia's Shenandoah Valley is one of the iconic landscapes of the American outdoors. Stretching from Harpers Ferry in the north, where the Shenandoah and Potomac rivers meet, to the James River in the south, the peaks and ridges of the Blue Ridge march into the characteristic blue mists produced by the mountains' lush and deep foliage. Between these ridgelines lie the fruitful valleys of the Shenandoah River, divided into its North and South forks, home to prosperous agriculture, rich horse land, and, more recently, promising vineyards.

This mountainous and rugged land is also a haven for hikers, serving as the backdrop for Shenandoah National Park, George Washington and Jefferson National Forests, the Blue Ridge Parkway, and a multitude of state and local parks, wild areas, and national monuments and recreation areas. The great trails run through it as well. More than 300 miles of the Appalachian Trail (AT) traverse the Shenandoah Valley, passing some of the AT's most iconic sights: Mary's Rock (Trip 15), Stony Man (Trip 16), Blackrock (Trip 31), and Spy Rock (Trip 44). And there are other trails to walk. The Tuscarora Trail begins its diversion from the AT toward Pennsylvania in the northern Shenandoah; Massanutten Trail (Section 5) runs a long circuit along the flat and rocky ridgelines of Massanutten Mountain; Wild Oak Trail passes a rugged course on the eastern edge of the Alleghenies. And where these great trails go, there are side trails, link trails, and blue and yellow blazes. You could hike for years and not see everything.

The hikes in this book can help you start such a journey. They range across the entire region. In truth, we extend a little beyond the Shenandoah Valley proper, giving you a taste for hiking along the Allegheny Plateau (the western Shenandoah boundary) and stretching to the top of the valley, with hikes in Harpers Ferry, where the Shenandoah and Potomac rivers meet. Together, our hikes include a little of everything, from big airy views to rocky scrambling, from bountiful waterfall hikes to cooling swimming dips. Though there are a few challenging, longer hikes, we have kept most of them short. Many of our trips are easy or moderate, and they can be hiked in just a few hours. We've tried to focus on the real reason for doing a particular hike—what makes it distinct from other hikes—instead of adding miles just for exercise. Thus, our hikes facilitate, we hope, photography, bird-watching, fishing, or whatever interests you.

Hiking Virginia is also an opportunity to explore the history of the United States, and we have selected hikes that visit a goodly array of historical sites, including Rapidan Camp (President Hoover's retreat in the Shenandoah), some of the first Civilian Conservation Corps projects, and locations that played a role in the Civil War and, in a few cases, even the Revolutionary War. Thomas Jefferson was, of course, a Virginian, and in his early life, surveyed land in the Shenandoah Valley. He knew this land better than most.

With a light pack and some rugged footwear, a bottle of water and a picnic lunch, hikers can explore this beautiful and storied land, finishing by exploring Virginia's wine country or touring rustic villages. The Shenandoah Valley is, truly, a garden and a superb destination for hikers of all levels of ability and of all inclinations.

HOW TO USE THIS BOOK

With 50 hikes to choose from, you may wonder how to decide where to go. The locator map at the front of this book will help you narrow down the trips by location, and the at-a-glance trip planner that follows the table of contents will provide more information to guide you toward a decision. Once you settle on a destination and turn to a trip in this guide, you will find a series of icons that indicate whether there are fees, whether the hike is good for kids, and whether dogs are allowed.

(For those hikes with the "good for kids" icon, the authors have used their best judgment, but of course children can surprise you with their hiking skills; it's not uncommon to see young hikers even on the summit of Old Rag [Trip 23, the most technically challenging hike in this book]. We have used the designation conservatively, basing suggestions on hikes we feel are appropriate for children whose families hike together regularly. Some of the hikes designated for kids visit waterfalls or cliffy lookouts; these can be great rewards for kids' efforts to get there but can also be hazardous. Ultimately, to determine whether a hike is appropriate for your family, gauge your children's level of interest, motivation, and ability.)

Information on the basics follows: location, rating, distance, elevation gain, estimated time, and maps. The ratings are based on the authors' perception and are estimates of what the average hiker will experience. You may find ratings to be easier or more difficult than stated. The distance and estimated hiking time shown are for the whole trip, whether it's an out-and-back hike (with distance noted as "round-trip") or a loop. The estimated time is also based on the authors' perception. Consider your own pace when planning a trip. The elevation gain is calculated from measurements and information from U.S. Geological Survey (USGS) topographic maps, landowner maps, and Google Earth. Information is included about the relevant USGS maps, as well as where you can find trail maps.

The boldface summary that accompanies the list of basics provides an overview of what you will see on your hike. The Directions explain how to reach the trailhead by car and include Global Positioning System (GPS) coordinates for parking lots. Whether or not you own a GPS device, it is wise to bring an atlas, such as the *DeLorme Atlas & Gazetteer* for Virginia, which shows small roads and forest roads in detail. In the Trail Description, you will find instructions on where to hike, the trails on which to hike, and where to turn. You will also learn about the natural and human history along your hike, as well as about flora, fauna, and any landmarks or objects you will encounter. The trail maps that accompany each trip will help guide you along your hike, but it would be wise to take an official trail map, which will show additional details of side trails and other information for the area, with you as well. Official maps are often—but not always—available for download or purchase online, at the trailhead, or at the visitor center. Each hike description also lists the best available topographic map of the area. We highly recommend that hikers purchase these maps.

Each trip ends with a "More Information" section that provides details about access times and fees, the property's rules and regulations, and contact information for the place where you will be hiking. The "Nearby" section offers suggestions for places to continue the experience when the hike is done and where to find the closest restaurants.

TRIP PLANNING AND SAFETY

Planning your trip well is the first step to having a safe hike. Some of the trips in this book ascend to higher elevations or summits where winds and lower temperatures necessitate extra clothing. Other hikes visit clifftops or waterfalls or have rocky stretches where you'll need to use extra caution with children and dogs. Learn about the terrain you will travel through so you can pack the right gear and prepare for the experience. Allow extra time in case you get lost. You will be more likely to have an enjoyable, safe hike if you plan ahead and take proper precautions. Before heading out for your hike, consider the following:

- Select a hike that everyone in your group is comfortable taking. Match the hike to the abilities of the least capable person in the group. If anyone is uncomfortable with the weather or is tired, turn around and complete the hike another day.
- Plan to be back at the trailhead before dark. Before beginning your hike, determine a turnaround time. Don't diverge from it, even if you have not reached your intended destination.
- Check the weather and assume it will be cooler and windier on the mountain than at the base. If you are planning a ridge or summit hike, start early so that you will be off the exposed area before the afternoon hours, when thunderstorms most often strike, especially in summer. Weather conditions can change quickly, and any changes are likely to be more severe the higher you are on the mountain.
- Bring a pack with the following items:
  - ✓ Water: Two quarts per person is usually adequate, depending on the weather and the length of the trip. On extended day hikes, consider carrying some method of water purification so you can refill your water bottles en route.
  - ✓ Food: Even if you are planning just an hour-long hike, bring some high-energy snacks, such as nuts, dried fruit, or snack bars. Pack a lunch for longer trips.
  - ✓ Map and compass: Be sure you know how to use them. A handheld GPS device may also be helpful but it is not always reliable.
  - ✓ Headlamp or flashlight, with spare batteries.
  - ✓ Extra clothing: waterproof/breathable rain gear, synthetic fleece or wool jacket, hat, and mittens or gloves.

- ✓ Sunscreen.
- ✓ First-aid kit, including adhesive bandages, gauze, nonprescription pain-killers, moleskin, and any necessary prescription medication, in case you are on the trail longer than expected.
- ✓ Pocketknife or multitool.
- ✓ Waterproof matches and a lighter.
- ✓ Trash bag.
- ✓ Toilet paper and double plastic bag to pack it out.
- ✓ Whistle.
- ✓ Insect repellent.
- ✓ Sunglasses.
- ✓ Cell phone: Be aware that cell phone service is unreliable in rural areas. If you are receiving a signal, use the phone only for emergencies to avoid disturbing the backcountry experience for other hikers.
- ✓ Trekking poles (optional).
- ✓ Binoculars (optional).
- ✓ Camera (optional).

- Wear appropriate footwear and clothing. Wool or synthetic hiking socks will keep your feet dry and help prevent blisters. Comfortable hiking boots or shoes will provide support and good traction. Avoid wearing cotton clothing, which absorbs sweat and rain and contributes to an unpleasant hiking experience. A synthetic or wool base layer (T-shirt, or underwear tops and bottoms) will wick moisture away from your body and keep you warm in wet or cold conditions. Synthetic zip-off pants that convert to shorts are popular. To help avoid bug bites, you may want to wear synthetic pants and a long-sleeve shirt.

- When you are ahead of the rest of your hiking group, wait at all trail junctions until the others catch up. This avoids confusion and keeps people from getting separated or lost.

- If you see downed wood that appears to be purposely covering a trail, it probably means the trail is closed due to overuse or hazardous conditions. If a trail is muddy, walk through the mud or on rocks, never on tree roots or plants. Staying in the center of the trail will keep it from eroding into a wide hiking highway.

- Leave your itinerary and the time you expect to return with someone you trust. If you see a logbook at a trailhead, be sure to sign in when you arrive and sign out when you finish your hike.

- After you complete your hike, check for deer ticks, which carry the dangerous bacteria that causes Lyme disease.

- Poison ivy is always a threat when hiking. To identify the plant, look for clusters of three leaves that shine in the sun but are dull in the shade. If you do come into contact with poison ivy, wash the affected area with soap as soon as possible.

- Wear blaze-orange items in hunting season. In Virginia, hunting begins in September, with various seasons extending throughout winter and spring. Yearly information, regulations, and fees are available at dgif.virginia.gov/hunting/regulations.

Check on trail or road closures with land managers prior to heading out in any season, particularly in winter. Winter conditions can lead to full or partial closures of Shenandoah's Skyline Drive. To get the most current status of Skyline Drive, call 540-999-3500; the park's Facebook and Twitter feeds are also great ways to check on the status of the drive. Certain forest roads may also be closed in the winter months; check with the relevant park agency to get updated information on gaining access to certain trailheads.

Winter hiking can be an enjoyable way to experience the Shenandoah Valley, but it requires extra gear and planning. All winter hikers need to bring more food and warm layers than they would in summer, and exercise more caution; fewer daylight hours, colder temperatures, and slower travel times magnify any problems that may occur, like getting lost or twisting an ankle. Near-freezing temperatures freeze hoses on hydration systems. Consider using insulated water bottles and packing them as close as possible to your body heat to keep your water from freezing during the day. Small-mouthed water bottles tend to freeze faster. Traction devices—such as Microspikes—can help you navigate icy stretches. Prudent winter travelers do not go out alone and make sure at least one person in the group has a sleeping bag and a small camp stove in case of emergency. When properly prepared, hikers can safely and comfortably experience the deep quiet and spectacular beauty of the Shenandoah Valley in winter.

When the weather warms up, the bugs start to come out. Mosquitoes can be a nuisance in some places, depending on seasonal and daily conditions. West Nile virus and eastern equine encephalitis (EEE) virus can be transmitted to humans by infected mosquitoes and cause rare but serious diseases. More prevalent, however, are deer ticks, which can transmit Lyme disease. Reduce your risk of being bitten by using insect repellent and wearing long sleeves and pants. Check yourself carefully for ticks when you finish your hike. A variety of options are available for dealing with bugs, ranging from sprays that include the active ingredient DEET, which can potentially cause skin or eye irritation, to more skin-friendly products. Head nets, which often can be purchased more cheaply than a can of repellent, are useful during especially buggy conditions.

APPALACHIAN MOUNTAIN CLUB'S POTOMAC CHAPTER

Founded in 1876, the Appalachian Mountain Club (AMC) promotes the protection, enjoyment, and understanding of the mountains, forests, waters, and trails of America's Northeast and Mid-Atlantic regions. AMC's 2,000-plus-member Potomac Chapter, established in 1984, is the southernmost of 12 regional chapters, each of which offers hundreds of annual outdoor activities open to the public, including day-hiking, backpacking, paddling, biking, and social get-togethers. AMC volunteers also lead outdoor skills workshops, promote stewardship of the region's natural resources, and, along with AMC staff, maintain 1,800 miles of trails along the East Coast, including portions of the Appalachian Trail. Read about AMC's work in the Mid-Atlantic on page 229 and learn more at outdoors.org.

APPALACHIAN TRAIL CONSERVANCY

The Appalachian Trail Conservancy (ATC), headquartered in Harpers Ferry, West Virginia, preserves and manages the Appalachian Trail from its origins in Georgia to its terminus in Maine. The ATC works cooperatively with volunteers, trail clubs, and other agencies to develop policies of trail design, and to protect the landscapes and cultural and natural resources along the Appalachian Trail. Their Appalachian Trail Guides include excellent, AT-focused text and maps; for coverage of this area, refer to the Maryland/Northern Virginia, Shenandoah National Park, and Central Virginia guides. For more information, visit appalachiantrail.org.

POTOMAC APPALACHIAN TRAIL CLUB

The volunteer-based Potomac Appalachian Trail Club, headquartered in Vienna, Virginia, was founded in 1927. Now the club partners with the National Park Service, the Appalachian Trail Conservancy, and other trail clubs and maintains and monitors more than 1,000 miles of hiking trails in the Mid-Atlantic region, as well as cabins, shelters, and hundreds of acres of conserved land. PATC also publishes indispensable resources for hiking in the region, including books and maps covering the Appalachian Trail, Massanutten Mountain, and Great North Mountain. For more information, visit PATC headquarters or patc.net.

SHENANDOAH NATIONAL PARK

Shenandoah National Park encompasses nearly 200,000 acres in Virginia. Almost 40 percent of the park is designated as Wilderness Areas, but its most well-known feature is Skyline Drive, which runs 105 miles through the length of the park and past 75 scenic overlooks. The park has approximately 500 miles of trails, including 101 miles of the Appalachian Trail. For more information, visit nps.gov/shen.

GEORGE WASHINGTON AND JEFFERSON NATIONAL FORESTS

Together, the George Washington and Jefferson National Forests form one of the largest areas of public land on the East Coast. Covering 1.8 million acres in Virginia, West Virginia, and Kentucky, the two forests are home to 2,000 miles of trails and 139,461 acres of designated Wilderness Areas. For more information, visit fs.usda.gov/gwj.

LEAVE NO TRACE

The Appalachian Mountain Club (AMC) is a national educational partner of Leave No Trace, a nonprofit organization dedicated to promoting and inspiring responsible outdoor recreation through education, research, and partnerships. The Leave No Trace program seeks to develop  wildland ethics—ways in which people think and act in the outdoors to minimize their impact on the areas they visit and to protect our natural resources for future enjoyment. Leave No Trace unites four federal land management agencies—U.S. Forest Service, National Park Service, Bureau of Land Management, and U.S. Fish and Wildlife Service—with manufacturers, outdoor retailers, user groups, educators, organizations such as AMC, and individuals.

The Leave No Trace ethic is guided by the following seven principles:

1. **Plan Ahead and Prepare.** Know the terrain and any regulations applicable to the area you're planning to visit, and be prepared for extreme weather or other emergencies. This will enhance your enjoyment and ensure that you've chosen an appropriate destination. Small groups have less impact on resources and on the experiences of other backcountry visitors.

2. **Travel and Camp on Durable Surfaces.** Travel and camp on established trails and campsites, rock, gravel, dry grasses, or snow. Good campsites are found, not made. Camp at least 200 feet from lakes and streams, and focus activities on areas where vegetation is absent. In pristine areas, disperse use to prevent the creation of campsites and trails.

3. **Dispose of Waste Properly.** Pack it in, pack it out. Inspect your camp for trash or food scraps. Deposit solid human waste in catholes dug 6 to 8 inches deep, at least 200 feet from water, camps, and trails. Pack out toilet paper and hygiene products. To wash yourself or your dishes, carry water 200 feet from streams or lakes and use small amounts of biodegradable soap. Scatter strained dishwater.

4. **Leave What You Find.** Cultural or historical artifacts, as well as natural objects, such as plants and rocks, should be left as found.

5. **Minimize Campfire Impacts.** Cook on a stove. Use established fire rings, fire pans, or mound fires. If you build a campfire, keep it small and use dead sticks found on the ground.

6. **Respect Wildlife.** Observe wildlife from a distance. Feeding animals alters their natural behavior. Protect wildlife from your food by storing rations and trash securely.

7. **Be Considerate of Other Visitors.** Be courteous, respect the quality of other visitors' backcountry experience, and let nature's sounds prevail.

AMC is a national provider of the Leave No Trace Master Educator course. AMC offers this five-day course, designed especially for outdoor professionals and land managers, as well as the shorter two-day Leave No Trace Trainer course, at locations throughout the Northeast.

For Leave No Trace information and materials, contact the Leave No Trace Center for Outdoor Ethics, P.O. Box 997, Boulder, CO 80306; 800-332-4100 or 302-442-8222; lnt.org. For a schedule of AMC Leave No Trace courses, see outdoors.org/education/lnt.

SECTION 1
HARPERS FERRY
AND NORTH VIRGINIA
PIEDMONT

The historic town of Harpers Ferry lies at the confluence of the Potomac and Shenandoah rivers, on the borders of Maryland, West Virginia, and Virginia. Known as the "psychological halfway point" on the Appalachian Trail, the town was taken eight times  during the Civil War and was the site of John Brown's famous raid—a bloody attempt to spark a slave revolt. A wealth of ruins and monuments on the area's trails commemorates these important events in U.S. history. Harpers Ferry National Historic Park encompasses 4,000 acres of protected land and has about 20 miles of hiking trails crossing Civil War battlefields and mountains alike. The Appalachian Trail passes through the park; the 184.5-mile C&O Canal Towpath can also be reached from the park by a footbridge over the Potomac. Two hikes in this book include the two highest cliffs overlooking Harpers Ferry—Maryland Heights (Trip 2) and Loudoun Heights (Trip 3)—showcasing where the Potomac and Shenandoah rivers meet.

The rolling hills and ridges of the Piedmont region stretch east to west, from the Potomac, Rappahannock, and James rivers to the Blue Ridge Mountains and run north to south, from North Carolina through central Virginia and into Maryland and Pennsylvania. From above, the Piedmont looks like a patchwork of secondary forests, pastures, and agricultural fields. Virginia pines and tulip trees are prevalent in the area's younger forests, which have begun to re-establish themselves after a history of repeated cutting and clearing. Mature forests in the area vary widely depending on topography and soil composition, supporting oak, hickory, beech, sycamore, silver maple, American elm, and eastern box elder. This section includes only a handful of the public lands in this region, focusing on features that lead into the Shenandoah Valley itself, including Raven Rocks (Trip 4), Shenandoah River State Park (Trip 5), and Sky Meadows State Park (Trip 6).

1

VIRGINIUS ISLAND

Take an archaeological tour of Harpers Ferry's manufacturing past with this stroll around Virginius Island.

DIRECTIONS

From I-270, Exit 32, take I-70 West for 1.0 mile to Exit 52 (US 340, Charles Town and Leesburg). Follow US 340 South/West for 22.0 miles into Harpers Ferry. Cross the Potomac and Shenandoah rivers. Turn left into the main entrance of Harpers Ferry National Historical Park and park near the visitor center. (Parking fees apply.) Park-operated shuttle buses run through Harpers Ferry frequently; check with the Park Service for current hours and schedule. *GPS coordinates: 39° 19.007′ N, 77° 45.381′ W.*

TRAIL DESCRIPTION

Harpers Ferry is famous for its role in the Civil War, but this easy hike showcases the town's manufacturing history as it winds past a number of archaeological sites. From the Shenandoah Street shuttle stop, turn left and head up the street until you arrive at the bridge connecting Harpers Ferry to Virginius Island. When the island was inhabited, multiple bridges connected it to the mainland to provide passage for residents and factory workers.

Cross the bridge and follow the path over train tracks and bear left—but note that this is an active track, so pay attention when crossing. As you follow the trail to the left, old building foundations come into view. Take some time to read the interpretive signs found throughout the trail. They offer information and background on the sites that can still be seen on the island, including the foundation of Island Mills, which ground and processed flour from the Shenandoah Valley that was then shipped to Baltimore.

As the trail approaches the Shenandoah River, bear to the right. Remains of the old river wall come into view.

LOCATION
Harpers Ferry National Historical Park, WV

RATING
Easy

DISTANCE
1.2 miles round-trip

ELEVATION GAIN
17 feet

ESTIMATED TIME
1-2 hours

MAPS
Harpers Ferry, Virginius Island Trail Guide (National Park Service): nps.gov/hafe/learn/education/upload/virginius%20island.pdf

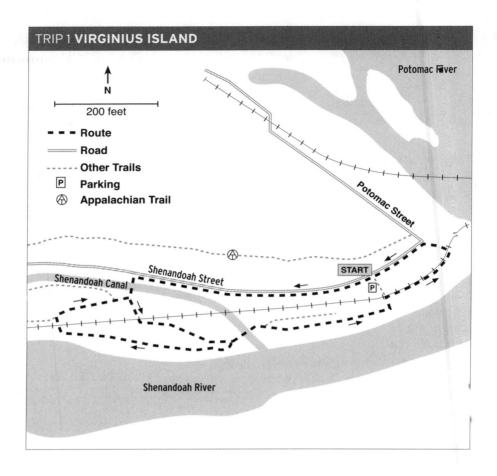

The Harpers Ferry & Shenandoah Manufacturing Company built this wall, and it served as part of the hydraulic system for the town and its mills. The head gates emerge into sight next; these helped control the island's water power. From here, the trail bends to the right and under the train tracks. Continue following and arrive back at the bridge.

You could cross the bridge here and retrace your steps back to town, but a more pleasant walk—and an opportunity to take in more sights—is to double back over the train tracks. This time, instead of bearing to the right, follow the trail to the left and explore the water tunnels, which helped increase power to the mills.

The path crosses a small bridge and then parallels the train tracks, passing more evidence of Harpers Ferry's thriving past: the foundations of a butcher shop, a boarding house, a market house, and an armory paymaster's house—a house where Meriwether Lewis might have stayed. The trail leads to a wooden staircase that brings you back to the town of Harpers Ferry and marks the end of your journey.

Exploring this island gives you a glimpse into Harpers Ferry's past, including a look at the remains of the water tunnels and river wall that powered the various mills on Virginius Island.

DID YOU KNOW?

Meriwether Lewis spent a few months in Harpers Ferry in 1803 to purchase equipment from the armory for his continental explorations. His shopping list, preserved by the National Park Service, included 15 rifles, 24 large knives, 15 powder horns and pouches, 40 fish gigs, a collapsible iron boat frame, and one small grindstone.

MORE INFORMATION

Harpers Ferry National Historical Park (nps.gov/hafe, 304-535-6029). The park is open year-round, except for Thanksgiving Day, Christmas Day, and New Year's Day. Entrance fees are collected for visitors arriving by foot, bicycle, or vehicle.

NEARBY

The town of Harpers Ferry is full of restaurants, ice cream shops, and more. If you're looking for another chance to stretch your legs and take on a bigger hiking challenge, consider nearby Maryland Heights (Trip 2) or Loudoun Heights (Trip 3), which are also accessible from Harpers Ferry.

2

MARYLAND HEIGHTS

Enjoy a trip through Harpers Ferry before heading up Maryland Heights for a great view of the town.

DIRECTIONS

From I-270, Exit 32, take I-70 West for 1.0 mile to Exit 52 (US 340, Charles Town and Leesburg). Follow US 340 South/West for 22.0 miles into Harpers Ferry. Cross the Potomac and Shenandoah rivers. Turn left into the main entrance of Harpers Ferry National Historical Park and park near the visitor center. (Parking fees apply.) Park-operated shuttle buses run through Harpers Ferry frequently; check with the Park Service for current hours and schedule. *GPS coordinates:* 39° 19.007′ N, 77° 45.381′ W.

TRAIL DESCRIPTION

This hike offers both historical interest and an impressive view of Harpers Ferry, but it is more demanding than you might think. The route crosses the Potomac, follows the C&O Canal, and then climbs to Maryland Heights. But because the trail drops down to the overlook, it will feel as if you're hiking uphill both ways!

A walk up Maryland Heights is a historical tour, starting and ending in Harpers Ferry and leading past several Civil War ruins. While there is parking in Harpers Ferry itself, it is hard to come by. The easiest way to reach the trailhead is to park at the Harpers Ferry Visitor Center and take the shuttle into town.

From the Shenandoah Street shuttle stop, turn right and follow the street past the restored shops. In the distance, Maryland Heights stretches above the town. Look for a white blaze on a signpost—the Appalachian Trail cuts through Harpers Ferry, and this route follows its path for a short distance. At the end of the street, 0.2 mile from the

LOCATION
Harpers Ferry National
Historical Park, WV

RATING
Strenuous

DISTANCE
4.4 miles round-trip

ELEVATION GAIN
1,378 feet

ESTIMATED TIME
2-3 hours

MAPS
Harpers Ferry,
Maryland Heights Trail Map
(National Park Service):
nps.gov/hafe/planyourvisit/
upload/Md-Hts2011-2.pdf

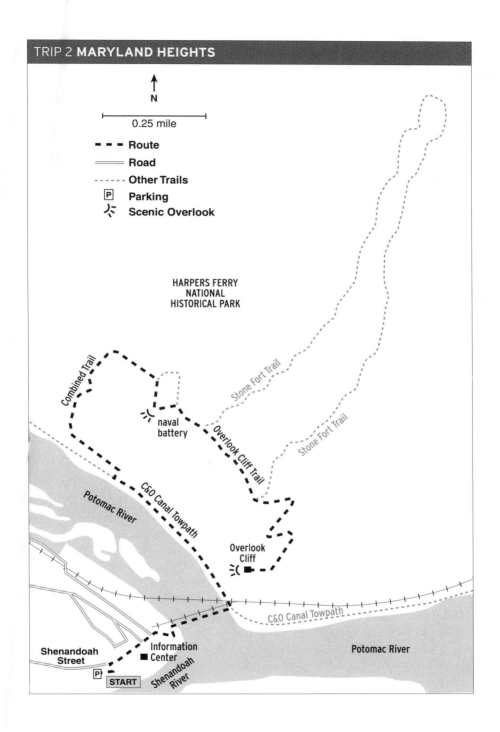

N

0.25 mile

- - - Route
═══ Road
----- Other Trails
P Parking
⅄ Scenic Overlook

HARPERS FERRY
NATIONAL
HISTORICAL PARK

Combined Trail

Stone Fort Trail

naval
battery

Overlook Cliff Trail

Stone Fort Trail

Potomac River

C&O Canal Towpath

Overlook
Cliff

C&O Canal Towpath

Potomac River

Shenandoah
Street

Information
Center

Shenandoah
River

P

START

The view of Harpers Ferry from the cliffs of Maryland Heights is one of the highlights of hiking in the Mid-Atlantic. Near the railway bridge, one can spot the foundations of the armory that John Brown raided in 1859.

shuttle stop, follow the wide gravel road, cross the railroad bridge over the Potomac, and descend the metal steps. These steps can be slippery when wet, and their open-grate surface can cause some pets to be reluctant to make the descent.

Turn left onto the wide C&O Canal Towpath. Walk along the Potomac for a spell, with the river on your left, the canal and Maryland Heights on your right. At 0.8 mile, cross the footbridge over the canal and then cross the road. Pass the gate and start heading uphill on green-blazed Combined Trail. The trail ascends rather quickly, giving views of the Potomac River to the left, before it swings to the right and enters the woods, still making its way uphill.

The trail comes to its first fork at 1.4 miles. Stay to the right to pass ruins of the Naval Battery, the first Union fortification built in Maryland Heights as protection against Stonewall Jackson's Valley Campaign. (Read "War in the Shenandoah Valley" on page 22 to learn more.) After seeing the ruins, follow the path back up the hill to where it rejoins Combined Trail and take a right. (You may also take a left from the fork to stay on Combined Trail. Both options lead you to the same point.)

The trail forks again at 1.6 miles. Blue-blazed Stone Fort Trail is to the left, but follow red-blazed Overlook Cliff Trail to the right. Overlook Cliff Trail continues the journey uphill. A final steep pitch leads to another intersection with Stone Fort Trail at 1.8 miles and the peak of the climb. Stay on Overlook Cliff Trail, which shortly turns to the right and starts to descend, switchbacking broadly. At 2.2 miles, the trail reaches a view of the Potomac and Shenandoah rivers meeting, as well as the town below—specifically the street on which you started the hike; descend the rocky area carefully for a nice spot to sit down.

After taking in the view, retrace your steps along the red- and green-blazed trails.

MORE INFORMATION

Harpers Ferry National Historical Park (nps.gov/hafe, 304-535-6029). The park is open year-round, except for Thanksgiving Day, Christmas Day, and New Year's Day. Entrance fees are collected for visitors arriving by foot, bicycle, or vehicle.

NEARBY

The town of Harpers Ferry is full of restaurants, ice cream shops, and more—perfect for replacing all the calories you just burned. If you're looking for another chance to stretch your legs, consider adding to this route blue-blazed Stone Fort Trail, which loops into the woods from the end point and adds about 2 miles to the trek as well as some more climbing. Virginius Island (Trip 1) and nearby Loudoun Heights (Trip 3) are also accessible from Harpers Ferry.

HARPERS FERRY

Harpers Ferry stands at the northernmost point of the Shenandoah Valley. Most modern-day visitors will marvel at the picturesque town perched between the Shenandoah and Potomac rivers, but its position has made it a key strategic point throughout much of American history, particularly during the Civil War. The town's importance was only increased by the U.S. government's decision in the nineteenth century to build an armory there—one of only two federal armories in the country.

In 1859, the abolitionist John Brown attacked Harpers Ferry with a band of 21 men, planning to seize the armory and escape to Virginia, where he hoped news of his actions would ignite a slave revolt. Brown and his followers were cornered in Harpers Ferry, however, after the surrounding townships were alerted. A force of marines under the command of Robert E. Lee and J.E.B. Stuart swiftly put down the revolt, and John Brown was hanged for treason on December 2, 1859. While Brown's actions thrust Harpers Ferry into national prominence, the meaning of his raid has always been hotly debated. Some saw Brown as a bloodthirsty vigilante; others regarded him as a martyr fallen to the cause of freedom. All should agree that his attack on the armory presaged the violence to come and was one of the crucial events leading up to the Civil War.

The beginning of the Civil War also spelled the end of prosperity for Harpers Ferry. The town changed hands no fewer than eight times during the battles that raged around the Washington, D.C., area. More recently, Harpers Ferry has been designated a National Historical Park and is known chiefly for tourism and outdoor activities. As it winds from Virginia to Maryland, the Appalachian Trail passes over the town's bridges and through its cobbled streets. Many thru-hikers pose for photos before the Appalachian Trail Conservancy Headquarters to indicate that they have completed half of the trail (though the true halfway point is in Pennsylvania). Other outdoors enthusiasts travel along the 184.5-mile Chesapeake & Ohio (C&O) Canal, which was built in the nineteenth century to enable trade from Washington, D.C., to Cumberland, Maryland. Today, the flat canal towpath is popular with cyclists, hikers, and runners.

Even if you're not traveling long distances, Harpers Ferry is an attractive destination for day hikes. Trip 1 in this book, Virginius Island, offers a walk back in time. Trip 2 takes you to Maryland Heights, where you can wander through Civil War ruins and peer down at the foundations of the old armory where John Brown made his last stand. Loudoun Heights, visited in Trip 3, also offers superb views of the town. If you visit in summer, be sure to enjoy a cooling float down the river!

3

LOUDOUN HEIGHTS

Quieter than Maryland Heights, this hike rewards you with stunning views and fewer crowds. A ramble through the town of Harpers Ferry takes you past some of the history in the area.

DIRECTIONS

From I-270, Exit 32, take I-70 West for 1.0 mile to Exit 52 (US 340, Charles Town and Leesburg). Follow US 340 South/West for 22.0 miles into Harpers Ferry. Cross the Potomac and Shenandoah rivers. Turn left into the main entrance of Harpers Ferry National Historical Park and park near the visitor center. (Parking fees apply.) Park-operated shuttle buses run through Harpers Ferry frequently; check with the Park Service for current hours and schedule. *GPS coordinates: 39° 19.007′ N, 77° 45.381′ W.*

TRAIL DESCRIPTION

Thomas Jefferson famously marveled at the views encountered along this hike: "It is as placid and delightful as that is wild and tremendous. For the mountains being cloven asunder, she [nature] presents to your eye, through the cleft, a small catch of smooth blue horizon, at an infinite distance in that plain country, inviting you, as it were, from the riot and tumult roaring around to pass through the breach and participate in the calm below." You may find yourself echoing these thoughts as you take in the views on this hike. Starting in Harpers Ferry, the trail leads to an overlook of the town and the confluence of the Shenandoah and Potomac rivers.

While there is parking in Harpers Ferry itself, it is hard to come by. The easiest way to reach the trailhead is to park at the Harpers Ferry Visitor Center and take the shuttle into town. From the Shenandoah Street shuttle stop, turn

LOCATION
Harpers Ferry National Historical Park, WV

RATING
Strenuous

DISTANCE
7.8 miles round-trip

ELEVATION GAIN
2,278 feet

ESTIMATED TIME
4-5 hours

MAPS
Map 7, Appalachian Trail in West Virginia and Northern Virginia, Potomac River & Harpers Ferry, WV to VA 7, 2013 (PATC): www.patc.net/PATC/ Our_Store/PATC_Maps.aspx

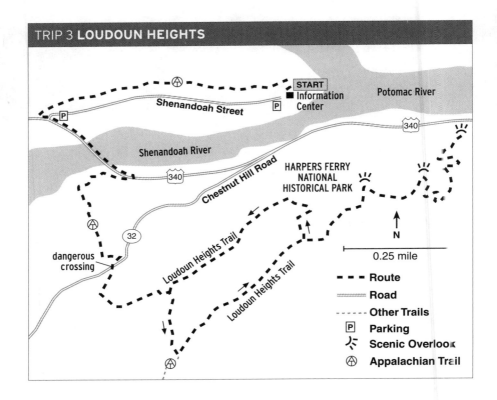

left onto Potomac Street toward the railroad station. Turn up Hog Alley. At the top, make a left and then a quick right up hand-carved rock steps; look for the white blaze of the Appalachian Trail (AT). These steps lead past St. Peter's Roman Catholic Church—its steeple being perhaps one of the most visible sights when entering Harpers Ferry—and the ruins of St. John's Church. Here, the white blazes of the AT become more visible, and the trail leaves the town and becomes more of a wooded path.

At 0.3 mile from the shuttle stop, just past the site of St. John's Church, the trail reaches Jefferson Rock. Thomas Jefferson, who stood here on October 25, 1793, wrote that this "scene is worth a journey across the Atlantic." Pillars now support the rock, but the view itself has not changed. Take some time to marvel at the vista, but avoid climbing on the rock (hikers are cautioned not to).

After taking in the scenery from Jefferson Rock, continue along the white-blazed AT. Side trails lead toward Harpers Cemetery and the Appalachian Trail Visitor Center, but keep following the white blazes. When the trail splits, stay to the right. Just before the trail reaches US 340, it descends along a series of rock steps. A secondary parking lot is nearby—this lot can fill quickly on weekends, and parking here would shorten the hike but lose the sights of Harpers Ferry.

Hikers can take in this iconic view of Harpers Ferry from the perches of Loudoun Heights.

Follow the trail to the left, and at 1.1 miles head over the US 340 bridge spanning the Shenandoah River. In warmer seasons, look for kayakers and rafters negotiating the rapids below.

At the end of the bridge, the trail descends down a staircase and back under the bridge, returning to a dirt path. Follow the white blazes as the trail climbs toward Loudoun Heights. It is easy to follow but does have occasional rocky patches and steep sections. At 1.9 miles, cross Chestnut Hill Road and continue to ascend. Pass an orange-blazed path at 2.2 miles (your return route) and turn left onto blue-blazed Loudoun Heights Trail at 2.4 miles. After climbing for just over 2 miles, the trail reaches a stretch of level walking. To the left and right, through the trees, you can glimpse the valley and town below, particularly in winter when the trees have lost their leaves. The trail passes another intersection with the orange-blazed trail before it descends to and ends at the overlook.

From here, gaze over Harpers Ferry. You might spot day-hikers enjoying the views from Maryland Heights (Trip 2) across the river. To continue your hike, head back along the blue-blazed path and turn right onto the orange-blazed trail at 4.9 miles. A quick and steep descent leads to some level walking and good views to the right of the river and Harpers Ferry. At 5.6 miles, arrive at the intersection with the AT you passed earlier in the trip. Turn right and follow the white blazes back down the mountain and into Harpers Ferry.

DID YOU KNOW?

The top slab of Jefferson Rock was so precariously balanced that hikers and tourists were able to move it with a gentle push. The pillars were placed under the slab between 1855 and 1860 to protect the town below.

MORE INFORMATION

Harpers Ferry National Historical Park (nps.gov/hafe, 304-535-6029). The park is open year-round, except for Thanksgiving Day, Christmas Day, and New Year's Day. Entrance fees are collected for visitors arriving by foot, bicycle, or vehicle.

NEARBY

The town of Harpers Ferry is full of restaurants, ice cream shops, and more—perfect for replacing all the calories you just burned. Nearby Virginius Island (Trip 1) and Maryland Heights (Trip 2) are also accessible from Harpers Ferry.

4

RAVEN ROCKS

On this portion of the Appalachian Trail's famous Roller Coaster section, a few dips and climbs lead to an outcropping that has an impressive view of the valley.

DIRECTIONS

From VA 267, Exit 1A, merge onto US 15 South/VA 7 West/Leesburg Bypass toward Leesburg/Warrenton. Follow VA 7 West for 18 miles, then turn right onto Pine Grove Road (VA 679) and look immediately to the right for the small parking area and trailhead. Parking rules here are strictly enforced. Obey the No Parking signs or risk being towed. An alternate parking lot can be found across VA 7 if this parking lot is full. *GPS coordinates: 39° 6.999′ N, 77° 51.143′ W.*

TRAIL DESCRIPTION

This hike is rated moderate for its distance, but the rocky terrain could be a challenge for hikers unused to rock hopping. This short route on a segment of the Appalachian Trail (AT) climbs and dips—and climbs and dips some more—as it makes its way up to the Raven Rocks Overlook. The route to the overlook covers a short portion of a notorious 13.5-mile stretch of the AT known as the Roller Coaster, which can tire even the hardiest of hikers. Taking on this challenging section of trail, however, will reward big effort with big views.

From the parking lot, look for the white blazes and an information post to signal the start of the hike. Head up the trail for the first climb of the day before the trail switchbacks steeply down. Near the end of this descent, at 0.6 mile, keep an eye out for a modest sign signaling the 1,000-mile marker for northbound thru-hikers of the AT. From here, the trail jogs slightly uphill, providing a relatively easy stretch of hiking for a while. Take some time to enjoy

LOCATION
Bluemont, VA

RATING
Moderate

DISTANCE
4.7 miles round-trip

ELEVATION GAIN
1,744 feet

ESTIMATED TIME
2-3 hours

MAPS
Map 7, Appalachian Trail in West Virginia and Northern Virginia, Potomac River & Harpers Ferry, WV to VA 7, 2013 (PATC): www.patc.net/PATC/Our_Store/PATC_Maps.aspx

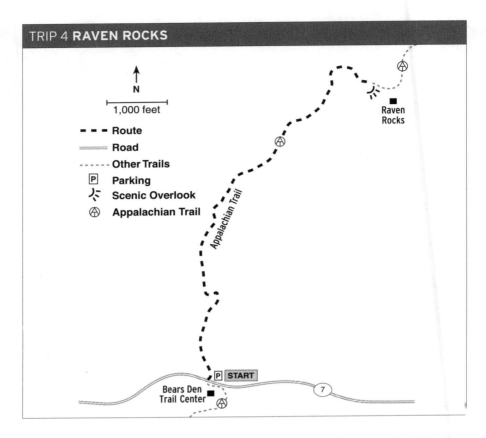

N

1,000 feet

- - - Route
===== Road
----- Other Trails
P Parking
⅄ Scenic Overlook
Ⓐ Appalachian Trail

Appalachian Trail

Raven
Rocks

P START

Bears Den
Trail Center

7

this section as the Roller Coaster isn't quite over yet. Another steep climb leads to a nice westerly view of the area, and then dips again at 1.9 miles to a rocky stream crossing. From here, the trail starts its final climb to Raven Rocks. Compared with the rockier stretches before, this portion of the trail may feel easier to navigate—or it may be that many hikers are used to rock hopping by this point.

At 2.2 miles, the trail passes a marker for the Virginia–West Virginia border. This sign signals that the end of the climb is near: the trail opens up dramatically and leads straight to the Raven Rocks area at 2.4 miles. Make sure to include time for a lunch break here as the large outcropping yields fantastic views of the Shenandoah Valley and the mountains beyond. This outcropping is popular not only with hikers but with rock climbers as well—looking below, you may be able to spot a few making their way up the rock.

After enjoying the views, retrace your steps back down (and up) along the rocky path to the parking lot.

DID YOU KNOW?

Experienced rock climbers flock to Raven Rocks—also known as Crescent Rocks—to take advantage of its nearly 30 climbs. Route names range from the

A hiker enjoys a flat stretch of trail before diving back into the famously hilly stretch, known as the Roller Coaster, that defines this rewarding hike.

ordinary (The Dish) to the fanciful (Litigiousness Psychosis), but all require experience and skill to get to the top safely.

MORE INFORMATION

Appalachian Trail Conservancy (appalachiantrail.org/hiking/trail-updates; 717-258-5771 [regional office]; 304-535-6331 [incident reports]). Local information may be available at Bears Den (see below) during trail center hours.

NEARBY

You're not too far from civilization along this hike. Heading in either direction on VA 7 will lead you to Winchester and Leesburg, which have shops and restaurants for all budgets and tastes. The Appalachian Trail Conservancy's 66-acre Bears Den property (bearsdencenter.org, 540-554-8708) is across VA 7 from the trailhead and offers a variety of overnight accommodations, including a lodge, campground, cottage, and hiker hostel. The trail center is open from 8 A.M. to 9 P.M.; the lodge and store are open from 5 to 9 P.M. unless there is an event. There is a small fee for parking in the day-use lot.

SHENANDOAH RIVER STATE PARK

Not to be confused with its national park sibling, Shenandoah River State Park has a little bit of everything for a hiker: a river walk, wide paths, woody climbs, and an overlook fit for a lunch break.

DIRECTIONS

From I-66, Exit 6 (Front Royal), turn left (south) onto US 340 and follow it through Front Royal. The park entrance is about 7.5 miles south of the junction of US 340 and VA 678. Turn right into the park (parking fees apply), and follow Daughter of Stars Drive to the Horsebarn Area. Park here for trailhead access. *GPS coordinates:* 38° 50.877' N, 78° 18.352' W.

TRAIL DESCRIPTION

Perfect for those looking for easy terrain while still getting in some miles, this lollipop route uses a number of trails in the park to take hikers for a meander along the Shenandoah River before heading up into the nearby woods. The park itself has more than 1,600 acres, with 5.2 miles along the shore of the Shenandoah River's South Fork.

Look for the information kiosk in the parking lot to find the trailhead; if you're facing the horse barn, the trail starts to the left. It quickly splits, with one fork heading to Bear Bottom Loop and another to Culler's Trail, your path forward. Follow the signs for Culler's Trail (orange blazes) as it wraps behind the barn and leads you into the woods.

The dirt trail crosses a road at 0.75 mile and changes to an open gravel path. Keep following this path and the signs for Culler's Trail, which heads closer to the Shenandoah River. Birdhouses dot the wooden fence that lines the way, and benches just off the trail invite sitting along

LOCATION
Bentonville, VA

RATING
Moderate

DISTANCE
6.5 miles round-trip

ELEVATION GAIN
1,368 feet

ESTIMATED TIME
3-4 hours

MAPS
Shenandoah River State Park Trail Map (dcr.virginia .gov/state-parks/ shenandoah-river.shtml)

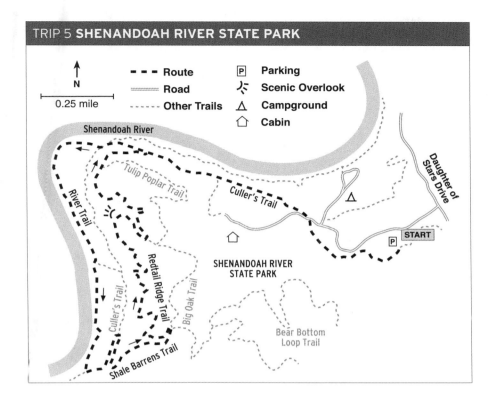

the river. Pass the intersection for Tulip Poplar Trail just ahead of the 1.5-mile point. At 1.6 miles, turn right onto River Trail (dark-green blazes).

This trail lives up to its name, drawing closer to the Shenandoah River and granting even better views of the water and nearby Massanutten Mountain. A connector trail comes in from the left, but stay alongside the river as long as possible in this pleasant stretch.

At 2.8 miles, River Trail meets up with Culler's Trail again. At this junction, take a left to return to Culler's Trail, but then rather quickly, at 3.0 miles, take a right onto gray-blazed Shale Barrens Trail. The path heads back into the woods and starts the only steep climb of the day—this is the workout portion of the hike. The trail switchbacks uphill and eventually reaches the top of the ridge. At 3.4 miles, turn left to follow Redtail Ridge Trail (red blazes). Good views of the river start to appear below, and the route mirrors the path you just took—although now from a higher vantage point. A short spur trail leads to a nice overlook at 4.2 miles, and a perfectly placed bench provides an excellent break spot.

Follow Redtail Ridge Trail just a bit farther, and then, at 4.5 miles, turn left onto pink-blazed Tulip Poplar Trail and follow as it wanders through the woods. Tulip Poplar Trail is a lollipop loop itself. Continue straight when you reach the trail's intersection with this loop at 5.5 miles to finish the hike. Turn right to

Hikers enjoy a gentle ramble as the route parallels the Shenandoah River.

rejoin Culler's Trail, giving another chance to enjoy the river views, to travel back along the gravel path, recross the road, and return to your car.

DID YOU KNOW?

The Shenandoah River flows for 55.6 miles and has two forks—North and South—that are each 100 miles long. A tributary of the Potomac River, the Shenandoah starts northeast of Front Royal where the North and South forks meet and eventually joins the Potomac near Harpers Ferry. Some historians credit George Washington with naming the river (and the valley) after Oskanondonha, an Oneida chief who helped Washington's troops during the Revolutionary War.

MORE INFORMATION

Shenandoah River State Park (dcr.virginia.gov/state-parks/shenandoah-river .shtml, 540-622-6840). The park is open from 8 A.M. to dusk and is a trash-free facility. A campground, bunkhouses, cabins, and a lodge are available for overnight stays; for reservations, contact ReserveAmerica at reserveamerica.com or 800-933-7275.

NEARBY

En route from I-66, you'll drive right past the entrance to Shenandoah National Park and Skyline Drive. Dickey Ridge (Trip 9) is just a short distance down Skyline Drive. Also nearby are Buzzard Rock (Trip 33) and Duncan Knob (Trip 35). The town of Front Royal has a number of stores, shops, and restaurants to fit most budgets and cuisine preferences.

WAR IN THE SHENANDOAH VALLEY

The Shenandoah Valley has always been known for its agriculture—even today the area is dotted with wineries, cideries, breweries, and restaurants that emphasize local produce—but its strategic importance for the South during the Civil War is less well known. Two major military campaigns were fought in the valley during the war, leaving the region devastated.

Long before the war, the valley's bounty was integral to the lives and lore of its native people. Later, the fertile soil lured German and Scots-Irish immigrants, who eventually called the area home. European settlers produced food in abundance and exported their surplus to cities on the East Coast. In this, the Shenandoah Valley was unique. Much of the economy of the South depended on growing cotton, sugar, and tobacco—in other words, crops that people couldn't eat. The Shenandoah Valley was the only major region in Virginia that had mixed agriculture, producing wheat and corn and raising livestock—a distinction that became incredibly important when war broke out.

Of equal importance was the pathway that the valley provided for the South during the Civil War as an invasion route to Maryland, Washington, D.C., and Pennsylvania. The Valley Pike—now known as VA 11—was used to transport food but also to quickly move troops and equipment. During the Shenandoah Valley campaign in 1862, Major General Stonewall Jackson deployed Confederate troops up and down the valley, guarding the area with his "foot cavalry" and using the gaps—Thornton, Swift Run, and others with names now familiar to hikers and park visitors—to surprise Union soldiers. Union leaders could only guess at the size of Jackson's forces and how fast they were moving. Jackson retained control of the valley for the first part of the war.

The Union was slow to realize the importance of the Shenandoah Valley, both agriculturally and strategically. In 1864, when Ulysses S. Grant was placed in charge of the Union Army, he and President Abraham Lincoln realized that the only way for the Union to defeat the Confederacy was to destroy the social and economic infrastructure of the South—and that included the Shenandoah Valley. Grant designed a plan to strike at the Confederacy from multiple directions, with an eye toward the Shenandoah Valley.

In the Valley campaigns of 1864, Grant designated a smaller army to parallel his movements south, but the Confederate general Jubal Early frustrated Grant's initial attempts by pushing the Union back up the valley, coming within striking distance of Washington, D.C. Grant then placed General Philip Sheridan in charge of the Army of the Shenandoah. Sheridan had served with Grant and Major General William Tecumseh Sherman in the West, and was appointed by Grant to strike at the Shenandoah Valley's infrastructure. As Sheridan's army moved through the valley, the troops laid waste to homes and burned farms, a precursor of Sherman's infamous march through Georgia. The valley was devastated but not completely destroyed. Although many residents left, some returned later to rebuild on the fertile soil.

6

SKY MEADOWS STATE PARK

Ramble through meadows on this moderate hike that gives grand views of the surrounding Virginia Piedmont area.

DIRECTIONS

From I-66, take Exit 23 (US 17 North/VA 55 West) and follow US 17 North for 6.4 miles. Turn left onto VA 710 to enter the park. Park in the main lot by Mount Bleak House. *GPS coordinates: 38° 59.478′ N, 77° 58.281′ W.*

TRAIL DESCRIPTION

This hike starts off with a climb to get your heart pumping; sweeping views open up during the latter half of the trip as the route wanders through woods and meadows. The 19 miles of hiking trails at Sky Meadows State Park meander through woodlands and the pastures of a historical farm. Designated trails are also available for bicycles and horses.

From the parking lot, head west to the start of the hike. Follow this gravel path past a wooden fence and then turn left onto graveled Boston Mill Road. Interpretive signs along the way offer background on the road, which was named after nearby Bosetyn's Mill and connected area villages to various local mills. Follow the road for 0.2 mile, passing through the intersection with Gap Run Trail to South Ridge Trail. Turn right and make a quick left to keep following South Ridge Trail. The climb starts here.

South Ridge Trail leads into the woods and past the ruins of the old Snowden homestead. The trail swings to the right, and the incline increases. At 1.0 mile, you arrive at George's Overlook, complete with a bench and views of the Piedmont—a welcome spot to take a break and enjoy the scenery.

Steep climbs are now behind you for the next mile or so. From the overlook, the trail heads to the right and back into the woods, all along a steady but gradual uphill

LOCATION
Delaplane, VA

RATING
Moderate

DISTANCE
5.1 miles round-trip

ELEVATION GAIN
995 feet

ESTIMATED TIME
2-3 hours

MAPS
Sky Meadows State Park Trail Map (Sky Meadows State Park): dcr.virginia.gov/state-parks/document/data/trail-guide-skymeadows.pdf

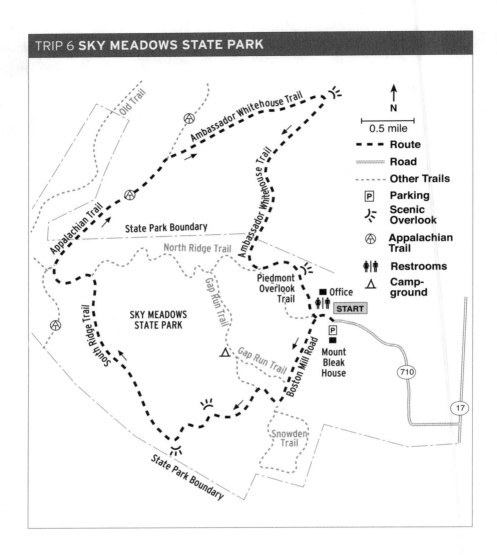

grade. Another bench along the way offers a place to rest if needed. At 1.9 miles, the path intersects North Ridge Trail; turn left for a short but steep climb to get your heart pumping again. The trail, which can be rocky at times, ends at the intersection with the Appalachian Trail at 2.5 miles. Turn right on the white-blazed Appalachian Trail, passing an intersection with purple-blazed Old Trail.

The trail slowly opens up into a wide meadow and remains relatively flat before arriving at the intersection with Ambassador Whitehouse Trail. Bear right to join Ambassador Whitehouse Trail and follow the broad, blue-blazed path through the meadow. The trail reaches Paris Overlook at 3.9 miles, with sweeping views you can enjoy from a perfectly situated picnic table.

Bucolic views of the Piedmont region make this hike a delight in any season.

From here, Ambassador Whitehouse Trail swings to the right and makes its way back into the woods. The trail passes a gas pipeline along the downhill slope and eventually meets up with North Ridge Trail at 4.5 miles. Make a left at this intersection and then another quick left onto red-blazed Piedmont Overlook Trail. A short 0.1-mile climb leads to a stile. Climb over the stile and enter the meadow for more views of the Piedmont from a well-placed bench.

When ready, follow the path down the meadow. (*Caution:* Cows sometimes graze this field and leave behind "mementos." Keep an eye on your footing.) The trail swings close to a wooden fence; pass through the stile on the right before crossing a short bridge. To the left, Boston Mill Road—the gravel road from the start of the hike—is within sight. Go down a set of steps to regain Boston Mill. Turn left and head back to your car.

DID YOU KNOW?

Sky Meadows is for the birds—bird-watching, that is. Bird-watchers flock to the park for its famous colony of red-headed woodpeckers, but they also can spy six other types of woodpeckers that are found in this part of Virginia: downy, hairy, red-bellied, and pileated woodpeckers; the northern flicker; and the yellow-bellied sapsucker.

MORE INFORMATION

For additional information, contact Sky Meadows State Park at 540-592-3556 or visit dcr.virginia.gov/state-parks/sky-meadows.shtml. The park is open daily, from 8:30 A.M. to dusk. All pets must be kept on a leash no longer than 6 feet. Year-round primitive hike-in camping is available at the designated camp-ground; for reservations, contact ReserveAmerica at reserveamerica.ccm or 800-933-7275.

NEARBY

Driving along VA 17 will take you past a few of Virginia's many wineries, perfect stops for sipping and snacking after the hike.

SECTION 2
SHENANDOAH NATIONAL PARK, NORTH DISTRICT

Shenandoah National Park's 200,000 protected acres encompass eight counties, 105 miles of Skyline Drive, and 101 miles of the Appalachian Trail—all within 75 miles of Washington, D.C. The park, one of the nation's most visited, welcomes more than 2 million people every year. It also has 79,579 acres that have been designated as Wilderness Areas. This designation, according to the 1964 Wilderness Act, is intended to preserve "the earth and its community of life" as "untrammeled by man, where man himself is a visitor who does not remain." Such Wilderness Areas also ensure that there are many wild places where hikers can escape the crowds who are just out for a scenic drive or stroll. (For a brief overview of park history, read the introduction to Section 3; for more on the park's ecology, read the introduction to Section 4.)

Shenandoah National Park's North District encompasses 25,000 acres of Wilderness Areas and stretches from Front Royal to Thornton Gap (from milepost 0 on Skyline Drive to just after milepost 31). Facilities in the area include the Dickey Ridge Visitor Center (between mileposts 4 and 5), 166 campsites in Mathews Arm Campground, and Elkwallow Wayside concession area and store (milepost 24). The Potomac Appalachian Trail Club maintains numerous cabins throughout the entire park, including Range View, which is off the Appalachian Trail, just east of Elkwallow Wayside (visit patc.net to make reservations). Throughout the park there are several overnight shelters on the Appalachian Trail or in its immediate vicinity.

Seventeen overlooks line Skyline Drive in this district; the highest peak here is Hogback Mountain (3,474 feet). The park's highest waterfall, at Overall Run (93 feet), is also here (Trip 10).

Several trips in this section begin at or pass through Elkwallow Wayside or Mathews Arm Campground, giving hikers direct access to concessions, carry-out food, and camping supplies without leaving the park.

7
COMPTON GAP

A short hike along the Appalachian Trail delivers a geological wonder along with western views.

DIRECTIONS

From I-66, take Exit 6 (Front Royal) and follow US 340 South for 2.1 miles. Turn left onto Skyline Drive (fee). The Compton Gap parking lot is located between mileposts 10 and 11. *GPS coordinates: 38° 49.424' N, 78° 10.233' W.*

TRAIL DESCRIPTION

The trail up to Compton Gap may be short, but it is well worth taking—and can deliver a bit of a challenge as it ascends nearly 500 feet along a sometimes rocky path to gain views of the surrounding area. From the parking lot, cross Skyline Drive and follow the white-blazed Appalachian Trail (AT), which is rather broad at this point and starts with a mild but steady gain. After passing a large boulder, the trail swings to the right and narrows slightly. More boulders dot the sides of the trail, which itself will get rocky at times as it steepens slightly and makes its way up stone steps and around rocky patches. Still, the route is easy to follow, despite a sharp left turn at 0.5 mile that can be tricky to spot. Keep an eye on the white blazes to assure you stay on the trail.

The trail maintains a steady climb to the ridge, steepening briefly at times. As it closes in on the summit, the trail swings to the right and starts to level out. Less than a mile from the start, you reach a concrete post that marks spur trails (both blazed blue) to the east and west. Both are less than 0.2 mile in length, and both are worth exploring.

The rocky western spur trail (to the right) briefly climbs before a slight dip that leads to an outlook with unobstructed views of the park, Skyline Drive, and Massanutten

LOCATION
North District, Shenandoah National Park, VA

RATING
Easy

DISTANCE
2.2 miles round-trip

ELEVATION GAIN
763 feet

ESTIMATED TIME
1-2 hours

MAPS
Map 9, Appalachian Trail and other trails in Shenandoah National Park, North District, 2015 (PATC): www.patc.net/PATC/ Our_Store/PATC_Maps.aspx

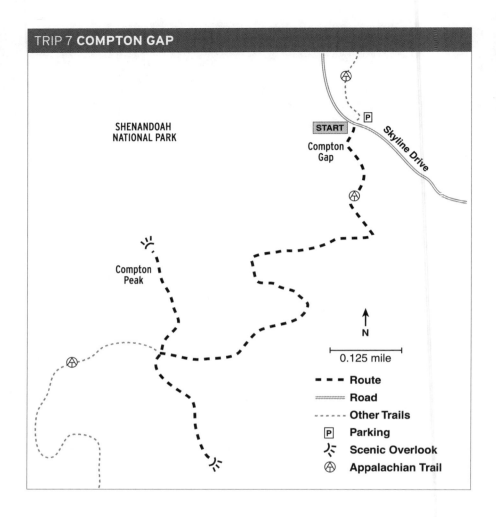

SHENANDOAH
NATIONAL PARK

START

Compton
Gap

Skyline Drive

Compton
Peak

P

N

0.125 mile

- - - Route
===== Road
----- Other Trails
P Parking
Scenic Overlook
Appalachian Trail

Mountain. Consider saving this spur trail as the second to explore, as it offers an excellent stopping point for lunch or a break.

Follow the eastern spur trail (to the left) for some geology. This trail dips down before arriving at a large boulder. It's possible to climb to the top for some views, but they are a bit obstructed. Continue past the boulder and descend rather steeply to see an example of a geologic phenomenon known as columnar jointing. This particular rock is part of the Catoctin Formation and is metamorphosed basalt formed around 700 million years ago. Rifting and other tectonic activity caused lava flows that cooled quickly when exposed, which led to the rock forming in distinct columns, rather than blocks. It's a marvel to see up close and well worth the effort to get there.

After exploring both spur trails, return to the concrete post and retrace your steps along the AT back to the parking lot and your car. If you want to know

You don't have to be a geology expert to be amazed by the dramatic example of columnar jointing that you'll see on this hike.

more about columnar jointing, check out a signpost in the parking lot that offers some information.

DID YOU KNOW?

The striking look of columnar jointing can be found across the world and in much larger arenas. The most famous example is the Giant's Causeway in Northern Ireland, which was featured as part of the artwork on Led Zeppelin's *Houses of the Holy* album.

MORE INFORMATION

Shenandoah National Park (nps.gov/shen, 540-999-3500, 800-732-0911 [for emergencies]). Park facilities are generally open from March through late November; a schedule is online. In cases of inclement weather and at night in deer-hunting season (mid-November through early January), call the park to confirm whether

Skyline Drive is open to vehicles. Overnight accommodations in the park include lodges, cabins, and campgrounds; visit nps.gov/shen/planyourvisit/lodging.htm or nps.gov/shen/planyourvisit/campgrounds.htm for more information.

NEARBY

The trails in this trip sit near the top of Skyline Drive, placing them close to Front Royal. This town has a number of stores, shops, and restaurants to fit most budgets and cuisine preferences. Consider pairing this hike with Dickey Ridge (Trip 9) if time allows.

SKYLINE DRIVE: BUILDING "A WONDER WAY"

When searching for a location to establish a national park in the eastern United States, many had their eyes on the Appalachian Mountains. These mountains fit the bill: A park along this range would be close enough to serve the 40 million Americans then living in cities on the East Coast, including Washington, D.C.

It wasn't easy, however, to open a national park in the East. Unlike the western half of the United States, there were not many public lands left. Decades—if not centuries—of logging also had taken their toll. Fears of a "timber famine" were mounting, as deforestation led to large swaths of cutover trees. The disappearance of these forests was causing wildfires, erosion, and flooding in nearby communities. The creation of the Forest Reserve Act in 1891 gave the president the authority to set aside public land to protect watersheds—lands that would eventually be known as national forests—but many people felt that more needed to be done. Citizens formed groups, such as the Appalachian National Park Association, begun in 1899, to urge the protection of natural resources. The group was renamed Appalachian National Forest Reserve Association in 1903 and disbanded just two years later, but its mission to create a national park in the Appalachians was taken up by the American Forestry Association.

Congress again stepped in to help. The Weeks Act of 1911, advocated for by the Appalachian Mountain Club and like-minded groups, paved the way for the creation of a national forest system in the eastern United States, allowing the U.S. Forest Service to start acquiring land. In the meantime, the idea of a national park in the Appalachian Mountains continued to gain steam. The U.S. Department of the Interior formed the Southern Appalachian National Park Committee in 1924 to study options for a national park. Concerns about deforestation had brought them to the Blue Ridge Mountains as a way to protect area resources. But the advent of—and fascination with—the automobile led to the additional suggestion of a "sky-line drive" that would provide tourists with views of the surrounding valleys.

Two years later, in 1926, Congress enacted a bill to create two national parks in the Appalachian Mountains: Great Smoky Mountains National Park and Shenandoah National Park. Officials broke ground on Skyline Drive in Shenandoah National Park in 1931. The project was largely an attempt to provide jobs and stimulate the economy during the Great Depression (see "Putting the Nation to Work," page 68). The goal was to create, as Senator Harry F. Byrd of Virginia put it, "a wonder way over which the tourist will ride comfortably in his car while he is stirred by a view as exhilarating as the aviator may see from the plane."

The groundwork for building a national park in Shenandoah was set, but hundreds of people still lived within the proposed boundaries. Some of them willingly sold their land to the government; others had to be forcibly displaced. A select few were allowed to live in the park for the remainder of their lives.

Annie Lee Bradley Shenk was the last of such residents with life tenancy; she passed away in 1979 at age 92. As families moved out of the area, the Civilian Conservation Corps (CCC) moved in to eradicate any visible sign of the former residents' existence. Keen-eyed hikers can still spot the remains of foundations and chimneys, but entire communities were removed from the region. The park encompasses at least 100 cemeteries, however, including the Fox Family Cemetery along Dickey Ridge (Trip 9) and Bolen Cemetery along Little Devils Stairs (Trip 11).

Work on the park and Skyline Drive moved quickly. The section of Skyline Drive from Thornton Gap to Swift Run Gap opened to the public on September 15, 1934. In 1936, the section from Thornton Gap to Front Royal opened, and the remaining sections—Swift Run to Jarman Gap and Rockfish Gap—opened in 1939. In total, Skyline Drive stretches 105 miles through Shenandoah National Park, featuring 75 overlooks and numerous hiking trails. Nearly 2 million people travel along the drive each year.

Read more about the creation of, and the debate behind, Skyline Drive in *Blazing Ahead: Benton MacKaye, Myron Avery, and the Rivalry That Built the Appalachian Trail*, by Jeffrey H. Ryan (AMC Books, 2017).

8

BIG DEVILS STAIRS

From Skyline Drive, descend into the steep canyon of Big Devils Stairs and peer down on the creek below.

DIRECTIONS

From I-66, take Exit 13 and follow VA 55 West for about 5 miles through Front Royal, then turn left onto US 340 South. In about 0.5 mile, turn left onto Skyline Drive and enter the park (fee). The Gravel Springs Gap parking lot is on the left, past milepost 17. *GPS coordinates:* 38° 46.071′ N, 78° 14.013′ W.

TRAIL DESCRIPTION

This fairly straightforward out-and-back hike is complicated slightly by the web of trails that weave around the Appalachian Trail (AT) and Gravel Springs Hut. In the parking lot, orient yourself by noting that the AT crosses Skyline Drive in the gap. You will not be walking on the AT for this trip.

Instead, head south on an old, grassy forest road leading straight out of the lot. This road bends sharply to your left in a little more than 0.1 mile. After the bend, keep an eye out to your left: At the next turn in the road (0.3 mile), a post marks a footpath. Head straight into the woods on that path and descend gently to the next intersection. A trail on the right leads to an AT shelter, which is not your destination. Yellow-blazed Bluff Trail, on the left (west) at 0.5 mile, continues toward Big Devils Stairs. A little farther along, a signpost marks Harris Trail—don't take that trail. Instead, swing left and stay on the yellow-blazed trail.

Heading west on Bluff Trail is comparatively smooth sailing. Over the next 1.4 miles, the path rolls some but generally stays level. At 1.8 miles, Bluff Trail intersects Big Devils Stairs Trail; turn right to follow the blue blazes. At first, Big Devils Stairs Trail is fairly flat as it passes a few improvised campsites tucked in among the rhododendrons, but the

LOCATION
North District, Shenandoah National Park, VA

RATING
Moderate

DISTANCE
4.7 miles round-trip

ELEVATION GAIN
1,313 feet

ESTIMATED TIME
2-4 hours

MAPS
Map 9, Appalachian Trail and other trails in Shenandoah National Park, North District, 2015 (PATC): www.patc.net/PATC/ Our_Store/PATC_Maps.aspx

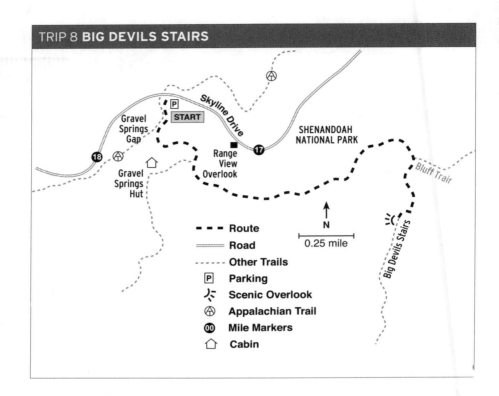

trail begins to lose elevation quickly. As it dives about 500 feet to the cliffs, the echoing sound of rushing water greets you. The trail brings you to the first overlook; follow a series of stone steps down to the best views. Explore a little farther along the cliffs to discover a few other vistas of the steep canyon walls and the creek below.

Big Devils Stairs Trail continues past these overlooks, but there is no access from the base of the park, and there are few sights, so the rarely walked section of trail becomes sketchy. If you're keen for some additional exercise, however, feel free to explore to the trail's end.

To return, climb Big Devils Stairs Trail back to Bluff Trail and take a left. As you approach Skyline Drive, two right-hand turns bring you to the parking lot.

If by chance you end up at Gravel Springs Hut instead, just continue until you reach the AT, then turn right to get to Skyline Drive and the parking lot.

DID YOU KNOW?

Big Devils Stairs Trail used to follow the course of the streambed, much like its cousin Little Devils Stairs (Trip 11). After the trail had been washed out repeatedly, however, the National Park Service decided to relocate it to the cliffs overlooking the gorge. Remnants of the old trail are still there, but they have not been maintained in many years.

Hikers take time out to relax and enjoy the view of the gorge on the Big Devils Stairs route.

MORE INFORMATION

Shenandoah National Park (nps.gov/shen, 540-999-3500, 800-732-0911 [for emergencies]). Park facilities are generally open from March through late November; a schedule is online. In cases of inclement weather and at night in deer-hunting season (mid-November through early January), call the park to confirm whether Skyline Drive is open to vehicles. Overnight accommodations in the park include lodges, cabins, and campgrounds; for more information, visit nps.gov/shen/planyourvisit/lodging.htm or nps.gov/shen/planyourvisit/campgrounds.htm.

NEARBY

There's plenty of additional hiking to be done in the northern Shenandoah. Consider hiking Little Devils Stairs (Trip 11), which offers quite a different experience, or branch out to try Overall Run (Trip 10) or Jeremy's Run (Trip 12). A little additional driving will take you to the riches of the Central District as well.

After any of these hikes, consider stopping in Front Royal, if you're leaving the park to the north, or Sperryville, if you're leaving from Thornton Gap.

9

DICKEY RIDGE

Located close to the park's northern entrance, this hike takes you on a tour of some local history as you pass remnants of Shenandoah's family farms.

DIRECTIONS

From I-66, take Exit 6 (Front Royal) and follow US 340 South for 2.1 miles. Turn left to enter Shenandoah National Park and Skyline Drive (fee). The Dickey Ridge Visitor Center is between mileposts 4 and 5. *GPS coordinates:* 38° 52.263′ N, 78° 12.260′ W.

TRAIL DESCRIPTION

This easy-to-moderate hike keeps it simple, following a well-marked trail past ruins of the Fox family farm on the first loop and Snead Farm on the second loop. Hikers seeking an even shorter option can pick one of the loops—both deliver an interesting peek into the park's history.

From the visitor center parking lot, cross Skyline Drive and head for the large sign to the trailhead. Follow the path to your left, which quickly intersects with blue-blazed Dickey Ridge Trail (marked by a concrete post). Head left again and follow Dickey Ridge Trail for 0.3 mile to its intersection with Fox Hollow Trail. Take a right onto Fox Hollow Trail.

This unblazed trail follows a rather obvious path down through the remains of the Fox homestead, passing the remains of old stone walls that were created by the family using rocks they cleared from the field. Before long, you arrive at the family cemetery. The path takes a sharp right turn after the cemetery and starts heading uphill, passing an old spring that was used by the family. If you look carefully, you'll also spot a millstone. At 1.2 miles, Fox Hollow

LOCATION
North District, Shenandoah National Park, VA

RATING
Easy to Moderate

DISTANCE
4.9 miles round-trip

ELEVATION GAIN
1,130 feet

ESTIMATED TIME
2-3 hours

MAPS
Map 9, Appalachian Trail and other trails in Shenandoah National Park, North District, 2015 (PATC): www.patc.net/PATC/ Our_Store/PATC_Maps.aspx

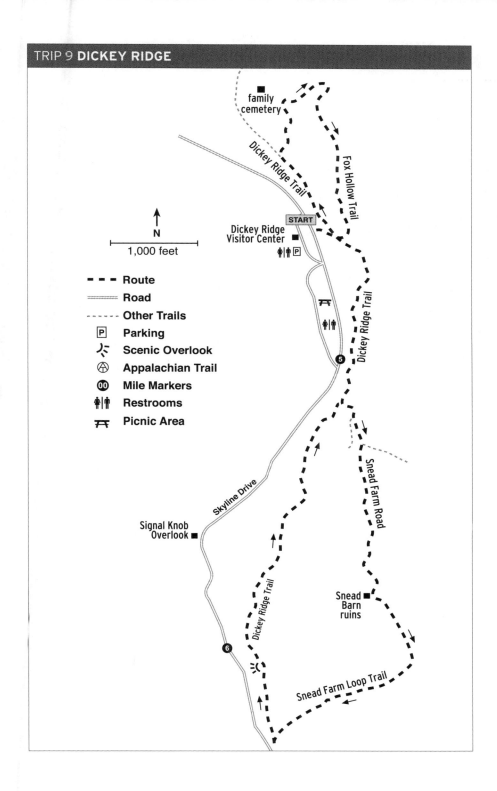

family
cemetery

Dickey Ridge Trail

Fox Hollow Trail

START

Dickey Ridge
Visitor Center

N

1,000 feet

- - - Route
===== Road
----- Other Trails
P   Parking
.ᶫ   Scenic Overlook
Ⓐ   Appalachian Trail
⓪⓪ Mile Markers
♦|♦ Restrooms
⊼   Picnic Area

Dickey Ridge Trail

5

Snead Farm Road

Skyline Drive

Signal Knob
Overlook ■

Snead
Barn
ruins

Dickey Ridge Trail

6

Snead Farm Loop Trail

Steps and a foundation are all that remain of the Snead Farm house. They serve as a reminder of the families who once resided in the area before the park was formed.

Trail returns to its previous intersection with Dickey Ridge Trail. Turn left to follow Dickey Ridge Trail for the second loop of the hike.

A brief and pleasant walk along the blue-blazed trail leads to an intersection with Snead Farm Road, a wide fire road, at 1.7 miles. Turn left, and in a few short steps you pass an intersection with a trail coming in from the woods on the right (your return route). Continue along Snead Farm Road, which has two well-marked forks in quick succession. At the first fork, stay to your left and head downhill. The second fork is just a short distance away; here, follow the path to the right that leads up the hill. At 2.4 miles, this grassy path arrives at the remains of Snead Farm, which was abandoned in the 1950s. The barn—one of the last non–National Park Service structures in the park— still stands, and you can see the stone foundation of the house.

After exploring the ruins, look for a concrete post and follow Snead Farm Loop Trail (blue-blazed) back into the woods. This path maintains a steady and mild uphill track and eventually leads to Dickey Ridge Trail at 3.1 miles. Turn right and continue to climb on Dickey Ridge Trail. Good views of the valley open on the left. Keep a lookout for a short spur trail at 3.3 miles that leads to a nice open outlook where you can take in the valley, the SouthFork of the Shenandoah River, and Massanutten Mountain.

The trail continues uphill for a short distance before descending on an easier grade and then regains the fire road at 4.3 miles. Turn left onto the fire road, and then make a quick right to stay on Dickey Ridge Trail. Retrace your steps back along this trail. At the intersection marked with the concrete post (4.8 miles), turn left to complete the hike and return to the visitor center.

Since this route follows a figure-eight shape, you can choose to shorten it by taking just one of the two loops. The first loop is roughly 1.2 miles, and the second loop is 3.7 miles.

DID YOU KNOW?

Four generations of the Fox family lived in Shenandoah before being displaced to make room for the creation of the park. Thomas and Martha Fox settled in Fox Hollow in 1856; Lemuel Fox Jr. and his wife, Martha, left in 1935.

MORE INFORMATION

Shenandoah National Park (nps.gov/shen, 540-999-3500, 800-732-0911 [for emergencies]). Park facilities are generally open from March through late November; a schedule is online. In cases of inclement weather and at night in deer-hunting season (mid-November through early January), call the park to confirm whether Skyline Drive is open to vehicles. Overnight accommodations in the park include lodges, cabins, and campgrounds; visit nps.gov/shen/planyourvisit/lodging.htm or nps.gov/shen/planyourvisit/campgrounds.htm for more information.

NEARBY

The trails in this hike sit at the top of Skyline Drive, placing them close to Front Royal. This town has a number of stores, shops, and restaurants to fit most budgets and cuisine preferences. If time permits, consider pairing this hike with Compton Gap (Trip 7), just a short distance down Skyline Drive.

10

OVERALL RUN

This ramble in Shenandoah's North District features one of the finest sights in the area: the 93-foot falls at Overall Run, which can be especially spectacular in spring.

LOCATION
North District, Shenandoah National Park, VA

RATING
Strenuous

DISTANCE
9.5-mile loop

ELEVATION GAIN
3,094 feet

ESTIMATED TIME
4-6 hours

MAPS
Map 9, Appalachian Trail and other trails in Shenandoah National Park, North District, 2015 (PATC): www.patc.net/PATC/Our_Store/PATC_Maps.aspx

DIRECTIONS
From I-66, Exit 43A, take US 29 South 13.2 miles to Warrenton. Turn right onto US 211 and drive for 34.0 miles. West of Sperryville, US 211 twists and turns before meeting the Thornton Gap park entrance (fee). Enter the park and drive north (right) on Skyline Drive for about 9 miles. After passing Elkwallow Wayside on your left, turn left onto Mathews Arm Road, a little farther down the road. Park in the hikers' lot on your right, near the Mathews Arm Campground gate. *GPS coordinates:* 38° 45.599′ N, 78° 17.837′ W.

TRAIL DESCRIPTION
This strenuous route essentially circumnavigates Mathews Arm Campground, descending the Blue Ridge on Heiskell Hollow Trail and then climbing back up again via Overall Run—Tuscarora Trail. When you're ready to begin hiking, walk on the pavement past the entrance to the campground—this is Mathews Arm Road. Beyond the entrance, bear left on Knob Mountain Road. Pass the hook-up station for RVs, walk around a gate, and then continue downhill on a road that turns to gravel. Shortly thereafter, at 0.5 mile, you'll see a post on the right indicating the Heiskell Hollow trailhead—the start of your route. On the left is a sign for Knob Mountain Trail.

Begin your descent of the western face of the Shenandoah by following yellow-blazed Heiskell Hollow Trail, which drops 1,500 feet over the next 2.4 miles into the drainage of Compton Run. The trail turns sharply to the right, then reaches an intersection with Weddlewood

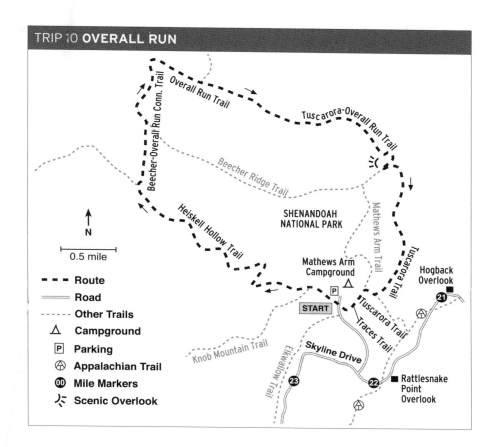

Trail, also blazed yellow, at 1.25 miles. This trail cuts across the mountain's shoulder and reaches Overall Run from above. However, your route turns sharply to the left as you continue on Heiskell Hollow Trail. As you descend, listen carefully for the sound of water on the left. Soon, the hollow flattens out, and the trail follows the stream before reaching an intersection on the right with Beecher Ridge Trail at 2.9 miles.

Turn right, cross the water several times in the stream bottom, and follow the yellow blazes as Beecher Ridge Trail traverses the western face of the Shenandoah at its knees. The path climbs some and becomes sandy. In spring, mountain laurels bloom around you. At 3.9 miles, the ascent tops out at an intersection on Beecher Ridge, where Beecher Ridge Trail heads right to follow the ridge back toward Skyline Drive. Instead, stay left and follow the blue-blazed Beecher Ridge–Overall Run Connector Trail as it descends into the Overall Run valley at 4.6 miles.

After a few creek crossings, the path reaches the very base of Overall Run Trail. Turn right to follow this blue-blazed trail as it rises toward Mathews Arm—almost 2,500 feet and 4.4 miles away. For the first section, the grade is fairly gentle as the route follows the run, which is on the right. At 5.25 miles, you

The view westward from Overall Run includes the South Fork of the Shenandoah River, as well as Massanutten Mountain. Kennedy Peak, Signal Knob, and Buzzard Rock are also visible from this perch.

pass a path leading off to the left, which is the Tuscarora Trail, headed out of the park. Continue straight onto what is now Overall Run–Tuscarora Trail. The footing becomes rocky, and you cross the run several times.

When the trail pulls away from the last water crossing to the left (6.25 miles), it gets serious about ascending the mountain, switchbacking very steeply for a section, then heading straight uphill. Thankfully, this difficult climb ends at 6.8 miles, rewarding you with a stunning view of Massanutten Mountain to the west, as well as of the valley out of which you've climbed. Take time to explore the outcroppings and a short spur trail farther down the path for opportunities to photograph and to get closer to the falls. The grade relents above this point, but the climbing continues.

Navigating the web of trails around Mathews Arm can be tricky, but never fear, because a serious error would be difficult to make. At 7.25 miles, you reach turnoffs to the left and the right, very close together, for Mathews Arm Trail. Ignore these and continue to follow Overall Run–Tuscarora Trail, which brings you to an intersection at 9.1 miles. At this intersection, bear right and then left to follow Traces Trail (unblazed, but very easy to follow) as it rounds the campground and brings you back to your vehicle.

If you are looking to shorten this loop, consider descending Beecher Ridge Trail instead of Heiskell Hollow Trail. A slightly longer trip could start from the Appalachian Trail parking lot near Hogback Overlook off Skyline Drive.

DID YOU KNOW?

As you're climbing Overall Run, for much of the distance you'll be walking on the first few miles of the Tuscarora Trail, a variant of the Appalachian Trail that starts in the Shenandoah and rejoins the Appalachian Trail just shy of Harrisburg, Pennsylvania (see "The Tuscarora Trail," page 174). As the Tuscarora Trail leaves the national park, it descends via the Overall Run valley to cross the Shenandoah River and then reach Massanutten Mountain.

MORE INFORMATION

Shenandoah National Park (nps.gov/shen, 540-999-3500, 800-732-0911 [for emergencies]). Park facilities are generally open from March through late November; a schedule is online. In cases of inclement weather and at night in deer-hunting season (mid-November through early January), call the park to confirm whether Skyline Drive is open to vehicles. Overnight accommodations in the park include lodges, cabins, and campgrounds, one of which is Mathews Arm Campground; visit nps.gov/shen/planyourvisit/lodging.htm or nps.gov/shen/planyourvisit/campgrounds.htm for more information.

NEARBY

This book describes a number of additional hikes in Shenandoah's Northern District, including Little Devils Stairs (Trip 11) and Jeremy's Run (Trip 12).

Once you've hiked to your heart's content, consider stopping at Elkwallow Wayside or Mathews Arm for a picnic or a snack. The nearest good-sized town is Front Royal (44 minutes via the north entrance), but Sperryville offers several eateries and shops (31 minutes via the Thornton Gap entrance). You can find a wider range of businesses in Warrenton (a little over an hour away and back in D.C.'s suburbs).

11

LITTLE DEVILS STAIRS

Winding its way between the steep cliffs of a gorge, Little Devils Stairs is a classic Virginia climb, renowned for its wildness and its backcountry feel, even though it is just steps away from the Appalachian Trail and Skyline Drive.

DIRECTIONS

From I-66, Exit 43A, take US 29 South 13.2 miles to Warrenton. Turn right onto US 211 and drive for 24.8 miles. About 2 miles shy of Sperryville, turn right onto VA 622/Gidbrown Hollow Road and proceed 1.9 miles. Then turn left onto VA 614/Keyser Hollow Run and drive about 3.1 miles. The parking lot on the right can hold about six cars. *GPS coordinates: 38° 43.836′ N, 78° 15.491′ W.*

TRAIL DESCRIPTION

In its first 2.0 miles, Little Devils Stairs Trail takes you on one of the most picturesque climbs in the Shenandoah as it twists and turns past waterfalls, steep rock faces, rockfalls, and dark forests. And climb it does—about 1,600 feet. At points the trail will be steep (as much as a 45 percent grade, though that stretch is mercifully short) and slick. If the mountains are at all wet, you may discover that the trail is colocated with the creek. (*Caution:* If there's been much rain or if there's any chance of ice, conditions in the gorge can become hazardous.) Don't forget your camera; many places along Little Devils Stairs make for excellent photographs.

From the parking lot, blue-blazed Little Devils Stairs Trail heads straight into the woods. Before you embark, however, note Keyser Run Fire Road on the left, as you'll be returning this way at the hike's end.

As the trail leads you into the forest, easily rock-hop to cross two streams. At first, the grade is moderate, but the

LOCATION
North District, Shenandoah National Park, VA

RATING
Strenuous

DISTANCE
5.7 miles round-trip

ELEVATION GAIN
1,940 feet

ESTIMATED TIME
3-5 hours

MAPS
Map 9, Appalachian Trail and other trails in Shenandoah National Park, North District, 2015 (PATC): www.patc.net/PATC/Our_Store/PATC_Maps.aspx

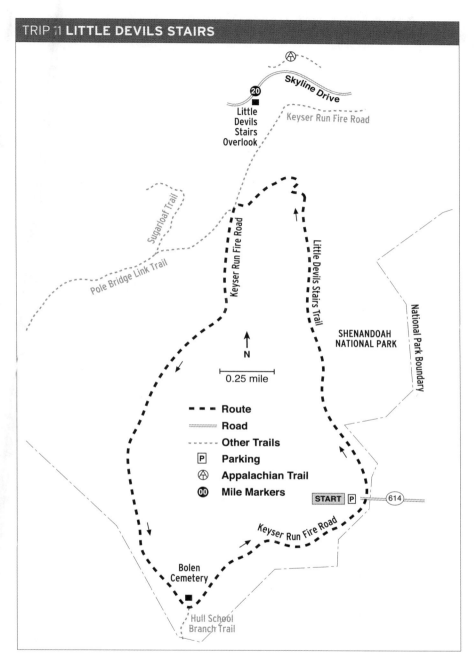

trail soon draws near Keyser Run, the stream that has eroded the gorge over time. Here, the climbing begins in earnest. Take your time, however, because the steepest areas are also the most scenic. The route crosses Keyser Run numerous times and ascends staircases of stone, passing between forbidding rock walls. Admire the waterfalls but keep an eye on the blue blazes. It's possible to stray off

The climb up the canyon of Little Devils Stairs is memorable for its beauty, as well as for the effort it requires. Here, a hiker ascends the rocky switchbacks.

the trail a bit, but you won't go far in this tight gulley. If you feel at all astray, just turn back to where you last saw a blaze.

At last, the trail crosses the run one final time and begins to veer leftward away from the gorge at 1.8 miles, climbing still, but at a less relentless grade as it switchbacks to the intersection known as Fourway (2.0 miles). Directly across this intersection, Pole Bridge Link Trail leads south toward Elkwallow, while Keyser Run Fire Road runs to the left and the right. Turning right here brings you to a small parking area off Skyline Drive. Turn left to continue your route and follow the fire road back to the trailhead.

The 3.5-mile descent down yellow-blazed Keyser Run Fire Road will be uneventful as it loses the elevation you worked so hard to gain. The road itself, however, takes a fairly moderate grade, so it will also be pleasant walking. Following the yellow blazes, pass Hull School Trail on your right at 4.3 miles and the Bolen Family Cemetery just a little farther on your left. Eventually, the trail passes a gate and arrives back at the parking lot.

If you're looking for a longer route (about 7.9 miles), consider taking Pole Bridge Link Trail from Fourway to Piney Branch Trail and then returning to Keyser Run Fire Road via Hull School Trail. Add Piney Ridge Trail to this for an even longer trip. These options keep to the footpaths and off the fire road, so some hikers may prefer them.

DID YOU KNOW?

The Bolen Family Cemetery, which is on the left as you descend Keyser Run Fire Road, is a reminder of the settlers who inhabited these hollows before the establishment of the national park in the 1930s. If you have a keen eye, you may be able to spot some remnants of old stone walls and foundations along Little Devils Stairs.

MORE INFORMATION

Shenandoah National Park (nps.gov/shen, 540-999-3500, 800-732-0911 [for emergencies]). Park facilities are generally open from March through late November; a schedule is online. In cases of inclement weather and at night in deer-hunting season (mid-November through early January), call the park to confirm whether Skyline Drive is open to vehicles. Overnight accommodations in the park include lodges, cabins, and campgrounds; visit nps.gov/shen/planyourvisit/lodging.htm or nps.gov/shen/planyourvisit/campgrounds.htm for more information.

NEARBY

Sperryville, a little farther west from the intersection of VA 622 and US 211, offers several eateries and shops. You can find a wider range of businesses in Warrenton (about 40 minutes from the trailhead back to D.C.). If it's more hiking you're after, the North District of Shenandoah will not disappoint. See Overall Run (Trip 10) and Jeremy's Run (Trip 12).

12

JEREMY'S RUN AND KNOB MOUNTAIN

The highlight of this wet and wild leg-stretcher is the walk along Jeremy's Run, with its abundant cascades, pools, and waterfalls, not to mention the many creek crossings for which the hike is justly famous.

LOCATION
North District, Shenandoah National Park, VA

RATING
Strenuous

DISTANCE
13.1 miles round-trip

ELEVATION GAIN
3,164 feet

ESTIMATED TIME
5–8 hours

MAPS
Map 9, Appalachian Trail and other trails in Shenandoah National Park, North District, 2015 (PATC): www.patc.net/PATC/Our_Store/PATC_Maps.aspx

DIRECTIONS

From I-66, Exit 43A, take US 29 South 13.2 miles to Warrenton. Turn right onto US 211 and drive for 34.0 miles. West of Sperryville, US 211 twists and turns before meeting the park's Thornton Gap entrance (fee). Drive north (right) on Skyline Drive for 7.2 miles to Elkwallow Wayside on your left. Park in the ample lot. *GPS coordinates: 38° 44.336' N, 78° 18.564' W.*

TRAIL DESCRIPTION

Because this route is a bit isolated from Skyline Drive at the Appalachian Trail, you'll need to make a good-sized loop using Knob Mountain Trail to see Jeremy's Run in its entirety. Before beginning this circuit, consider conditions carefully: You'll be crossing the creek many times, and if the water is particularly high, you won't be able to stay dry. In warm weather, the cold water will feel refreshing, but no matter how steamy the summer heat, it is probably not prudent to attempt this hike if there's been a great deal of recent rainfall. In colder weather, resign yourself to chilly feet if you undertake this hike.

From the parking lot, look past the concession shop, to the north, to see the blue-blazed trail leading into the forest. A few feet into the woods, the trail joins the Appalachian Trail (AT). Turn left and follow the white blazes southbound, gently downhill, for about 0.6 mile.

Soon enough, you reach an intersection where the AT heads left (south), and blue-blazed Jeremy's Run Trail continues straight (west). Follow the blue blazes as the

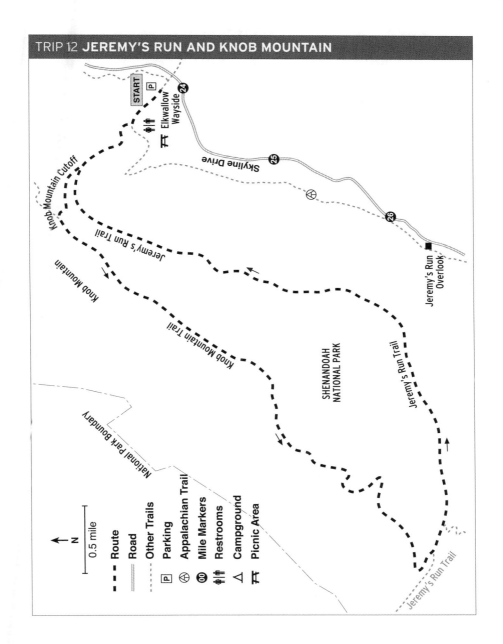

trail descends into the run's drainage. At an intersection at 1.3 miles, Jeremy's Run Trail reaches the creek and continues its descent straight ahead, but Knob Mountain Cutoff Trail branches right. Both are blazed blue, but there is a signpost that displays the trail names. (Take note of this intersection; you'll return to it near the end of the hike.) Take Knob Mountain Cutoff Trail to the right, cross the creek, and begin a short but sometimes steep climb to Knob Mountain Trail.

A hiker fords one of the many stream crossings on Jeremy's Run. If there has been much rain at all, you will find it quite a challenge to keep your feet dry.

At 1.9 miles, reach a saddle and turn left onto yellow-blazed Knob Mountain Trail. Over the next 2.1 miles, the path climbs about 680 feet, primarily along an old forest road, before it reaches a post marking the summit of Knob Mountain at 3.9 miles. Oddly, the post is a little short of the mountain's true summit so you still have a few more feet to climb. This significant mountain fences in Jeremy's Run on its westward flanks. Though the peak is fairly prominent compared with its neighbors, its summit is wooded and has few views. You may, however, be able to catch occasional glimpses of the valley below and of Massanutten Mountain to the west.

From Knob Mountain's summit, begin the 1,600-foot descent to the water. Though this is a considerable dropoff, the path is well graded and not especially rocky or treacherous. Eventually, the stream becomes audible, and at 6.9 miles the route forces you to ford the run for the first of many crossings. On the far side, turn left to follow the blue-blazed Jeremy's Run Trail and immediately pass the intersection for Neighbor Mountain Trail on the right. This route offers an opportunity for a different circuit hike (be warned, though, that it is a little longer, at almost 15 miles, and certainly a little harder).

For the next 5.0 miles, the path follows the fairly gentle walk up Jeremy's Run, the highlight of this trip and one of the finest hikes in the park. In the beginning of this section, the trail passes a large waterfall, which makes an excellent spot for a break. (Note the large campsite across the stream.) Each crossing provides an excellent opportunity to admire the pools and other features of the creek. You may also spot wildlife: Deer and black bears are common in this expansive valley.

Fourteen crossings later (but who's counting?), at 11.9 miles, the route regains the intersection with Knob Mountain Cutoff Trail. Bear right, and continue following the blue blazes of Jeremys Run Trail until you reach the AT at 12.5 miles. Follow the white blazes until you are virtually at the Elkwallow Wayside. Turn right to enter the parking lot.

If 13.0 miles seems a bit much, check with the National Park Service, as there's a lower trailhead near US 340 that would enable you to walk up the run as far as you like, then return back down. As this book when to press, access to the park via this route was closed due to a dispute with a landowner, but the Park Service was working to resolve the problem, so we've included the directions. Just off VA 611, which leaves VA 340 to head east toward the park, there is a parking lot that will enable you to reach the bottom of Jeremy's Run, as described here, after just 1.3 miles of walking. By walking out and back from this trailhead, you can get an idea of what the trail is like without having to commit to such a demanding loop. Of course, always respect the rights of landowners, and don't attempt this option without contacting the Park Service to see if the dispute has been resolved.

DID YOU KNOW?

Jeremy's Run features some of the best fishing in the park. To learn more about the rules for fishing in Shenandoah National Park, see the Park Service's flyer on the topic at nps.gov/shen/planyourvisit/upload/FishingRegulations.pdf.

MORE INFORMATION

Shenandoah National Park (nps.gov/shen, 540-999-3500, 800-732-0911 [for emergencies]). Park facilities are generally open from March through late November; a schedule is online. In cases of inclement weather and at night in deer-hunting season (mid-November through early January), call the park to confirm whether Skyline Drive is open to vehicles. Overnight accommodations in the park include lodges, cabins, and campgrounds; visit nps.gov/shen/planyourvisit/lodging.htm or nps.gov/shen/planyourvisit/campgrounds.htm for more information.

NEARBY

This book describes a number of additional hikes in the North District, including Overall Run (Trip 10) and Little Devils Stairs (Trip 11). Of course, the park's Central District is not far, either.

The little store at the Elkwallow Wayside sells a number of treats, and you can also find concessions at Mathews Arm, a few miles north along Skyline Drive. If you're in pursuit of more substantial fare, then your best bet is to drive north to Front Royal (45 minutes) or south to Sperryville (26 minutes) or Luray (27 minutes).

13

BLUFF-A.T.-MOUNT MARSHALL TRAILS

Stretch your legs along this challenging trip with two epic views from North and South Marshall mountains.

DIRECTIONS

From I-66, take Exit 6 (Front Royal) and follow US 340 South for 2.1 miles. Turn left onto Skyline Drive (fee). The Jenkins Gap parking lot is between mileposts 12 and 13. *GPS coordinates: 38° 48.235' N, 78° 10.492' W.*

TRAIL DESCRIPTION

Although on the long side, this hike is an excellent option if you're interested in trying out high-mileage days. Hiking it clockwise allows you to warm up your legs on a relatively flat stretch before the climb—and the views—begin.

From the Jenkins Gap parking lot, cross Skyline Drive and walk south (0.2 mile) until you come to the turn for Mount Marshall Trail. Go left here and follow the yellow-blazed trail as it makes its way down the mountain. To the left, a stream gurgles within sight, and you eventually arrive at an easy crossing. Overall, the hiking along this stretch is relatively easy—a wide, flat trail with a few stream crossings, none of which are too difficult. It's a nice way to begin a lengthy trek.

Before too long, about 3.8 miles into the hike, Bluff Trail intersects with Mount Marshall Trail. Bear to the right to pick up yellow-blazed Bluff Trail. From here, the route gets a little more complicated, with short climbs and descents that weave around rock outcroppings. Pass the intersection with the blue-blazed trail for Big Devils Stairs (Trip 8) around the 6.0-mile mark and continue along Bluff Trail, which now settles into a mild but steady ascent.

As the trail approaches Gravel Springs Hut, it swings to the right and heads uphill, eventually transitioning into a

LOCATION
North District, Shenandoah National Park, VA

RATING
Strenuous

DISTANCE
13.5-mile loop

ELEVATION GAIN
2,089 feet

ESTIMATED TIME
6-7 hours

MAPS
Map 9, Appalachian Trail and other trails in Shenandoah National Park, North District, 2015 (PATC): www.patc.net/PATC/Our_Store/PATC_Maps.aspx

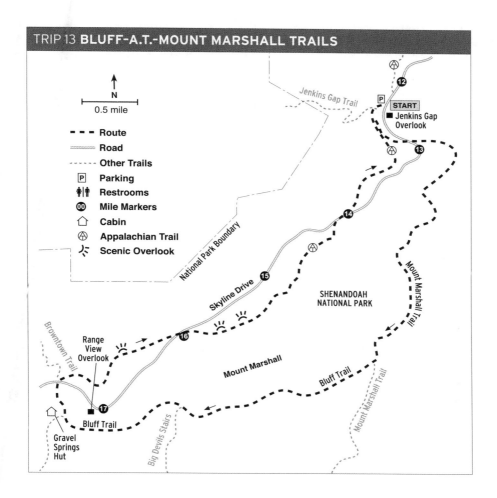

fire road. Off to the left, another trail—the white-blazed Appalachian Trail (AT)—starts to parallel your path. Stay on the yellow-blazed trail and cross Skyline Drive (7.6 miles) to arrive at an intersection with the AT. Turn right here to start following the AT. The trail climbs slowly at first, then more earnestly as it nears one of two outstanding views along this section: an overlook on South Marshall, the first of Mount Marshall's two summits, that yields a vista of the Shenandoah Valley, the winding forks of the Shenandoah River, and Massanutten Mountain in the distance.

After enjoying the scenery—and perhaps even some lunch or snacks—proceed along the AT. Side trails lead to smaller overlooks, providing even more opportunities to pause and take in the sights, and the trail soon crosses Skyline Drive again, now heading toward North Marshall, the second of Mount Marshall's two summits. Follow the white blazes as the path becomes rockier and then climbs steadily, at one point along stone steps, before arriving at a rock

A hiker approaches one of the viewpoints located along Mount Marshall.

outcropping (9.9 miles) where adventurous hikers can scramble to check out more views, this time to the east of the valley below.

From here, the trail climbs a bit more before easing out again, crossing Skyline Drive one more time. The route passes through Hogwallow Flats and then by the foundation of a planned comfort station for park visitors that was never completed. It gently descends to an intersection with yellow-blazed Jenkins Gap Trail. Turn right onto Jenkins Gap Trail and follow it just a few steps to return to the parking lot and to your car.

DID YOU KNOW?

Mount Marshall is named after the Marshall family who lived in the area. The most famous member of this family is John Marshall, who was both the longest-serving chief justice of the United States and the longest-serving justice on the Supreme Court.

MORE INFORMATION

Shenandoah National Park (nps.gov/shen, 540-999-3500, 800-732-0911 [for emergencies]). Park facilities are generally open from March through late November; a schedule is online.

In cases of inclement weather and at night in deer-hunting season (mid-November through early January), call the park to confirm whether Skyline Drive is open to vehicles. Overnight accommodations in the park include lodges, cabins, and campgrounds; visit nps.gov/shen/planyourvisit/lodging.htm or nps.gov/shen/planyourvisit/campgrounds.htm for more information.

NEARBY

The trails in this trip sit at the top of Skyline Drive, placing them close to Front Royal, which has a number of stores, shops, and restaurants to fit most budgets and cuisine preferences.

SECTION 3
SHENANDOAH NATIONAL PARK, CENTRAL DISTRICT

Though European settlers only reached the heights of what is now Shenandoah National Park as recently as 300 years ago, evidence of human habitation here goes back 8,000 to 9,000 years. However, Native people were more often visitors than residents, combing the mountains for resources, including wild game, nuts and berries, and stone for tools. Around 1750, however, the first settlers began homesteading in the hollows, quickly opening doors for a community of farmers, loggers, and hunters. By the early twentieth century, these residents were a barrier to the protection of this land as a national park. In the 1930s at least 500 families were relocated, and the Civilian Conservation Corps (CCC) began constructing Skyline Drive, overlooks, and other facilities that make the park what it is today. The CCC's construction work took years, beginning in 1933, two years before the park was officially established; the last CCC camp was disbanded in 1942, shortly after America entered World War II. Much of this human history is still preserved along the trails, particularly in Nicholson, Corbin, and Weakley hollows, where cellar holes and stone walls are ghostly reminders of what these hills were before the park came to be. (For a brief overview of the park and its Wilderness Areas, read the introduction to Section 2; for more on the park's ecology, read the introduction to Section 4; to learn more about the communities

Facing page: Hawksbill Summit provides commanding views of the surrounding countryside.

displaced by the creation of the park, see "Skyline Drive: Building a 'A Wonder Way,'" on page 33.)

Shenandoah National Park's central district encompasses more than 21,000 acres of designated Wilderness between Thornton Gap and Swift Run Gap (just after milepost 31 on Skyline Drive to milepost 65.5). Many of the park's overnight options are in this area, including Skyland Resort (milepost 41.7), Big Meadows Lodge and Campground (milepost 51), Lewis Mountain Campground and Cabins (milepost 57.5), and four Potomac Appalachian Trail Club cabins: Corbin, Jones Mountain, Rock Spring, and Pocosin (visit patc.net to make reservations). The Byrd Visitor Center is located at milepost 51. Picnic areas include Pinnacles (milepost 36.5) and South River (milepost 62.5). The segment of Skyline Drive in this district boasts 32 overlooks, as well as access to the park's highest peak, Hawksbill (Trip 21, 4,051 feet).

14

LIMBERLOST

Designed to meet Americans with Disabilities Act (ADA) standards, Limberlost Trail packs in spring blooms, chances to see wildlife, and a bit of geology for those who explore this path.

DIRECTIONS

From I-66, Exit 43A, take US 29 South 13.2 miles to Warrenton. Turn right onto US 211 and drive for 34.0 miles. West of Sperryville, US 211 twists and turns before meeting the park's Thornton Gap entrance (fee). Enter the park and drive south on Skyline Drive to the Limberlost Parking Area (milepost 43). *GPS coordinates:* 38° 34.482′ N, 78° 22.523′ W.

TRAIL DESCRIPTION

Limberlost Trail is a fully accessible route in Shenandoah National Park, complete with stone benches and numerous resting areas throughout its 1.4 miles.

From the parking area, look for the information board. The trail starts and ends here. To make the trip counterclockwise, look to your right for the start of Limberlost Trail. The walkway is made up of crushed greenstone, making for a relatively flat and packed surface.

Limberlost Trail makes its way through the woods, passing mountain laurels, a truly stunning sight in late May or early June when the white flowers bloom. The route crosses a bridge about 0.5 mile into the hike before reaching an intersection with the Crescent Rock Trail. A number of trails crisscross your path, including White Oak Canyon Trail (at 0.9 mile and again at 1.3 miles) and Old Rag Fire Road (1.0 mile). Just stay on the greenstone to maintain your course.

Look for a basalt formation that resembles columns near the second intersection with White Oak Canyon Trail. This phenomenon, called columnar jointing, is evidence

LOCATION
Central District, Shenandoah National Park, VA

RATING
Easy

DISTANCE
1.4-mile loop

ELEVATION GAIN
91 feet

ESTIMATED TIME
1-2 hours

MAPS
Map 10, Appalachian Trail and other trails in Shenandoah National Park, Central District, 2013 (PATC): www.patc.net/PATC/ Our_Store/PATC_Maps.aspx

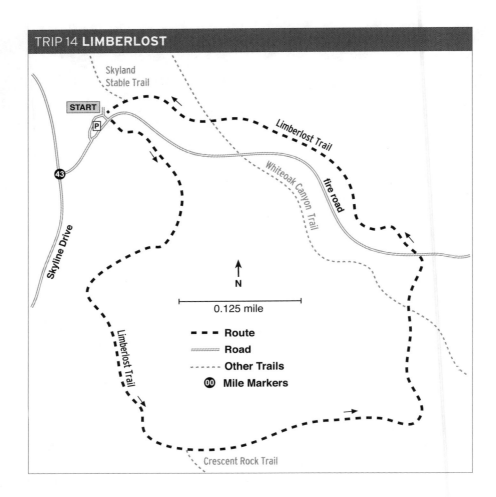

of the park's geologic roots: as lava flowed and then started to form basalt, it cracked into these unique hexagonal shapes.

After passing through this last intersection, Limberlost Trail nears its end. Continue to follow the path through the woods until you arrive back at the parking area.

Those hiking with children—or who are children at heart—can pick up an activity brochure by the trailhead or download it online from kidsinparks.com/shenandoah-national-park-limberlost-trail.

DID YOU KNOW?

The Pollock family was instrumental in Shenandoah National Park's history. George Freeman Pollock built Skyland, and he and his wife, Addie Pollock, were instrumental in trying to preserve the hemlocks that existed in Shenandoah National Park, buying 100 of the large trees near Skyland to save them from

This peaceful and easy route is for nature lovers, giving visitors a chance to take in the surroundings as they navigate the flat path. Photo by Meryl Huxham, Creative Commons on Flickr.

loggers. The area was named "Limberlost" after the book *A Girl of the Limberlost* by Gene Stratton-Porter.

MORE INFORMATION

Shenandoah National Park (nps.gov/shen, 540-999-3500, 800-732-0911 [for emergencies]). Park facilities are generally open from March through late November; a schedule is online. In cases of inclement weather and at night in deer-hunting season (mid-November through early January), call the park to confirm whether Skyline Drive is open to vehicles. Overnight accommodations in the park include lodges, cabins, and campgrounds, such as Big Meadows Lodge and Campground; for more information, visit nps.gov/shen/planyourvisit/lodging.htm or nps.gov/shen/planyourvisit/campgrounds.htm. Big Meadows Wayside—which offers full-service dining, groceries, camping supplies, gasoline, and more—is open Sunday through Thursday from 8 A.M. to 5:30 P.M. and Friday and Saturday from 8 A.M. to 7 P.M. between April and early November; visit goshenandoah.com for additional concession information.

NEARBY

Skyline Drive is dotted with hikes and overlooks, and Big Meadows Campground serves as a good base to explore the area. Nearby hikes include Lewis Falls (Trip 17), Rose River Falls (Trip 19), and Dark Hollow Falls (Trip 20).

15

MARY'S ROCK

Get your pulse racing on this climb to the top of the eighth-highest peak in Shenandoah National Park. Stunning 360-degree views and rock-scrambling opportunities await.

DIRECTIONS

From I-66, Exit 43A, take US 29 South 13.2 miles to Warrenton. Turn right onto US 211 and drive for 34.0 miles. West of Sperryville, US 211 twists and turns before meeting the park's Thornton Gap entrance (fee). Drive south on Skyline Drive to the Meadow Spring Parking Area between mile markers 33 and 34. *GPS coordinates:* 38° 38.300′ N, 78° 18.823′ W.

TRAIL DESCRIPTION

At 3,487 feet, Mary's Rock is the eighth-highest point in Shenandoah. The views from this peak looking over the park and the surrounding valleys earn this hike its popularity.

From the parking area, cross Skyline Drive and head left up the path. One of the park's ubiquitous concrete trail markers indicates the trailhead. Turn right here onto blue-blazed Meadow Spring Trail, and start with a steady climb. The first 0.25 mile is the toughest, as the path gains about 650 feet in elevation, but the route takes you through a tunnel of mountain laurels—a stunning sight when they bloom in spring.

At 0.4 mile, pass the remains of an old homestead as the trail winds up the mountain. Soon, at 0.6 mile, arrive at a three-way intersection with the Appalachian Trail (AT). Turn right and begin to follow the AT's white blazes. The trail continues uphill just a bit longer but starts to dip and eventually levels out just beyond 0.75 mile. Great views of the Shenandoah Valley stretch left as you walk along the

LOCATION
Central District, Shenandoah National Park, VA

RATING
Moderate

DISTANCE
2.7 miles round-trip

ELEVATION GAIN
1,043 feet

ESTIMATED TIME
1-2 hours

MAPS
Map 10, Appalachian Trail and other trails in Shenandoah National Park, Central District, 2013 (PATC): www.patc.net/PATC/ Our_Store/PATC_Maps.aspx

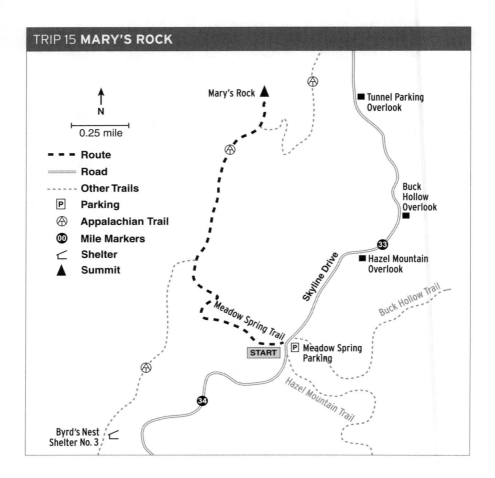

ridge. Short side trails take you to overlooks, but the real prize is ahead at 1.1 miles as you get your first look at the base of Mary's Rock.

The AT loops to the right of Mary's Rock to a junction with Mary's Rock Lookout Trail at 1.2 miles. Take a left onto this spur trail (the AT descends to the right). In just 0.1 mile, the views open up at Mary's Rock itself. To the west, you can see more of the Shenandoah Valley and Massanutten Mountain. To the north, the Thornton Gap park entrance is visible below a few of the park's northern peaks. A short scramble to the top of Mary's Rock earns you even more stunning views of the surrounding area, as well as a spectacular 360-degree panorama.

To return, simply retrace your steps back to the parking lot.

DID YOU KNOW?

Legends abound about how Mary's Rock got its name, each with its own twist. The first is for the romantics: Francis Thornton brought his wife, Mary, to the top of the mountain to show her the lands they would own together. A more adventurous version says that Thornton's daughter Mary climbed the mountain

On a winter's morning, Shenandoah hikers can be rewarded with sweeping views like this one of Mary's Rock from Oventop Mountain.

when she was young and returned with a bear cub under her arm. The last story keeps it simple: The peak was named after Mary Barbee, the wife of sculptor William Randolph Barbee, who was from the area.

MORE INFORMATION

Shenandoah National Park (nps.gov/shen, 540-999-3500, 800-732-0911 [for emergencies]). Park facilities are generally open from March through late November; a schedule is online. In cases of inclement weather and at night in deer-hunting season (mid-November through early January), call the park to confirm whether Skyline Drive is open to vehicles. Overnight accommodations in the park include lodges, cabins, and campgrounds; visit nps.gov/shen/planyourvisit/lodging.htm or nps.gov/shen/planyourvisit/campgrounds.htm for more information.

NEARBY

You'll find no shortage of hikes along Skyline Drive, including Stony Man (Trip 16), and numerous overlooks to give you additional views of the surrounding valleys. Nearby Sperryville has restaurants and small shops, and VA 211 is dotted with wineries, perfect spots for post-hike snacking and sipping.

PUTTING THE NATION TO WORK

The Civilian Conservation Corps (CCC) was the United States' largest public work relief program and contributed to forming much of the national park system we enjoy today. One of the most popular components of President Franklin D. Roosevelt's New Deal, the CCC was created to address the devastating and lingering impacts of the Great Depression. When Roosevelt took office, one-quarter of the nation's workers were unemployed, most of them young men with limited employment opportunities.

The CCC was established in 1933 and in operation until 1942. Its main goal was to provide employment opportunities primarily for unemployed and unmarried men, ages 18 to 25, from families who had difficulty finding work. Each participant received $30 a month, $25 of which had to go back to support his parents, siblings, or other dependents. In addition, the men were housed in camps, where they received food, shelter, medical care, and clothing. They had to work for one six-month period and could serve up to four periods over two years if they continued to have difficulty finding employment. More than 3 million men participated in the CCC during its nine-year existence. Nationally, they planted nearly 3 billion trees, helped create more than 800 parks, and supported construction of buildings and roadways.

The earliest CCC camps were in Virginia: Camp Roosevelt (a side trip from Trip 34) was the first to be created. Shenandoah National Park was home to the first two CCC camps in national parks: Skyland and Big Meadows. In total, Virginia had more than 80 camps, with ten either in or near Shenandoah National Park, ranking fourth among states for the number of camps. In Virginia, more than 107,000 men worked for the CCC.

The primary objective of the CCC in Virginia was to control erosion and support reforestation, but the most visible legacy may be the contribution to the development of a state park system—Virginia had none before 1932—and the work in Shenandoah National Park. The men built overlooks, picnic areas, campgrounds, comfort stations, visitor and maintenance buildings, and signs. They removed most evidence of human habitation in the park, a change that stirs some debate today (see "Skyline Drive: Building a 'A Wonder Way,'" page 33). CCC participants also built many of the stone walls along the drive and overlooks. (Some of these walls have since been rebuilt, using the original stone.)

World War II and higher employment rates led to the termination of the CCC in 1942, but the work that was accomplished has lasted for decades. In its final report on the CCC, the state of Virginia noted: "In no state did the CCC make a greater or more lasting contribution to the well-being of its citizens than it did in Virginia."

16

STONY MAN

Ascending Shenandoah's second-tallest mountain is a short and rewarding trek, probably one of the nicest circuits in the park. Arrive early to avoid the crowds; this is also one of the park's most popular hikes.

DIRECTIONS

From I-66, Exit 43A, take US 29 South 13.2 miles to Warrenton. Turn right onto US 211 and drive for 34.0 miles. West of Sperryville, US 211 twists and turns before meeting the park's Thornton Gap entrance (fee). Enter the park and drive south on Skyline Drive to the Skyland parking lot (between mileposts 41 and 42). *GPS coordinates:* 38° 35.555′ N, 78° 22.535′ W.

TRAIL DESCRIPTION

This short hike delivers a quick reward as you climb to the top of Stony Man Mountain, Shenandoah's second-tallest peak (4,014 feet). It's one of the easier and more pleasant hikes in the park, which explains its popularity. A few trails may make navigation more complicated than on other hikes with an easy rating, but just keep an eye on the blazes to stay headed in the right direction.

From the parking lot, look for the well-marked trailhead that leads to the white-blazed Appalachian Trail (AT). At the start, blue-blazed Stony Man Loop Trail and the AT share the same path. The route starts off with an easy and mild climb. Pass several numbered posts, which are part of a self-guided interpretative nature walk; instructions are available from nearby Skyland Resort if you wish to take advantage of that option.

Arrive at an intersection at 0.4 mile. The AT turns to the right, but follow blue-blazed Stony Man Trail straight. The trail quickly splits; going in either direction will get you to the top. (The yellow-blazed Stony Man Horse Trail can

LOCATION
Central District, Shenandoah National Park, VA

RATING
Easy

DISTANCE
1.5 miles round-trip

ELEVATION GAIN
407 feet

ESTIMATED TIME
1-2 hours

MAPS
Map 10, Appalachian Trail and other trails in Shenandoah National Park, Central District, 2013 (PATC): www.patc.net/PATC/Our_Store/PATC_Maps.aspx

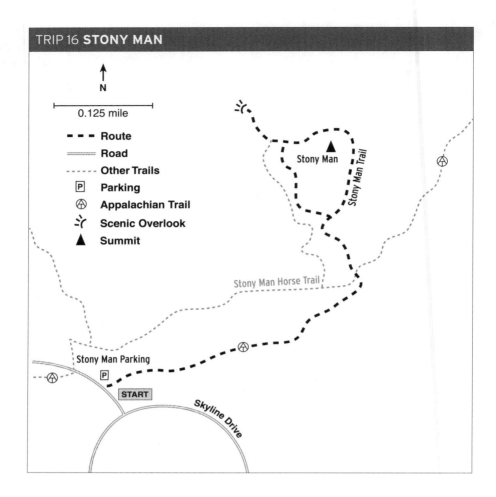

create a bit of confusion along this loop; continue following the Stony Man Trail's blue blazes to stay on track.) From the AT intersection, the path begins to climb more steadily up the mountain. A well-placed sign at the top directs you to the main vista. From here on a clear day, you can see the town of Luray and the Shenandoah Valley below, and Massanutten Mountain in the distance. If you're looking for more solitude, explore some of the side trails, which lead to equally stunning but less-crowded views.

To complete the loop, continue along blue-blazed Stony Man Loop Trail, which descends steadily and then arrives back at the intersection with the AT at 1.0 mile. Turn right onto the AT, and retrace your path back to the parking lot.

DID YOU KNOW?

Skyland, a resort once known as Stony Man Camp, was built before Shenandoah National Park existed. George Freeman Pollock designed it for wealthy vacationers.

A hiker studies the topography of Shenandoah Valley from Stony Man's summit.

Constructed in 1895, the property was first advertised as a dude ranch, and vacationers arrived by horse or wagon. Shenandoah National Park took over the resort in 1931, and eventually expanded it to what visitors see and enjoy today. Skyline Drive, which was built right past the resort, reaches its highest elevation here.

MORE INFORMATION

Shenandoah National Park (nps.gov/shen, 540-999-3500, 800-732-0911 [for emergencies]). Park facilities are generally open from March through late November; a schedule is online. In cases of inclement weather and at night in deer-hunting season (mid-November through early January), call the park to confirm whether Skyline Drive is open to vehicles. Overnight accommodations in the park include lodges, cabins, and campgrounds; visit nps.gov/shen/planyourvisit/lodging.htm or nps.gov/shen/planyourvisit/campgrounds.htm for more information. Pets are not allowed on Stony Man Trail.

NEARBY

Skyline Drive is dotted with hikes and overlooks, and Big Meadows Campground serves as a good base to explore the area. Nearby hikes include Lewis Falls (Trip 17), Rose River Falls (Trip 19), and Dark Hollow Falls (Trip 20).

17

LEWIS FALLS

Lewis Falls is just one of the attractions along this pleasant walk near Big Meadows Campground. Tack on a quick scramble to Blackrock Cliffs for great views of the valley.

DIRECTIONS

From I-66, Exit 43A, take US 29 South 13.2 miles to Warrenton. Turn right onto US 211 and drive for 34 miles. West of Sperryville, US 211 twists and turns before meeting the park's Thornton Gap entrance (fee). Enter the park and drive south on Skyline Drive to the gated service road just south of Big Meadows (milepost 51). The main lot can hold just a few cars; if it is full, head back toward Big Meadows for additional parking options. *GPS coordinates: 38° 31.019′ N, 78° 26.518′ W.*

TRAIL DESCRIPTION

This ramble near Big Meadows has a bit of everything for the day-hiker: a waterfall, good views, and a climb up to Blackrock for even better views. It's an enjoyable walk, one well worth taking.

From the parking lot, pass the yellow gate and start to descend along a yellow-blazed fire road. Continue straight on the fire road through the intersection with the white-blazed Appalachian Trail (AT). To the right, a padlocked door appears on the side of the trail: While an odd sight for a day hike, this door covers a spring, which supplies much of the water for facilities in the Big Meadows area.

At 0.25 mile, arrive at blue-blazed Lewis Spring Falls Trail, and turn left on the trail to continue the hike. The route narrows from the wide fire road and starts to descend along several switchbacks before reaching Overlook Trail at 0.9 mile. Walk to the left here to get a good look at the falls.

LOCATION
Central District, Shenandoah National Park, VA

RATING
Moderate

DISTANCE
3-mile loop

ELEVATION GAIN
997 feet

ESTIMATED TIME
1-2 hours

MAPS
Map 10, Appalachian Trail and other trails in Shenandoah National Park, Central District, 2013 (PATC): www.patc.net/PATC/Our_Store/PATC_Maps.aspx

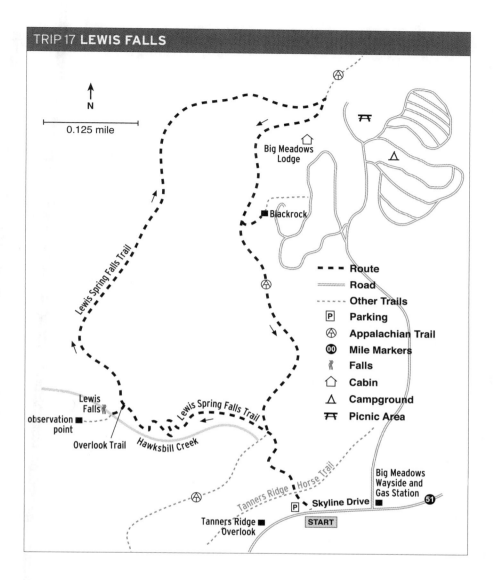

A rock outcropping just a few steps into Overlook Trail offers the first view of Lewis Falls and of the valley below. To reach it, continue along the trail, across a stream, and down a very rocky path. These rocks can be slippery when wet, but a handrail provides extra support as you make your way to the overlook. From here, admire the excellent vista of the 81-foot-tall Lewis Falls as it plunges to the valley below.

To continue the hike, return to the intersection with Overlook Trail and turn left onto Lewis Spring Falls Trail. The trail steadily ascends back up to the ridge—a moderate climb that can get steep at times, but the scenery along the

This pleasant hike leads to views of the 81-foot Lewis Falls.

way provides a good excuse to pause and enjoy the surroundings. At 2.0 miles, turn right onto the AT and follow the white blazes along a relatively flat path. To your left, evidence of nearby Big Meadows Campground is visible as the AT skirts close to the lodge.

A rocky overlook provides a good resting point to pause and take in views of the valley. To get even higher, turn left at the intersection with blue-blazed Blackrock Trail at 2.4 miles and follow it uphill to the Blackrock Cliffs for more vistas. (Continuing past the cliffs brings you to Big Meadows Lodge, which lies a short distance away. When open, the lodge has tempting food and drink for hungry hikers.) To continue your trek, retrace your steps back to the AT. Turn left onto the AT, which starts to descend and eventually leads back to the intersection with the fire road you entered on. Turn left and retrace your steps to the parking lot.

DID YOU KNOW?

Big Meadows Lodge, within sight of the Lewis Falls loop, has a long history. Built in 1939, the lodge is listed on the National Register of Historic Places. It was constructed with stones cut from nearby Massanutten Mountain, and the interior—the paneling, in particular—was made from the wood of American chestnut trees that are now nearly extinct.

MORE INFORMATION

Shenandoah National Park (nps.gov/shen, 540-999-3500, 800-732-0911 [for emergencies]). Park facilities are generally open March through late November; a schedule is online. In cases of inclement weather and at night in deer-hunting season (mid-November through early January), call the park to confirm whether Skyline Drive is open to vehicles. Overnight accommodations in the park include lodges, cabins, and campgrounds, such as the Big Meadows Lodge and Campground, which typically open in May and close in November; for more information on opening and closing dates, visit nps.gov/shen/planyourvisit/lodging.htm or nps.gov/shen/planyourvisit/campgrounds.htm. Big Meadows Wayside—which offers full-service dining, groceries, camping supplies, gasoline, and more—is open Sunday through Thursday from 8 A.M. to 5:30 P.M. and Friday and Saturday from 8 A.M. to 7 P.M. between April and early November; visit goshenandoah.com for additional concession information.

NEARBY

Skyline Drive is dotted with hikes and overlooks, and Big Meadows Campground serves as a good base for further explorations of the area. For a longer outing, this hike can be coupled with nearby Rose River Falls (Trip 19) and Dark Hollow Falls (Trip 20) to create the popular Three Falls Loop.

18

SOUTH RIVER FALLS

Descend—and then descend some more—to enjoy views of South River Falls, one of the loveliest cascades in the park.

DIRECTIONS

From I-66, Exit 43A, take US 29 South 13.2 miles to Warrenton. Turn right onto US 211 and drive for 34.0 miles. West of Sperryville, US 211 twists and turns before meeting the park's Thornton Gap entrance (fee). Enter the park and drive south on Skyline Drive to the South River Falls Picnic Area (milepost 63). *GPS coordinates: 38° 22.875′ N, 78° 31.078′ W.*

TRAIL DESCRIPTION

Like many hikes in Shenandoah National Park, the South River Falls loop starts with a descent and ends with an ascent. The views of the waterfall, however, lend themselves to a long break before you start climbing. In warmer weather, the base of the falls provides a pleasant place for wading and relaxing.

The blue-blazed South River Falls Trail starts next to the restrooms at the South River Falls Picnic Area. Follow the path into the woods, and quickly arrive at an intersection with the Appalachian Trail (AT). Go straight through the intersection, following the blue blazes. The route will descend along a fairly rugged path, with some decent stretches of rock-hopping.

In 1.0 mile, you get your first look at the 83-foot waterfall. An outcropping provides a good vantage point, but head for the overlook just a few steps away. From here, catch a nice view of the plunging waterfall below.

A more impressive sight farther along the path requires some extra work to get there. From the overlook, continue down South River Falls Trail and arrive at a concrete post. Turn right to follow a fire road down to the base of the falls.

LOCATION
Central District, Shenandoah National Park, VA

RATING
Moderate

DISTANCE
4.9-mile loop

ELEVATION GAIN
1,914 feet

ESTIMATED TIME
2–3 hours

MAPS
Map 10, Appalachian Trail and other trails in Shenandoah National Park, Central District, 2013 (PATC): www.patc.net/PATC/Our_Store/PATC_Maps.aspx

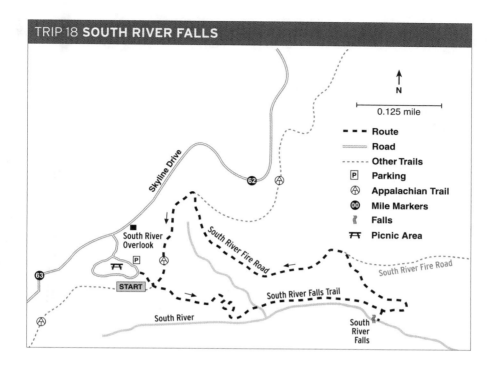

The fire road appears to end at the river. Look upstream to spot a rocky path that leads to the base of the falls and some pools perfect for wading (2.3 miles).

After enjoying the falls, follow the fire road back up the hill and arrive again at the concrete post. Continue straight on the yellow-blazed fire road. (Turning left takes you back to the overlook.) At the intersection with South River Fire Road, keep going straight, following the yellow blazes. The trail makes a long, steady ascent before arriving at an intersection with the AT. Turn left onto the white-blazed AT and follow its relatively flat path back to the intersection with South River Falls Trail. Turn right and arrive back at your vehicle.

DID YOU KNOW?

Hikers can enjoy the impressive waterfalls, but birders are in luck here as well. According to the Virginia Department of Game and Inland Fisheries, this area is one of the prime spots for breeding birds along Skyline Drive. Bird-watchers can encounter many species along this route, including cerulean, Blackburnian, and black-throated blue warblers; northern Parula; Louisiana waterthrush; American redstart; white-breasted nuthatch; red-eyed and blue-headed vireos; scarlet tanager; rose-breasted grosbeak; and eastern towhee.

MORE INFORMATION

Shenandoah National Park (nps.gov/shen, 540-999-3500, 800-732-0911 [for emergencies]). Park facilities are generally open March through late November;

Make sure to follow the side trail to the base of South River Falls, which affords a better view—and better photo opportunities.

a schedule is online. In cases of inclement weather and at night in deer-hunting season (mid-November through early January), call the park to confirm whether Skyline Drive is open to vehicles. Overnight accommodations in the park include lodges, cabins, and campgrounds, including Big Meadows Lodge and Campground; for more information, visit nps.gov/shen/planyourvisit/lodging.htm or nps.gov/shen/planyourvisit/campgrounds.htm. Big Meadows Wayside—which offers full-service dining, groceries, camping supplies, gasoline, and more—is open Sunday through Thursday from 8 A.M. to 5:30 P.M. and Friday and Saturday from 8 A.M. to 7 P.M. between April and early November; visit goshenandoah.com for additional concession information.

NEARBY

Skyline Drive is dotted with hikes and overlooks, and Big Meadows Campground serves as a good base to explore the area. If you want more waterfalls, nearby hikes include Lewis Falls (Trip 17), Rose River Falls (Trip 19), and Dark Hollow Falls (Trip 20).

19

ROSE RIVER FALLS

Go chasing waterfalls with this outing that's bookended by a glimpse of Dark Hollow Falls near the beginning and the cascades of Rose River Falls near the end.

DIRECTIONS

From I-66, Exit 43A, take US 29 South 13.2 miles to Warrenton. Turn right onto US 211 and drive for 34.0 miles. West of Sperryville, US 211 twists and turns before meeting the park's Thornton Gap entrance (fee). Enter the park and drive south on Skyline Drive to the Fishers Gap Parking Area. *GPS coordinates: 38° 31.842′ N, 78° 26.380′ W.*

TRAIL DESCRIPTION

The Rose River and Dark Hollow loop is a mild one, providing plenty of opportunities to pause and enjoy the scenery.

From the parking area, cross Skyline Drive and follow the fire road past a gate. The road will split here. Bear to the right to follow Rose River Fire Road. While only intermittently blazed yellow, this wide path is an easy one to follow as it makes a gentle descent.

About 0.5 mile from the start, a path to the Cave Family Cemetery will come into view on the right. It's worth a quick detour here to see one of the 100 family cemeteries that remain within the park.

The fire road continues its descent, and before too long, you can hear the sound of rushing water. At 1.26 miles into the hike, arrive at the base of lovely Dark Hollow Falls.

From here, follow the fire road for a few steps before reaching the intersection with blue-blazed Rose River Loop Trail. Bear to the left to start following this trail, which runs alongside the Hogcamp Branch of Rose River. As the trail continues to descend, the river will tempt you with numerous spots to stop and soak your feet—a treat on a warm day.

LOCATION
Central District, Shenandoah National Park, VA

RATING
Moderate

DISTANCE
4.4-mile loop

ELEVATION GAIN
1,189 feet

ESTIMATED TIME
2-3 hours

MAPS
Map 10, Appalachian Trail and other trails in Shenandoah National Park, Central District, 2013 (PATC): www.patc.net/PATC/ Our_Store/PATC_Maps.aspx

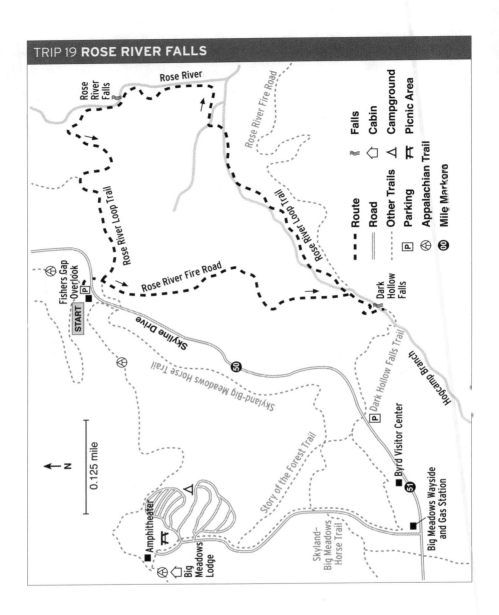

At about 2.3 miles, cross a bridge over the Hogcamp Branch. The trail then works its way into the woods and passes the remains of the foundation of an old copper mine before arriving at a concrete post. Bear to the left here. The route, now paralleling Rose River, will climb slightly before arriving at Rose River Falls. The waters cascade down 67 feet—and after heavy rains there could be as many as four cascades, according to park information.

The trail continues to climb, now more earnestly, and eventually veers away from the water that has been your companion for most of the hike. Arrive at a concrete post and turn left to continue following Rose River Loop Trail.

The trail along Hogcamp Branch is one of the highlights of this hike, dotted with numerous spots to take a break and enjoy the burbling water.

After more climbing, the trail eventually swings to the right before arriving at another concrete post, this time marking the intersection with the Skyland-Big Meadows Horse Trail. Turn left here to follow the yellow-blazed horse trail, which maintains its steady ascent for the next 0.5 mile before arriving back at the gate and Skyline Drive.

DID YOU KNOW?

There are more than 70 streams and 38 species of fish in Shenandoah National Park, making it an attractive destination for anglers. The brook trout is the most elusive quarry, being easily spooked, so anglers aim to arrive early and find a quiet stretch alongside one of the streams to see if they can catch one. Make sure to follow the park's current fishing regulations, which are available on its website (nps.gov/shen/planyourvisit/upload/FishingRegulations.pdf).

MORE INFORMATION

Shenandoah National Park (nps.gov/shen, 540-999-3500, 800-732-0911 [for emergencies]). Park facilities are generally open from March through late November; a schedule is online. In cases of inclement weather and at night in deer-hunting season (mid-November through early January), call the park to confirm whether Skyline Drive is open to vehicles. Overnight accommodations in the park include lodges, cabins, and campgrounds, such as Big Meadows Lodge and Campground; for more information, visit nps.gov/shen/planyourvisit/lodging.htm or nps.gov/shen/planyourvisit/campgrounds.htm. Big Meadows Wayside—which offers full-service dining, groceries, camping supplies, gasoline, and more—is open Sunday through Thursday from 8 A.M. to 5:30 P.M. and Friday and Saturday from 8 A.M. to 7 P.M. between April and early November; visit goshenandoah.com for additional concession information.

NEARBY

Skyline Drive is dotted with hikes and overlooks, and Big Meadows Campground serves as a good base to explore the area. For an added challenge, consider tacking on Lewis Falls (Trip 17) and Dark Hollow Falls (Trip 20) to form the bigger hiking loop known as Three Falls.

20

DARK HOLLOW FALLS

This delightful hike takes you on a journey next to one of Shenandoah's loveliest waterfalls. Lest you think the trek is too easy, the climb back up ensures you get a good workout— surrounded by great views, of course.

DIRECTIONS

From I-66, Exit 43A, take US 29 South 13.2 miles to War-renton. Turn right onto US 211 and drive for 34.0 miles. West of Sperryville, US 211 twists and turns before meeting the park's Thornton Gap entrance (fee). Enter the park and drive south on Skyline Drive to the Dark Hollow Parking Area Trailhead (near milepost 51). *GPS coordinates:* 38° 31.114′ N, 78° 25.513′ W.

TRAIL DESCRIPTION

This short hike packs a punch, first with views of Dark Hollow Falls as you descend alongside it and then with the climb back up. It's a trip well worth taking, but it is also a popular one, so plan to arrive early to beat the crowds and fully enjoy the views.

Dark Hollow Falls Trail starts directly from the parking lot. It is easy to follow and descends rather mildly at first. This pleasant stretch becomes even more delightful when the route begins to parallel the Hogcamp Branch of Rose River, which burbles alongside your walk. Signs caution hikers not to go off trail—the slippery rocks by the falls can be quite dangerous—so be sure to keep to the path.

Before too long, the descent starts to steepen a bit more and arrives at the upper falls viewing area in just 0.5 mile. In early spring or just after a storm, the upper falls are impressive. Take some time to enjoy the sight.

There is more to come, though. Keep walking a bit farther—the trail descends more steeply and then arrives at the base of the lower falls in 0.7 mile from the start. It's

LOCATION
Central District, Shenandoah National Park, VA

RATING
Easy

DISTANCE
1.5 miles round-trip

ELEVATION GAIN
445 feet

ESTIMATED TIME
1-2 hours

MAPS
Map 10, Appalachian Trail and other trails in Shenandoah National Park, Central District, 2013 (PATC): www.patc.net/PATC/ Our_Store/PATC_Maps.aspx

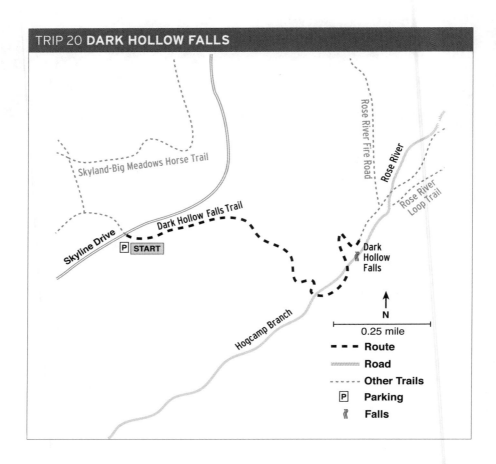

another impressive sight and an excellent spot to take a break and soak in the scenery. The base of the falls is also near this trail's intersection with Rose River Loop Trail, however, so this area can get quite busy.

The way back is straight up the trail you descended. The climb is steep at times but rewards you with another look at the upper falls as you follow the trail back to the parking area.

Be aware that dogs are not allowed on Dark Hollow Falls Trail. If you are traveling with a dog, the Rose River Falls hike (Trip 19) will allow you to take your furry friend to see the base of the falls—a lovely sight.

DID YOU KNOW?

Nearby Big Meadows has its place in history: President Franklin D. Roosevelt dedicated the park and Skyline Drive here in 1935. But the land itself has an even longer history, one that is still being discovered. Archaeologists have found evidence of human habitation as early as 2000 BCE.

This hike is a classic for a reason: the dramatic falls that are present throughout your journey from their crest to their base.

MORE INFORMATION

Shenandoah National Park (nps.gov/shen, 540-999-3500, 800-732-0911 [for emergencies]). Park facilities are generally open from March through late November; a schedule is online. In cases of inclement weather and at night in deer-hunting season (mid-November through early January), call the park to confirm whether or not Skyline Drive is open to vehicles. Overnight accommodations in the park include lodges, cabins, and campgrounds, such as Big Meadows Lodge and Campground; for more information, visit nps.gov/shen/planyourvisit/lodging.htm or nps.gov/shen/planyourvisit/campgrounds.htm. Big Meadows Wayside—which offers full-service dining, groceries, camping supplies, gasoline, and more—is open Sunday through Thursday from 8 A.M. to 5:30 P.M. and Friday and Saturday from 8 A.M. to 7 P.M. between April and early November; visit goshenandoah.com for additional concession information.

NEARBY

Skyline Drive is dotted with hikes and overlooks, and Big Meadows Campground serves as a good base to explore the area. For an added challenge, consider tackling Lewis Falls (Trip 17) and Rose River Falls (Trip 19) to form the bigger hiking loop known as Three Falls.

21

HAWKSBILL

Challenge yourself with a short, steep climb to Shenandoah National Park's highest peak. The reward: great views and a return route that's all downhill.

DIRECTIONS

From I-66, Exit 43A, take US 29 South 13.2 miles to Warrenton. Turn right onto US 211 and drive for 34.0 miles. West of Sperryville, US 211 twists and turns before meeting the Thornton Gap park entrance (fee). Enter the park and drive south on Skyline Drive to the Hawksbill Gap Parking Area, between mileposts 45 and 46, on the right. *GPS coordinates: 38° 33.372' N, 78° 23.207' W.*

TRAIL DESCRIPTION

The distance may be short, but the first mile of this hike is certainly a challenge as you gain more than 600 feet to reach the summit of Shenandoah's highest peak.

Small parking lots are on either side of Skyline Drive, but the trailhead is on the western side, marked by an informational sign. Follow the wide and graveled blue-blazed trail as it starts to thread its way steadily up the mountain.

The top is tantalizingly in view as the climb continues. Stone steps mark the halfway point, and the trail levels out for a bit, giving you a chance to catch your breath. Keep pressing forward. At 0.7 mile, a concrete post marks the end of the ascent. Ahead to the right is the Byrd's Nest Shelter No. 2 (day use only), and the top of Hawksbill (4,051 feet). Pass in front of the shelter and enjoy the scenery. A viewing platform, just a bit beyond the shelter at 0.8 mile, gives even better vistas to the west, north, and east. Skyline Drive is within sight below, the rocky crags of Old Rag (Trip 23) are to the east, and the Shenandoah Valley and Massanutten Mountain are to the west.

LOCATION
Central District, Shenandoah National Park, VA

RATING
Moderate

DISTANCE
2.8-mile loop

ELEVATION GAIN
1,089 feet

ESTIMATED TIME
1-2 hours

MAPS
Map 10, Appalachian Trail and other trails in Shenandoah National Park, Central District, 2013 (PATC): www.patc.net/PATC/Our_Store/PATC_Maps.aspx

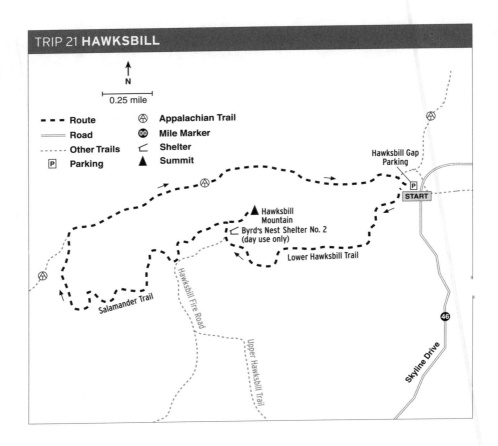

To continue the hike, head back past the shelter to the concrete post. (You can shorten the described route by heading to the left at the post and retracing your steps back down the trail.) Make a slight turn to the right and follow the blue blazes, and quickly arrive at another concrete post at 0.9 mile. Turn right here to gain Salamander Trail, also blue-blazed, which enters the woods. Pass several nice viewing points, and follow the trail as it winds its way around the mountain.

Salamander Trail makes its way gently downhill until it intersects with the Appalachian Trail (AT), which you'll see coming in from the left at 1.7 miles. Another concrete post marks the intersection. Turn right onto the AT, and follow the white blazes as it continues around the mountain. Good views of Hawksbill greet you as you start on the AT, and rock formations provide interest on the right. Three talus fields in short succession at 2.2 miles offer a bit of rock-hopping. The trail remains rugged for a bit but eventually levels out.

Skyline Drive and the parking lot will pop into sight as you round the last bend of the trail. Resist the temptation to cut through the trees to get to your car faster; in just a few minutes, a concrete post at 2.7 miles marks a spur trail to the parking area.

Hawksbill's summit marks the highest point in Shenandoah National Park and offers an impressive panoramic view of the area, including such features as Old Rag and Stony Man.

DID YOU KNOW?

Peregrine falcons and balsam firs are two unique finds on Hawksbill's summit. In an attempt to restore the peregrine population, the Park Service launched the Peregrine Falcon Restoration Project and had a successful nesting attempt at Hawksbill. These falcons were removed from the Endangered Species List in 1999 but are still considered to be a threatened species. Hawksbill is also one of the few places outside of northern New England where balsam firs can be found.

MORE INFORMATION

Shenandoah National Park (nps.gov/shen, 540-999-3500, 800-732-0911 [for emergencies]). Park facilities are generally open from March through late November; a schedule is online. In cases of inclement weather and at night in deer hunting season (mid-November through early January), call the park to confirm whether Skyline Drive is open to vehicles. Overnight accommodations in the park include lodges, cabins, and campgrounds; for more information, visit nps.gov/shen/planyourvisit/lodging.htm or nps.gov/shen/planyourvisit/campgrounds.htm.

NEARBY

Nearby Sperryville has restaurants and small shops, and VA 211 is dotted with wineries, perfect spots for post-hike snacks and sips. If you're looking for a strenuous outing, couple this hike with Whiteoak and Cedar Run (Trip 25). Consider starting the climb up Cedar Run, crossing Skyline Drive, and continuing up to Hawksbill before descending back to the drive and then down Whiteoak.

22
RAPIDAN CAMP

Visit President Hoover's retreat and enjoy a picturesque stretch of the Appalachian Trail along Hazeltop Mountain.

DIRECTIONS
From I-66, Exit 43A, take US 29 South 13.2 miles to Warrenton. Turn right onto US 211 and drive for 34.0 miles. West of Sperryville, US 211 twists and turns before meeting the park's Thornton Gap entrance (fee). Enter the park and drive south on Skyline Drive to the parking lot for Milam Gap (between mileposts 52 and 53). *GPS coordinates:* 38° 30.025′ N, 78° 26.732′ W.

TRAIL DESCRIPTION
Toward the back of the parking lot, on the south side, you should find a spur trail that takes you, in very short order, to the Appalachian Trail (AT). Turn left (south) onto the white-blazed AT and cross Skyline Drive. On the opposite side of the road, the AT heads to the right, while blue-blazed Mill Prong Trail (your route) heads to the left, toward Rapidan Camp.

Go left, following the blue blazes, to start a pleasant descent. About a mile later, the route arrives at an intersection with Mill Prong Horse Trail. Bear right to follow the yellow-blazed horse trail and continue the descent. At 1.5 miles, pass Big Rock Falls on your right—a bonus on this hike, as the waterfalls are lovely and the pool deep enough for a dip—then cross the creek. A forest road cuts across your path at 1.8 miles. Note this point: when you return from visiting Rapidan Camp, your route on Laurel Prong Trail will head south.

To reach the camp, continue straight ahead on the paved path and past a post. Though only a few buildings remain, the camp is still a striking historical site, with its rustic structures appearing out of the foliage. A number of signs

LOCATION
Central District, Shenandoah National Park, VA

RATING
Moderate

DISTANCE
7.5 miles round-trip

ELEVATION GAIN
1,623 feet

ESTIMATED TIME
3-5 hours

MAPS
Map 10, Appalachian Trail and other trails in Shenandoah National Park, Central District, 2013 (PATC): www.patc.net/PATC/ Our_Store/PATC_Maps.aspx

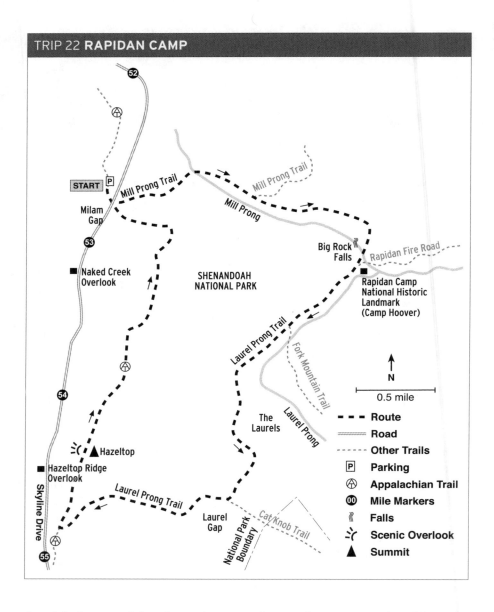

The map shows trail routes, roads, and landmarks including:

- 52
- START / P
- Mill Prong Trail
- Milam Gap
- 53
- Naked Creek Overlook
- Mill Prong
- Mill Prong Trail
- Big Rock Falls
- Rapidan Fire Road
- Rapidan Camp National Historic Landmark (Camp Hoover)
- SHENANDOAH NATIONAL PARK
- Laurel Prong Trail
- Fork Mountain Trail
- 54
- The Laurels
- Laurel Prong
- Hazeltop
- Hazeltop Ridge Overlook
- Laurel Prong Trail
- Skyline Drive
- Laurel Gap
- Cat Knob Trail
- National Park Boundary
- 55

N
0.5 mile

- **– – –** Route
- ══ Road
- - - - Other Trails
- P Parking
- Ⓐ Appalachian Trail
- 00 Mile Markers
- Falls
- Scenic Overlook
- ▲ Summit

detail the history of this place, where President Herbert Hoover relaxed from the stress of governing the country during the Great Depression. The White House physician of the day called the camp "one of the most relaxing places that I have ever known." Conversely, the leader of the Marine Corps construction team that worked on the site between 1929 and 1932 described the job as one of the most challenging in his career because of the surrounding terrain.

Once you've completed your walking tour, return to the post where the pavement ends at the forest road, and turn south (left) to begin Laurel Prong Trail.

Seeking shelter on a rainy day, a hiker checks out the buildings of Rapidan Camp's historic presidential retreat.

Pass a placard on the right for Five Tents, and then reach a somewhat confusingly marked fork in the trail on the edge of Rapidan Camp at 2.2 miles. Do not take the footpath to the left (it leads to a dam and a dead end); instead, follow the forest road (Laurel Prong Trail) to the right. Blue blazes appear eventually, and the trail climbs gently to an intersection with Fork Mountain Trail at 2.7 miles.

Beyond this intersection, Laurel Prong Trail makes its way through a beautiful woodland section known as the Laurels. At 3.4 miles, pass a campsite at a sharp right-hand bend, and begin a steeper climb. Just beyond 4.0 miles, you reach a ridgeline where Cat Knob Trail heads east, also on blue blazes. Turn right to stay on Laurel Prong Trail and continue climbing, but more gently, as the path works its way along the contour lines of Hazeltop Mountain. You may see some views here, depending on the time of year.

At last, Laurel Prong Trail ends at the AT at 5.0 miles, just south of the summit of Hazeltop Mountain. Turn right and complete the hike up this mountain. Beyond its summit is a spur trail at 5.5 miles that leads to an impressive view westward that makes the short side trip entirely worthwhile. The AT continues northward and makes for a pleasant walk as it descends toward Milam Gap.

At 7.4 miles, the trail returns to Milam Gap and the intersection with Mill Prong Trail. Cross Skyline Drive and return to your vehicle.

DID YOU KNOW?

Rapidan Camp, or Camp Hoover, was the Camp David of its day; President Herbert Hoover used the camp to host visiting luminaries throughout the 1930s. President Franklin Roosevelt found the surroundings too rugged for his liking and had Camp David constructed for his presidential retreat. Jimmy Carter was the last president to visit Rapidan Camp. (Rapidan Camp exhibits are open intermittently; check at Byrd Visitor Center for current hours.)

MORE INFORMATION

Shenandoah National Park (nps.gov/shen, 540-999-3500, 800-732-0911 [for emergencies]). Park facilities are generally open from March through late November; a schedule is online. In cases of inclement weather and at night in deer-hunting season (mid-November through early January), call the park to confirm whether Skyline Drive is open to vehicles. Overnight accommodations in the park include lodges, cabins, and campgrounds; visit nps.gov/shen/planyourvisit/lodging.htm or nps.gov/shen/planyourvisit/campgrounds.htm for more information.

To learn more about Rapidan Camp, visit nps.gov/shen/historyculture/rapidancamp.htm; for ranger-led tour information, visit nps.gov/shen/planyourvisit/rangerprograms.htm.

NEARBY

There is no shortage of excellent hikes in the Central District of Shenandoah National Park. The waysides at Big Meadows (milepost 51) and Skyland (between mileposts 41 and 42) are great spots for a break or a snack. If you're heading back to the D.C. metropolitan area, consider stopping in Sperryville or Warrenton.

PRESIDENTS IN SHENANDOAH

"The passage of the Patowmac [*sic*] through the Blue Ridge is perhaps one of the most stupendous scenes in Nature. You stand on a very high point of land. On your right comes up the Shenandoah, having ranged along the foot of the mountain a hundred miles to seek a vent. On your left approaches the Patowmac [*sic*] in quest of a passage also. In the moment of their junction they rush together against the mountain, rend it as under and pass off to sea.... This scene is worth a voyage across the Atlantic."

—Thomas Jefferson, *Notes on the State of Virginia* (1785)

Given the proximity of the Shenandoah Valley to Washington, D.C., it is no surprise that the land has left its mark on the writings and biographies of more than a few American presidents. In the eighteenth century, Thomas Jefferson admired the view of the confluence of the Potomac and Shenandoah rivers, where the settlement of Harpers Ferry now stands. Modern-day hikers can visit Jefferson Rock in Trip 3, or enjoy other awe-inspiring views from Maryland Heights or Loudoun Heights (Trips 2 and 3).

Not only were several of the nation's early presidents—George Washington, Thomas Jefferson, and James Madison—Virginians who knew the Shenandoah Valley intimately, others also made homes in the Blue Ridge and Shenandoah Valley. In the late 1920s and early 1930s, before Shenandoah National Park was founded, Herbert Hoover established Rapidan Camp as a summer retreat where he could escape the heat and turmoil of the city, enjoy the mountain air, and indulge his favorite pastime of fishing. Long before George W. Bush called Crawford, Texas, home and before Barack Obama relaxed at Martha's Vineyard, Hoover's modest "Brown House" was a fact of the political landscape. Visit Rapidan Camp, also known as Camp Hoover, on Trip 22.

On July 3, 1936, Franklin Delano Roosevelt dedicated Shenandoah National Park, describing it as part of a larger social project of ending "involuntary idleness of thousands of young men" through the work of the Civilian Conservation Corps (CCC). Roosevelt reportedly found Rapidan Camp too primitive for his tastes, but he established CCC camps throughout the Blue Ridge. Camps throughout the Shenandoah Valley were models for the rest of the nation during Roosevelt's New Deal, which brought Americans back to work. (See "Putting the Nation to Work," page 68, for more on the Civilian Conservation Corps.)

23

OLD RAG

No other hike in the Shenandoah Valley rivals the fame of the scramble along Old Rag's Ridge Trail. If you're going to do only one hike in the area, this should be it. But come prepared: The Class 3 terrain at the top is as challenging as it is rewarding.

DIRECTIONS

From I-66, Exit 43A, take US 29 South 13.2 miles to Warrenton. Turn right onto US 211 west toward Sperryville. In 27.0 miles, take a left onto US 522 South, cross Thornton River, and then take another left to remain on US 522 South. About 0.7 mile later, turn right onto VA 231 South. In 7.8 miles, turn right onto VA 600. Follow VA 600 for 3.2 miles to the end of public access. A parking lot is on your left, and there is a small ranger station in the corner of the lot. *GPS coordinates:* 38° 34.233′ N, 78° 17.187′ W.

TRAIL DESCRIPTION

Old Rag is one of the best hikes in the region, and everybody knows it. Midmorning on a beautiful spring day, count on finding the parking lot filled to bursting, and expect to encounter a few thousand of your best friends on the mountain. For more solitude, come on a weekday, very early in the morning, or when the weather is less than ideal. Even then, you can probably expect to wait in lines at some of the obstacles. The terrain at the ridgeline is challenging and will likely require you to use your hands to pull yourself up and over the rocks, so if you're uncomfortable with very rocky terrain, this may not be an ideal hike for you.

The hike at Old Rag is justly famed for the approximately mile-long scramble atop the ridgeline, but for the first 0.9 mile, the trail is simply a road that goes by a few

LOCATION
Central District, Shenandoah National Park, VA

RATING
Strenuous

DISTANCE
9 miles round-trip

ELEVATION GAIN
2,812 feet

ESTIMATED TIME
4-7 hours

MAPS
Map 10, Appalachian Trail and other trails in Shenandoah National Park, Central District, 2013 (PATC: www.patc.net/PATC/Our_Store/PATC_Maps.aspx

Old Rag Area (National Park Service)

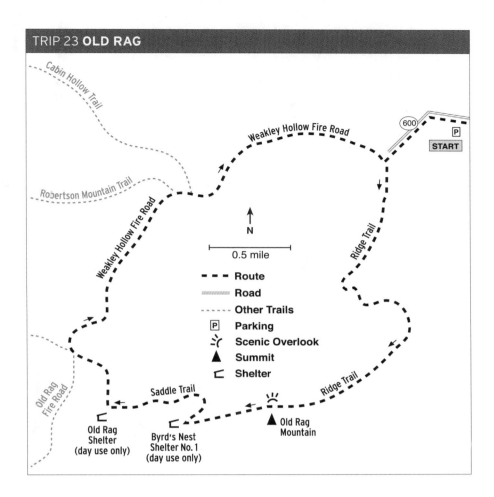

cottages. Pass Nicholson Hollow Trail on the right at 0.5 mile and then, at 0.9 mile, arrive at the trailhead for blue-blazed Ridge Trail, which you follow to Old Rag's summit. Note this location carefully: you're about to head south on Ridge Trail now, but you'll return to this point from the west on Weakley Hollow Fire Road.

A good amount of climbing awaits you, with 3.0 miles and 2,400 feet of gain to the summit. Ridge Trail begins by ascending gently through the forest, but it soon starts to switchback along some rather typical Virginia hollows. In the upper reaches, there are fewer switchbacks, but the trail continues to climb. Just before the ridgeline, it becomes quite steep and rocky. The path reaches a viewpoint, and then shortly thereafter, at nearly 3.0 miles, you meet the first obstacle: an awkwardly angled rock slab you must either crawl through or clamber up.

From this point forward, over the next 0.8 mile, you must scramble to reach the summit. Although the ascent does continue over this stretch, it won't feel

Hikers clamber through this narrow notch and crawl under the wedged boulder. This is one of the many obstacles that will test your determination as you scramble toward Old Rag's summit.

especially vertical, as you'll be concentrating on the moves necessary to overcome the obstacles. Lower yourself into cracks, edge out around shelves, pass through a cave or two, climb chimneys, jump over fissures, and embrace many, many rocks. Throughout this section, keep your eye open for the blue blazes, which can be tricky to find in some of the areas with more slabs. But never fear—there are often several ways to pass an obstacle (some more scrambly than others), and it would be quite hard to lose the ridgeline.

The terrain on the ridge is considered Class 3 in the Yosemite Decimal System, which means that you periodically need your hands to advance but ropes are not required. There is little exposure to speak of, and none of the moves aspire to Class 4 (the first class that the Yosemite Decimal System truly considers "climbing," which is often aided by ropes). If you have trekking poles, affix them to your pack, as they are more encumbrances than aids when scrambling. Make sure that you always have three points in firm contact with rock before moving a fourth.

Old Rag's summit is at 3.9 miles, just beyond the stretch of scrambles. Clamber up any one of a number of boulders for expansive views of the Shenandoah region. Relax and enjoy a snack (and perhaps a nap) before it's time to complete this classic trip.

Your descent begins with a series of switchbacks, which takes you just over 0.6 mile and 550 vertical feet down to Byrd's Nest Shelter No. 1 (day use only). Turn hard right here, and traverse left, then right, across the mountain, losing 670 feet before reaching Old Rag Shelter at 5.3 miles. From here, walk just 0.4 mile farther on a forest road to reach Weakley Hollow Fire Road. Turn right and follow the fire road past Robertson Mountain Trail at 6.7 miles and Corbin Hollow Trail at 6.8 miles, both on the left. The route eventually crosses a few bridged creeks before returning to the trailhead for Ridge Trail, just beyond 8.0 miles.

Follow the road for 1.0 mile back to the parking lot and your vehicle.

DID YOU KNOW?

Old Rag, the mountain's official name, is actually a shorter version of "Old Raggedy Top," as it is sometimes still referred to. As you're driving in on US 211 toward Shenandoah National Park, you should be able to spot the distinctive ragged line of Old Rag's rocky summit, which stands out against the more typical wooded Mid-Atlantic peaks.

MORE INFORMATION

Shenandoah National Park (nps.gov/shen, 540-999-3500, 800-732-0911 [for emergencies]). Park facilities are generally open from March through late November; a schedule is online. In cases of inclement weather and at night in deer-hunting season (mid-November through early January), call the park to confirm whether Skyline Drive is open to vehicles. Overnight lodging in the park includes lodges, cabins, and campgrounds; visit nps.gov/shen/planyourvisit/lodging.htm or nps.gov/shen/planyourvisit/campgrounds.htm for more information.

If you want to have Old Rag's summit all to yourself (albeit by means of an overnight trip), consult *AMC's Best Backpacking in the Mid-Atlantic*.

Should you arrive at the Old Rag parking lot and find it entirely full (it happens), some enterprising neighbors may allow you to park on pasture land—for a small fee.

NEARBY

Sperryville is the closest town, and there are a few eateries there, but the nearest town with a full array of services is Warrenton. Hikes in the vicinity of Old Rag include Hawksbill (Trip 21), Mount Robertson (Trip 24), Whiteoak and Cedar Run (Trip 25), and many others.

24

MOUNT ROBERTSON, CORBIN HOLLOW

Climb a Shenandoah peak next door to Old Rag with equally excellent views but none of the crowds.

DIRECTIONS

From I-66, Exit 43A, take US 29 South 13.2 miles to Warrenton. Turn right onto US 211 west toward Sperryville. In 27.0 miles, take a left onto US 522 South, cross Thornton River, and then take another left to remain on US 522 South. About 0.7 mile later, turn right onto VA 231 South. In 7.8 miles, turn right onto VA 600. Follow this road for 3.2 miles to the end of public access. A parking lot is on your left, and there is a small ranger station in the parking lot's corner. *GPS coordinates: 38° 34.233' N, 78° 17.187' W.*

TRAIL DESCRIPTION

Starting in the Old Rag parking lot near Nethers, this teardrop-shaped loop takes you up and over Mount Robertson, a peak neighboring Old Rag, and then down through Corbin Hollow to return to the Weakley Hollow fire road and your car. There's no scrambling, and you certainly won't see anything like the number of hikers climbing Old Rag on this relatively secluded peak, but the trek is steep and demanding.

Just like the hike up Old Rag, you begin in the parking lot. Pay your entry fee at the ranger station and begin walking east into the park on the blacktop. You'll pass a number of houses and eventually Nicholson Hollow Trail (0.5 mile) on the right. The road turns to gravel and climbs gradually. Reach the intersection with Old Rag's Ridge Trail on the left (0.86 mile) and go around the vehicle gate. Cross a few little footbridges spanning tributaries to the river. For the next 1.5 miles, you walk up the Weakley Hollow fire road with the river on your left.

LOCATION
Central District, Shenandoah National Park, VA

RATING
Strenuous

DISTANCE
9 miles round-trip

ELEVATION GAIN
2,136 feet

ESTIMATED TIME
4–6 hours

MAPS
Map 10, Appalachian Trail and other trails in Shenandoah National Park, Central District, 2013 (PATC): www.patc.net/PATC/Our_Store/PATC_Maps.aspx

Old Rag Area (National Park Service)

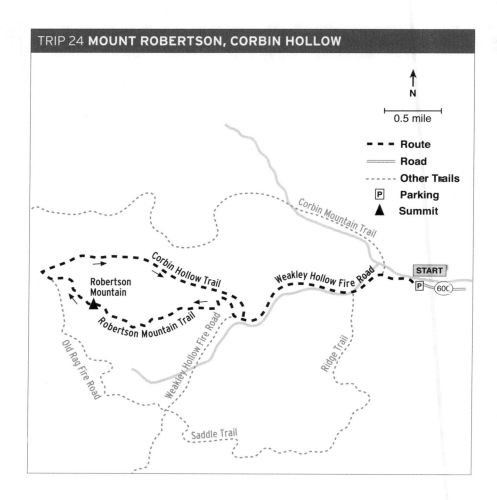

N

0.5 mile

- - - Route
═══ Road
----- Other Trails
P Parking
▲ Summit

Corbin Mountain Trail

Corbin Hollow Trail

Weakley Hollow Fire Road

START

P 60C

Robertson Mountain

Robertson Mountain Trail

Weakley Hollow Fire Road

Old Rag Fire Road

Ridge Trail

Saddle Trail

At 2.3 miles, you reach a bend in the road where two trails meet the road on the right, first Corbin Hollow Trail and then Robertson Mountain Trail. Both are marked by concrete posts. Note this intersection well, as you'll be returning here toward the end of the hike. For now, take the second intersection and the blue-blazed Robertson Mountain Trail, which starts by following Brokenback Run, but quickly swings to the left and starts its climb up Robertson Mountain.

And what a climb it is. Over the next 1.7 miles, you ascend 1,800 feet to reach the summit, with the trail never really relenting more than a few degrees. In the lower reaches, be sure to look out to the left for partial views of Old Rag. Once you finally reach the mountain's flat shoulder, walk for a few hundred feet on the broad back of the mountain with the summit on your left. Keep your eye out on the left for an unmarked spur trail that will lead you to the rocky summit (4.1 miles), which sports a few small camping sites and boundless views. From there, you have only to soak it in.

Mount Robertson offers up a fine view of Shenandoah National Park's Central District, without the crowds that frequent Old Rag.

When you're ready to continue, head east, getting back on Robertson Mountain Trail, which descends, not especially precipitously, through several switchbacks before flattening out as you emerge from the trees at the Old Rag fire road (4.7 miles). Turn right and walk a few hundred feet to a post that marks the beginning of blue-blazed Corbin Hollow Trail. Turn right again and continue your descent. The trail is not especially steep and includes some nice views of the falls and rapids of Brokenback Run, on your left.

As you near the bottom of the hollow, you need to cross the run twice. The first crossing can be accomplished by using a fallen log that acts as an impromptu bridge, but be careful and keep watching for the blue blazes. Walk for a bit more with the creek on your right, and then you can easily hop across the water on a few big boulders. Soon enough, you return to the three-way intersection you started from (6.8 miles).

From that point, turn left and retrace your steps down the Weakley Hollow fire road to the Old Rag parking lot.

DID YOU KNOW?

Outdoorspeople often say that mountains make their own weather. Science has a name for this phenomenon. An "orographic" effect is a change in the weather caused by changes in elevation, such as might occur when a mountain affects the atmosphere. With the right weather conditions, Mount Robertson is an excellent spot to observe such an effect. When warm western winds push moist air up the far side of the Shenandoah Valley, that air can condense into clouds that, from the vantage point atop Robertson, look as if a witch's cauldron is boiling on the far side of the mountain. With some luck, you may see a similar effect in the park.

MORE INFORMATION

Shenandoah National Park (nps.gov/shen, 540-999-3500, 800-732-0911 [for emergencies]). Park facilities are generally open from March through late November; a schedule is online. In cases of inclement weather and at night in deer-hunting season (mid-November through early January), call the park to confirm whether Skyline Drive is open to vehicles. Overnight accommodations in the park include lodges, cabins, and campgrounds; visit nps.gov/shen/planyourvisit/lodging.htm or nps.gov/shen/planyourvisit/campgrounds.htm for more information.

NEARBY

Sperryville is the closest town, and there are a few eateries there, but the nearest town with a full array of services is Warrenton. Of course, there are many hikes in the vicinity of Mount Robertson. Old Rag (Trip 23) is the closest, but there are also Hawksbill (Trip 21), Whiteoak and Cedar Run (Trip 25), and a number of others.

25

WHITEOAK AND CEDAR RUN

This hike is not only one of the great classics of Shenandoah National Park—and of Virginia, in general—but also a strong contender for the best waterfall hike in the state.

DIRECTIONS

From I-66, Exit 43A, take US 29 South 13.2 miles to Warrenton. Turn right onto US 211 west toward Sperryville. In 27.0 miles, take a left onto US 522 South, cross Thornton River, and then take another left to remain on US 522 South. About 0.7 mile later, turn right onto VA 231 South and drive 10.0 miles to the junction with VA 643. Turn right here at a sign for Whiteoak. After about 4 miles, take a right onto Weakley Hollow Road. The parking lot for Whiteoak and Cedar Run is about 3.6 miles away, on the left. This lot can become quite crowded when the weather is good, but there is some overflow parking nearby. *GPS coordinates: 38° 32.316′ N, 78° 20.878′ W.*

TRAIL DESCRIPTION

To begin this classic and much-loved Shenandoah hike, start by walking to the back of the parking lot past the ranger station. A bridge takes you over Cedar Run. At this point, you're walking on blue-blazed Whiteoak Trail, which quickly arrives at an intersection. The left fork leads up Cedar Run, the described route; the right goes up Whiteoak Canyon. Though you can certainly walk Whiteoak Canyon first, Cedar Run is the steeper trail, so you'll likely be more comfortable climbing it and then descending the less steep, though certainly challenging, Whiteoak Canyon Trail.

Bear left and begin climbing Cedar Run Trail, which is also blue-blazed. At first, it ascends fairly gently through the run's lower reaches, with the water on your left. At 0.6

LOCATION
Central District, Shenandoah National Park, VA

RATING
Strenuous

DISTANCE
8-mile loop

ELEVATION GAIN
2,720 feet

ESTIMATED TIME
3-6 hours

MAPS
Map 10, Appalachian Trail and other trails in Shenandoah National Park, Central District, 2013 (PATC): www.patc.net/PATC/Our_Store/PATC_Maps.aspx

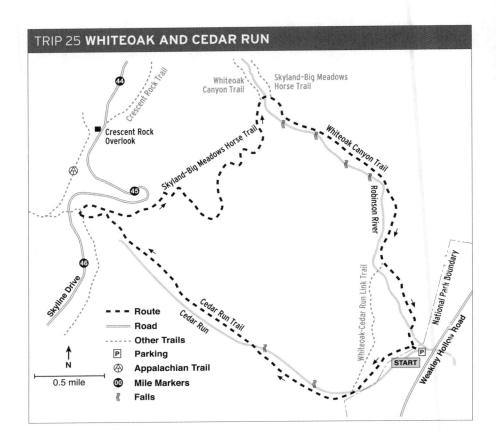

mile, the route reaches an intersection with Cedar Run–Whiteoak Link Trail. Continue straight ahead.

Cedar Run Trail reaches the creek, crosses to the left, bears sharply left, and begins switchbacking its way up the mountain, at times very steeply. Over the next 2.4 miles, you'll climb 2,020 feet and enjoy quite a good workout. The trail alternates between climbing and easing off for stretches before arriving at the falls of Cedar Run. In places, the creek passes over slabs of rock at a low angle, forming natural waterslides that intrepid hikers sometimes slide down into the waiting pools. Take time to enjoy the slides, as they are the highlight of this portion of the trail. The slide at 1.5 miles, in particular, is often crowded with hikers cooling themselves in its pool.

Beyond this slide, the trail crosses the creek again to the right. It continues to climb steadily, but the steepest parts mercifully are over. The forest opens out as the trail emerges from the narrow hollow and eventually veers away from the creek. At 3.1 miles, just a few feet shy of Skyline Drive, Skyland–Big Meadows Horse Trail appears on the right; from this point, the horse trail leads 2.2 miles to its junction with Whiteoak Canyon Trail.

The waterfalls along Cedar Run and Whiteoak make this circuit one of the finest waterfall hikes in Virginia. If the weather is hot, keep your eye out for the swimming holes, especially on the lower reaches of Whiteoak.

Turn right onto the yellow-blazed horse trail and begin the trek to Whiteoak Canyon. Pass a spur trail to a parking lot on your left at 3.7 miles. Eventually, at 5.2 miles, the big, broad, and easy path reaches the creek that flows down toward the falls of Whiteoak Canyon. Rock-hop across to join blue-blazed Whiteoak Canyon Trail. If the water is high, there is a bridge a little farther upstream. To reach it, walk to the creek and turn sharply left. You should spot it a few yards ahead.

The next 1.5 miles of descent are the highlight of this hike. Whiteoak Canyon Trail plummets down the canyon, sometimes rather steeply, bringing you several fine views of the cascades. At times it veers away to make its way past the steepest cascades, then brings you back to the water. Take some time to explore. There are not only excellent spots for photography and relaxing but also a number of good swimming holes. Pass the upper falls at 5.75 miles and then the lower at 6.5 miles. The trail crosses a tributary creek and follows it through the lower reaches of the canyon. Though the falls here are less dramatic, the swimming holes more than make up for it.

When the trail becomes nearly flat, you're almost at the hike's end. Pass Cedar Run–Whiteoak Link Trail at 7.1 miles and then rejoin Cedar Run itself at 7.8 miles. Bear left. The parking lot is just ahead at 8.0 miles.

DID YOU KNOW?

While the highest waterfall in Shenandoah National Park is 93-foot Overall Run (Trip 10), you won't feel shorted by the falls of Cedar Run or Whiteoak. Lower and Upper White Falls, in particular, will not disappoint, as you're able to get much better vantage points than with Overall Run. Of course, the highest waterfall in Virginia is Jefferson National Forest's Crabtree Falls (Trip 45), with five major cascades that fall a total of more than 1,000 feet. The highest single drop is 400 feet.

MORE INFORMATION

Shenandoah National Park (nps.gov/shen, 540-999-3500, 800-732-0911 [for emergencies]). Park facilities are generally open from March through late November; a schedule is online. In cases of inclement weather and at night in deer-hunting season (mid-November through early January), call the park to confirm whether Skyline Drive is open to vehicles. Overnight accommodations in the park include lodges, cabins, and campgrounds; visit nps.gov/shen/planyourvisit/lodging.htm or nps.gov/shen/planyourvisit/campgrounds.htm for more information.

NEARBY

The variety and quality of hikes near the Central District of Shenandoah National Park may be among the best on the East Coast. If you want to increase the difficulty of this hike, consider adding on a stretch to Hawksbill's summit (see Trip 21), which means that you'll have climbed from the base of the valley to its highest point. Start by climbing Cedar Run, crossing Skyline Drive, and continuing to climb up to Hawksbill before descending back to the Drive and then down Whiteoak. For a much more challenging option, from Hawksbill, descend to the Appalachian Trail, hike north to Skyland, and then descend Whiteoak Canyon Trail (about 13 miles).

Sperryville is the closest town, but if you're headed back toward Washington, D.C., a wider range of goods and services is available in Warrenton (a little over an hour away).

26

BEARFENCE

Don't be lulled by the short distance and mild elevation gain. This rock scramble has you climb and hoist your way to 360-degree views of the park.

DIRECTIONS

From I-66, Exit 43A, take US 29 South 13.2 miles to Warrenton. Turn right onto US 211 and drive for 34.0 miles. West of Sperryville, US 211 twists and turns before meeting the park's Thornton Gap entrance (fee). Enter the park and drive south on Skyline Drive to the Bearfence Parking Area located between mileposts 56 and 57. *GPS coordinates:* 38° 27.091' N, 78° 28.014' W.

TRAIL DESCRIPTION

This hike packs a punch in just over a mile, with a rock scramble that leads to 360-degree views of the park. If you are nervous about heights, consider avoiding the scramble and staying on the Appalachian Trail for an out-and-back trip to an outlook that affords equally nice, if not panoramic, views.

From the parking lot, cross Skyline Drive and follow blue-blazed Bearfence Loop Trail up a series of wooden steps. At 0.1 mile from the start, arrive at the intersection with the white-blazed Appalachian Trail. Proceed straight through the intersection and continue to follow the blue-blazed path as it works its way uphill a bit more and then bends to the right.

Teasers for what lies ahead begin to pop up as you clamber around and over various rock formations. Before too long, arrive at the first of several obstacles that require using your hands to help you climb up and over the rock formations. A few can feel rather exposed, so take your time here to evaluate the best path to move forward.

LOCATION
Central District, Shenandoah National Park, VA

RATING
Moderate to Strenuous

DISTANCE
1.2-mile loop

ELEVATION GAIN
300 feet

ESTIMATED TIME
1–2 hours

MAPS
Map 10, Appalachian Trail and other trails in Shenandoah National Park, Central District, 2013 (PATC): www.patc.net/PATC/Our_Store/PATC_Maps.aspx

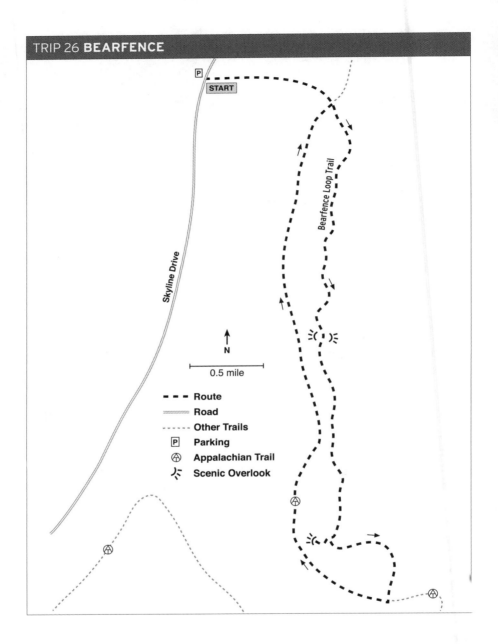

The scramble is worth it, however, especially when you reach the high point and the views of the surrounding area. Take some time to enjoy it, despite the sometimes brisk wind.

Although not as daunting as earlier, a few more obstacles present themselves going forward, and at one point the trail feels like a maze. It eventually eases out and then arrives at a concrete post 0.5 mile into the hike. You can shorten the

A hiker navigates one of the challenging rock scrambles along this short but difficult hike.

hike by turning to the right here and picking up the Appalachian Trail to complete the trek.

It's worthwhile, however, to go straight and stay on Bearfence Loop Trail for another more scenic spot. In just a little farther than 350 feet, reach an overlook that faces west, giving views of the park below. The trail passes over Bearfence Mountain and begins to descend just as it intersects with the Appalachian Trail at 0.6 mile. Turn right here and follow the white blazes. Before long, the trail passes underneath the scramble, providing an alternate view of the rocks above.

At 1.0 mile, the Appalachian Trail intersects with Bearfence Loop Trail—your starting point. Turn left here to retrace your steps back to the parking lot and your car.

DID YOU KNOW?

The Yosemite Decimal System was developed to help rate the difficulty of hikes and climbs. Classes 1, 2, and 3 are frequently used to describe hikes: Class 1 describes a walk with a low chance of injury; Class 2 involves some rock scrambling; Class 3 includes hikes that involve obstacles where you need to use your hands to advance and with portions that are exposed. Class 4 moves into rock climbing territory, and Class 5 has subclasses to further break out the difficulty of such climbs.

MORE INFORMATION

Shenandoah National Park (nps.gov/shen, 540-999-3500, 800-732-0911 [for emergencies]). Park facilities are generally open from March through late November; a schedule is online. In cases of inclement weather and at night in deer-hunting season (mid-November through early January), call the park to confirm whether Skyline Drive is open to vehicles. Overnight accommodations in the park include lodges, cabins, and campgrounds, including Big Meadows Lodge and Campground; for more information, visit nps.gov/shen/planyourvisit/lodging.htm or nps.gov/shen/planyourvisit/campgrounds.htm. Big Meadows Wayside—which offers full-service dining, groceries, camping supplies, gasoline, and more—is open Sunday through Thursday from 8 A.M. to 5:30 P.M. and Friday and Saturday from 8 A.M. to 7 P.M. between April and early November; visit goshenandoah.com for additional concession information.

NEARBY

Skyline Drive is dotted with hikes and overlooks, and Big Meadows Campground serves as a good base to explore the area. Nearby hikes include Lewis Falls (Trip 17), South River Falls (Trip 18), and Dark Hollow Falls (Trip 20).

SECTION 4
SHENANDOAH NATIONAL PARK, SOUTH DISTRICT

Shenandoah National Park's South District, which stretches from Swift Run Gap to Rock-fish Gap, encompasses more than 33,000 acres of designated Wilderness, most of which are in the western part of the district. The southernmost 39 miles of Skyline Drive

traverses this district, from milepost 65.5 to milepost 104.6. Park facilities are sparser here: a ranger station is located at Simmons Gap (milepost 73), and the Dundo Group Camp is located farther south at milepost 83.5. The most developed area in the district is Loft Mountain, which includes 219 campsites and an information center. The Potomac Appalachian Trail Club operates a number of cabins in the area, including the Doyles River Cabin (visit patc.net to make reservations). Thirty-one overlooks dot Skyline Drive in this stretch of the park. Hightop Mountain (Trip 27), the district's highest peak at 3,587 feet, is just south of the Swift Run Gap entrance station.

The full park's nearly 200,000 acres lie between the Virginia Piedmont and the Shenandoah Valley, providing a diverse array of habitats that shelter migratory birds, originate headwaters of three river drainages, and nurture a host of rare and notable plant and animal species.

When Shenandoah National Park was founded in 1940, 85 percent of the land was forested; the rest was either natural grassland or had been cultivated previously. As of surveys in 1987 and 2009, 95 percent of the park was forested, although the types of trees had changed, due to disease, extreme weather, and pests, such as the gypsy moth and the hemlock woolly adelgid (a type of insect similar to aphids; see "Invasive Species in Virginia," page 201). Most of the park supports oak–hickory forests, but chestnut–red oak forests also occur, as do tulip poplar, cove hardwood, and small sections of spruce–fir forests. In the understory, look for hepatica, bloodroot, trillium, purple and yellow violets, pink lady's slippers, bluets, columbine, oxeye daisy, milkweed, and 852 other species of wildflowers. Visit in June to see the mountain laurel in bloom. Ferns, grasses, lichens, mosses, and liverworts fill the spaces between, flourishing on the forest floor, on dry cliff faces, in muddy streambeds, and in the acidic soils at higher elevations. If you're visiting in the wet seasons of spring or fall, you'll likely see the park's 400 mushroom species at their peak of development.

More than 200 species of animals either reside in or pass through Shenandoah National Park. Most visitors see the abundant white-tailed deer, but black bears, bobcats, big brown bats, and other smaller, elusive species are present. Approximately 100 species of birds breed in the park; common species include the broad-winged hawk, Carolina wren, ovenbird, and eastern towhee, among many others. Ten species of amphibians reside here, including the endangered Shenandoah salamander, which is found only in the park. (For a brief overview of the park and its Wilderness Areas, see the introduction to Section 2; for more on the park's history, see the introduction to Section 3.)

PRESERVING THE NIGHT SKY

At night from the many overlooks in Shenandoah National Park, visitors can gaze at the towns lighting up the valley below. For some people, this is an added attraction, but to others, it is a sign that our night skies are disappearing. In North America in 2017, 80 percent of people lived in areas where they could not see the Milky Way and other night sky features. Look at any map that tracks light pollution, and the East Coast shines brilliantly. (Visit www.darksky.org for information, maps, and images.)

Disappearing night skies have an impact beyond humans having fewer stars to enjoy. Light pollution also affects the nocturnal habits of some animals. For example, migrating birds rely on stars for navigation, and some scientists believe that some moth populations are being affected by unnatural light—moths are drawn to the light but may be killed by the hot surface.

As national parks become one of the few places where night skies are visible, the National Park Service has taken up the charge of preserving not only the environment around us but also the one above us. Since 2001, its Night Skies Team has been measuring the impact of light pollution in 100 parks, finding that every park has been affected by light pollution. Fortunately, there are solutions at hand. Park officials have joined with local communities to reduce the impact of light pollution. In the Shenandoah Valley, officials have erected zoning codes to reduce light use.

In Shenandoah National Park itself, the staff has been looking at ways to reduce light pollution. For example, light fixtures at Big Meadows Wayside now have shields on them to reduce glare, and staff members are looking at other ways to improve area and walkway lights. Since 2000, Big Meadows has been hosting programs to raise awareness of the night sky and of what park visitors can do to make a difference. The Night Sky Festival, launched in 2016 and held annually, features ranger activities and educational programs in celebration of dark skies.

Stretch your legs on this steady uphill hike to Hightop Mountain and a scenic spot for a good long break.

DIRECTIONS

From I-66, Exit 43A, take US 29 South 54.5 miles to its junction with VA 33 in Ruckersville. Turn right (west) onto VA 33 and continue 14.4 miles to the park's Swift Run Gap entrance (fee). Head left (south) on Skyline Drive to the Smith Roach Gap Parking Area (between mileposts 69 and 70). *GPS coordinates: 38° 19.717′ N, 78° 34.498′ W.*

TRAIL DESCRIPTION

Hightop Mountain may not be one of the better-known hikes in Shenandoah National Park, but this lovely stretch on the Appalachian Trail (AT) is a perfect introduction to the trails in the southern part of the park, which tend to be less crowded and a little wilder. Starting the trip from the Smith Roach Gap Parking Area rather than the Hightop Parking Area makes for a longer hike, but this approach gives a more gradual climb to the top. With an easy path that isn't too rocky, this is a perfect route for a leisurely stroll.

To start, head past the yellow gate in the parking area and then make a quick left turn onto the white-blazed AT. The path maintains a steady climb until you reach the top, giving you a chance to take your time and enjoy your surroundings as you meander up the mountain.

At a little less than a mile, the AT intersects Smith Roach Gap Fire Road; pass through the intersection and stay on the AT. Shortly after this intersection, a blue-blazed spur trail departs on the left. Your route lies straight ahead on the AT, but if you're interested in a quick diversion, follow the blue blazes to and from Hightop Hut, one of the many

LOCATION
South District, Shenandoah National Park, VA

RATING
Easy

DISTANCE
3.5 miles round-trip

ELEVATION GAIN
999 feet

ESTIMATED TIME
2-3 hours

MAPS
Map 11, Appalachian Trail and other trails in Shenandoah National Park, South District (PATC): www.patc.net/PATC/ Our_Store/PATC_Maps.aspx

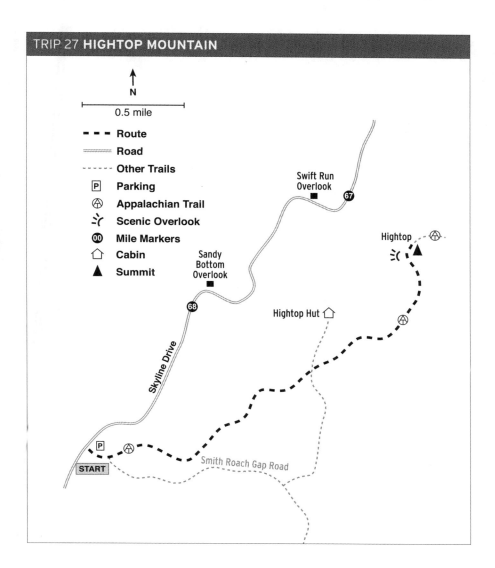

N

0.5 mile

- **- - -** Route
- ═══ Road
- ----- Other Trails
- P Parking
- Appalachian Trail
- Scenic Overlook
- 00 Mile Markers
- Cabin
- ▲ Summit

Swift Run Overlook

67

Sandy Bottom Overlook

68

Hightop

Hightop Hut

Skyline Drive

Smith Roach Gap Road

START

P

shelters along the AT in Shenandoah. This shelter is a mile shy from a milestone for AT thru-hikers, sitting 899 miles from Springer Mountain, Georgia. Katahdin, Maine, is only another 1,293 miles away.

The trail continues to steadily climb the mountain, passing a covered spring to the right. Shortly after the spring, the path flattens out slightly. Some paths lead off to campsites, but keep an eye on the white blazes to stay straight on the AT. Arrive at an overlook at 1.7 miles that greets with views of Skyline Drive and some of the peaks farther south in the park.

After enjoying the scenery, retrace your steps back down the mountain and to the parking lot.

These stone posts are an omnipresent sight throughout the park, marking both the Appalachian Trail and the numerous other trails that crisscross its path.

DID YOU KNOW?

Swift Run Gap, near this hike, has an important place in history. In 1716, British colonial governor Alexander Spotswood led 62 men and 74 horses on an expedition to explore the interior of what was then the colony of Virginia. They reached Swift Run Gap on September 5, 1716, and then toasted their success in the Shenandoah Valley near what is now Elkton. Spotswood continued the celebration by giving each member a golden horseshoe pin inscribed in Latin with *Sic jurat transcendere montes* ("Thus he swears to cross the mountains"). This group became known as the Knights of the Golden Horseshoe, and a plaque marks the site of their crossing.

MORE INFORMATION

Shenandoah National Park (nps.gov/shen, 540-999-3500, 800-732-0911 [for emergencies]). Park facilities are generally open from March through late November; a schedule is online. In cases of inclement weather and at night in deer-hunting season (mid-November through early January), call the park to confirm whether Skyline Drive is open to vehicles. Overnight accommodations in the park include lodges, cabins, and campgrounds, including Loft Mountain Campground; visit nps.gov/shen/planyourvisit/lodging.htm or nps.gov/shen/

planyourvisit/campgrounds.htm for more information. Loft Mountain Wayside (milepost 79.5) sells groceries, camping and hiking supplies, and gifts and is open daily from 9 A.M. to 6 P.M. between mid-April and early November; visit goshenandoah.com for additional concession information.

NEARBY

The towns of Harrisonburg and Crozet are good stopping points for hikers on their way into or out of Shenandoah National Park. The hikes in this section (Trips 27–32) are all within about 30 minutes of one another and within an hour's drive of the Central District hikes on Skyline Drive (Trips 14–26).

28

DOYLES RIVER, JONES RUN FALLS

In spring, the falls along Doyles River and Jones Run make for one of the most attractive waterfall walks in Virginia.

DIRECTIONS

From the north: From I-66, Exit 43A, take US 29 South 54.5 miles to its junction with VA 33 in Ruckersville. Turn right (west) onto VA 33 and continue 14.4 miles to the park's Swift Run Gap entrance (fee). Enter the park and head left (south) on Skyline Drive to the Jones Run trailhead parking lot on the left, near milepost 84.

From the south: From I-64, take Exit 99 (US 250) and follow signs for Skyline Drive. Enter the park through the Rockfish Gap entrance (fee). Drive north on Skyline Drive for 21.2 miles, then turn right into the Jones Run trailhead parking lot, near milepost 84. *GPS coordinates:* 38° 13.802′ N, 78° 43.577′ W.

TRAIL DESCRIPTION

The first 2.4 miles of this loop descend 1,272 feet, past Jones Run Falls and to a low point in the valley; the second 2.2 miles vault you higher as you gain 1,506 feet on what is by far the most strenuous part of this route. The incredible views of Doyles River Falls make it worth the effort, and the final 3.4 miles on the Appalachian Trail (AT) roll along far more placidly.

Starting in the parking lot, follow the blue-blazed trail from the back of the lot to an intersection with the white-blazed AT, which crosses your path from left to right. Note this intersection; you return to it at the end of the hike.

Continue on the blue-blazed Jones Run Trail, as it drops through a fairly mild series of switchbacks as it approaches Jones Run Falls. This is one of the most popular trails in this part of the park, so it is well maintained and well graded.

LOCATION
South District, Shenandoah National Park, VA

RATING
Moderate

DISTANCE
8 miles round-trip

ELEVATION GAIN
2,267 feet

ESTIMATED TIME
3–5 hours

MAPS
Map 11, Appalachian Trail and other trails in Shenandoah National Park, South District (PATC): www.patc.net/PATC/ Our_Store/PATC_Maps.aspx

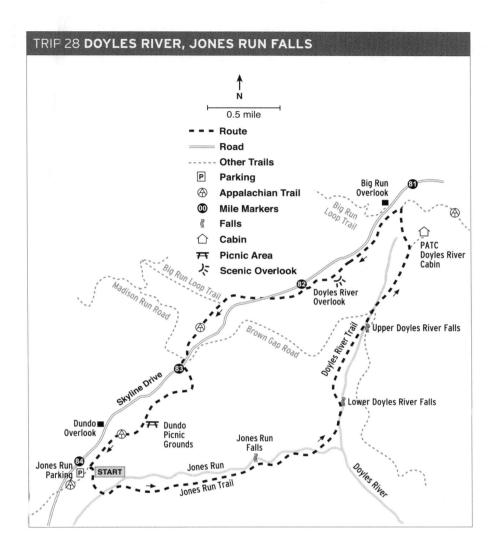

Eventually, the trail approaches the creek more closely and reaches an area where the water forms a steep slide over the stone. The trail switchbacks over a broad rim and brings you down into the bowl of Jones Run Falls itself at 1.6 miles. This is one of the better places to photograph a waterfall in Shenandoah National Park.

Follow the trail as it parallels the creek, which is on the left. Don't forget to stop and look back uphill—the cascades and little falls are quite scenic. At 2.4 miles, Jones Run Trail finally arrives at the intersection with Doyles River Trail, also blue-blazed, which has descended the mountain from the left. The V-shaped valley you are now in is the lowest point on the trail; the big climb lies ahead.

Follow Doyles River Trail's blue blazes back up the mountain. The path first arrives at Lower Doyles River Falls at 3.1 miles. Take a steep spur trail down to

This route along Doyles River and Jones Run provides excellent waterfall views in Shenandoah National Park's South District. Canine hikers are especially keen to splash about in the creeks.

explore. Although you may find it difficult to believe, Upper Doyles River Falls is even more attractive. To judge for yourself, continue up Doyles River Trail another 0.4 mile; a short path leads to the base of the two terraces over which the water cascades. If you like, get close enough to feel the spray. (*Caution:* Approaching the waterfall involves some scrambly moves on rocks that may be slick.)

From here, the climb becomes a bit more of a chore as the trail leaves the falls and ascends—step by laborious step—toward Skyline Drive and the AT. Pass Brown Gap Road at 3.8 miles. In another 0.5 mile, your route intersects a trail on the right that leads to the Potomac Appalachian Trail Club's Doyles River Cabin; continue on Doyles River Trail, which can be steep at times, but is very frequently walked and quite well maintained. At 4.6 miles, just shy of the parking lot on Skyline Drive, the path intersects the AT. Turn left (south) to follow the white blazes. You may want to pause here to catch your breath.

Though this final section is fairly gentle, it does involve some rolling terrain. At first, the trail runs along the left (east) side of Skyline Drive. Pass through the parking lot at Doyles River Overlook, cross the drive, and hike to Brown Gap at

6.7 miles. From this point, the AT crosses Skyline Drive, climbs slightly, and then passes alongside the Dundo Picnic Grounds at 7.4 miles. In another 0.6 mile of easy walking, you reach the intersection with the Jones Run Trail from which you started. Turn right to return to the parking lot.

DID YOU KNOW?

Although Jones Run and Doyles River lay claim to some of the most attractive waterfalls in Shenandoah National Park, these falls are not the tallest. That honor goes to Overall Run (Trip 10), which at 93 feet measures higher than any other falls in the park. Unfortunately, Overall Run suffers dry spells and is not as easily viewed. In nearby Jefferson National Forest, Apple Orchard Falls (Trip 46) is particularly dramatic. Crabtree Falls (Trip 45), also in Jefferson National Forest, claims the honor of being not only the highest falls in Virginia but also the highest east of the Mississippi.

MORE INFORMATION

Shenandoah National Park (nps.gov/shen, 540-999-3500, 800-732-0911 [for emergencies]). Park facilities are generally open from March through late November; a schedule is online. In cases of inclement weather and at night in deer-hunting season (mid-November through early January), call the park to confirm whether Skyline Drive is open to vehicles. Overnight accommodations in the park include lodges, cabins, and campgrounds, such as Loft Mountain Campground; for more information, visit nps.gov/shen/planyourvisit/lodging .htm or nps.gov/shen/planyourvisit/campgrounds.htm.

NEARBY

You won't lack for hiking opportunities in the wild South District of Shenandoah National Park. The hikes in this area (Trips 27–32) are all within about 30 minutes of one another and within an hour's drive of the Central District hikes on Skyline Drive (Trips 14–26). The trailhead for Blackrock (Trip 31) is just another mile south on Skyline Drive.

Harrisonburg, to the north, and Staunton, to the south, offer a broad array of goods and services.

29

BIG RUN, BROWN MOUNTAIN LOOP

Reachable only by circuitous routes, Big Run's most picturesque pools, cascades, and falls are hidden gems of Shenandoah National Park.

DIRECTIONS

From the north: From I-66, Exit 43A, take US 29 South 54.5 miles to its junction with VA 33 in Ruckersville. Turn right (west) onto VA 33 and continue 14.4 miles to the park's Swift Run Gap entrance (fee). Head left (south) onto Skyline Drive to Brown Mountain Overlook on the right (between mileposts 76 and 77).

From the south: From I-64, Exit 99 (US 250), follow signs for Skyline Drive and enter the park through the Rockfish Gap entrance (fee). Drive north on Skyline Drive for 28.5 miles to Brown Mountain Overlook, on the left. *GPS coordinates: 38° 17.537' N, 78° 39.477' W.*

TRAIL DESCRIPTION

Take time before beginning the hike to survey your route from the overlook. Directly ahead of you, spot the rocky ridgeline of Brown Mountain. You will descend to the saddle beneath you, then reascend to this ridgeline, which you'll follow westward until you drop down to Big Run. From there, the route doubles back on itself, following Big Run east toward Skyline Drive. Directly beneath you is Rocky Mountain Run, which you'll follow as it climbs away from Big Run, to the saddle, and then back to the overlook where you stand. You'll need to ford a few runs on this route. In drier seasons, you might be able to rock-hop over these fords and reach the other side with dry feet, but always be prepared to get your feet wet, no matter the conditions. If there's been considerable rainfall recently, be extra cautious at these crossings.

LOCATION
South District, Shenandoah National Park, VA

RATING
Moderate

DISTANCE
9.3-mile loop

ELEVATION GAIN
2,464 feet

ESTIMATED TIME
4-7 hours

MAPS
Map 11, Appalachian Trail and other trails in Shenandoah National Park, South District (PATC): www.patc.net/PATC/ Our_Store/PATC_Maps.aspx

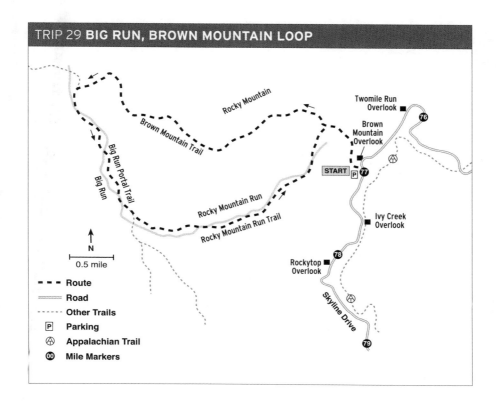

Legend
- - - Route
═══ Road
----- Other Trails
P Parking
Ⓐ Appalachian Trail
⓪⓪ Mile Markers

Once you start hiking, you'll descend about 500 feet over 0.6 mile, following the blue blazes of Brown Mountain Trail, to reach the intersection with Rocky Mountain Run Trail on the left, also blue-blazed. Take careful note of this point, as you'll return here near the end of the hike. For now, climb away from the saddle on Brown Mountain Trail, which switchbacks its way to the ridgeline, gaining about 450 feet. The footway opens out to a series of rocky views. Scramble up for a look back toward Skyline Drive.

Over the next 1.3 miles, Brown Mountain Trail generally follows this ridgeline as it weaves its way westward toward the park's periphery. Generally, the terrain is rolling. Keep your eye out for side paths that will take you to various interesting viewpoints. Eventually, the trail runs out of mountain and begins to switchback vigorously down toward Big Run. Scope out the rock slides on the northern face of Rockytop, and listen for the sound of rushing water. After about 1,700 feet of total descent and 4.6 total miles, the path reaches two park posts and passes by the metal bridge leading over the river, on the right, to Rockytop Trail.

Stay left and follow Big Run Portal Trail, blazed in yellow. At first, this trail stays to the north of the stream, passing by a few campsites. Soon enough, it

As the biggest watershed in Shenandoah National Park, the Big Run area is dotted with pools that tempt hikers to take a break and enjoy their surroundings.

crosses the run at the first of four fords. The trail crosses first to the south, then the north, then the south, and finally the north once again over the next 1.5 miles. The hiking here is generally easy, as it follows an old road grade that stays fairly flat. Take time to explore, as Big Run is the star of this hike.

After the fourth ford, at 6.0 miles, the trail reaches a truly magnificent swimming hole that stays deep enough to enjoy even in fairly dry weather. Seize this opportunity for a break, a dip, and a picnic. Don't leave until you're refreshed, as you have the climb back to Skyline Drive ahead of you.

Immediately after you leave the swimming hole, the route intersects blue-blazed Rocky Mountain Run Trail on the left. Turn left, leave Big Run, and begin to climb. At first, the path's grade is gentle as it cuts through a deep and dark valley that sees few visitors. In season, you might find berries and bears along the path. The trail passes by a nice campsite at the base of a little waterfall. Then, grin and bear it as the climbing becomes steeper, the path eventually switch-backing—quite indirectly—as it nears the saddle, noted above.

At 8.6 miles, the trail reaches the saddle. Turn right onto Brown Mountain Trail and climb the remaining 500 feet and 0.6 mile to the overlook.

DID YOU KNOW?

Big Run is the park's largest drainage, emptying a vast watershed and draining into the North Fork of the Shenandoah River. To get a sense of how large the valley that Big Run occupies is, climb Blackrock (see Trip 31). From its summit, you can see Big Run's capacious valley to the north, guarded to the west by Rockytop and Brown Mountain.

MORE INFORMATION

Shenandoah National Park (nps.gov/shen, 540-999-3500, 800-732-0911 [for emergencies]). Loft Mountain Wayside (milepost 79.5) sells groceries, camping and hiking supplies, and gifts and is open daily from 9 A.M. to 6 P.M. between mid-April and early November; visit goshenandoah.com for additional concession information. Park facilities are generally open from March through late November; a facilities schedule is online. In cases of inclement weather and at night in deer-hunting season (mid-November through early January), call the park to confirm whether Skyline Drive is open to vehicles. Overnight lodging in the park includes lodges, cabins, and campgrounds, including Loft Mountain Campground; for more information, visit nps.gov/shen/planyourvisit/lodging .htm or nps.gov/shen/planyourvisit/campgrounds.htm.

NEARBY

The hikes in this section (Trips 27–32) are all within about 30 minutes of one another and within an hour's drive of the Central District hikes on Skyline Drive (Trips 14–26). Nearby trips include Hightop Mountain (Trip 27) and Doyles River and Jones Run Falls (Trip 28).

For supplies, visit the Loft Mountain Wayside or campground store, or leave the park to shop at Harrisonburg, the nearest city.

30

TRAYFOOT MOUNTAIN AND PAINE RUN LOOP

Another gem of Shenandoah National Park's South District, this hike includes a ridgeline walk that is one of the nicest in the park and delivers one highlight early with the near-360-degree vista from Blackrock.

DIRECTIONS

From the north: From I-66, Exit 43A, take US 29 South 54.5 miles to its junction with VA 33 in Ruckersville. Turn right (west) onto VA 33 and continue 14.4 miles to the park's Swift Run Gap entrance (fee). Enter the park and head left (south) on Skyline Drive to the Blackrock Gap Parking Area (between mileposts 87 and 88).

From the south: From I-64, Exit 99 (US 250), follow signs for Skyline Drive and enter the park through the Rockfish Gap entrance (fee). Drive north on Skyline Drive for 25.9 miles, then turn right into the Blackrock Gap Parking Area (between mileposts 87 and 88). *GPS coordinates:* 38° 12.405′ N, 78° 44.983′ W.

TRAIL DESCRIPTION

The Trayfoot Mountain and Paine Run loop is another excellent example of southern Shenandoah National Park's rugged hiking. This route starts and ends with a climb, making it a good trek if you're looking for a challenge. Save most of your energy for the end, however, as the trail ascends steadily for more than 3.0 miles back to the parking lot.

From the parking lot, cross Skyline Drive and look for the concrete post marking the Appalachian Trail (AT). Turn left onto the white-blazed AT and follow it uphill. The trail crosses Skyline Drive again and continues to climb steadily. Stay straight on the AT, passing an

LOCATION
South District, Shenandoah National Park, VA

RATING
Strenuous

DISTANCE
9.2-mile loop

ELEVATION GAIN
2,500 feet

ESTIMATED TIME
5–6 hours

MAPS
Map 11, Appalachian Trail and other trails in Shenandoah National Park, South District (PATC): www.patc.net/PATC/ Our_Store/PATC_Maps.aspx

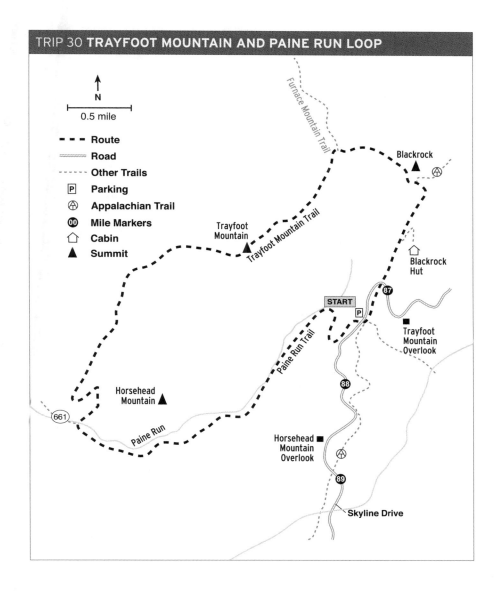

intersection with a spur trail at 0.7 mile. (The blue-blazed spur leads to Black-rock Hut, one of the shelters along the AT in the park.)

The trail continues to ascend and at 1.1 miles intersects Trayfoot Mountain Trail. Stay on the AT and keep following the white blazes. Famed Blackrock, both a mountain summit and unique geologic formation known as a talus slope, with its jumble of rocks lies just past this intersection, and it is well worth taking a break here to scramble to the top for 360-degree views of the park and out to the valley.

A hiker pauses for a worthy photo opportunity, capturing these scenic eastward views.

After you have enjoyed the scenery, continue on the AT as it loops around Blackrock and arrives at Blackrock Spur Trail at 1.25 miles. Turn left onto the blue-blazed spur trail, which leads through a maze of slabs to an intersection with blue-blazed Trayfoot Mountain Trail at 1.4 miles. Bear right and follow Trayfoot Mountain Trail as it makes its way farther up the mountain, passing an intersection with Furnace Mountain Trail at 2.0 miles and eventually arriving at Trayfoot's 3,371-foot summit (2.2 miles).

The next stretch of the route is pleasant, running up and down along the ridge and passing interesting rock formations. Occasional, but obscured, views across the valley emerge. Don't despair, though, as another outlook awaits. Eventually, at 5.2 miles, the trail arrives at an outcropping that offers a good view of Buzzard Rock and the valley below.

From here, the route turns sharply to the left and heads downhill. Arrive at yellow-blazed Paine Run Trail at 5.8 miles, and turn left to start following it. Paine Run Trail crosses Paine Run a few times as it makes its way uphill. The climb at first is a mild one, and the wide path switches from a sandy and rocky surface to one more packed down. This part of the trail also can be rather exposed to the sun, especially in summer, because the area is still recovering from a forest fire that occurred several years ago.

The mild climb eventually gets a little tougher as the route makes a sharp turn to the right and begins a series of long, steep switchbacks before arriving at the parking lot.

DID YOU KNOW?

Little evidence remains of Blackrock Springs Hotel, which was located along Paine Run Road. The first mention of this resort appeared in a newspaper in 1835, and its seven springs were touted as able to heal gout and even baldness. The property switched hands several times over the years, and cottages and a boardinghouse sprang up nearby. In 1909, the hotel and cottages were destroyed in a fire, but the boardinghouse was spared. It—and its bowling alley—remained in operation until Shenandoah National Park was established.

MORE INFORMATION

Shenandoah National Park (nps.gov/shen, 540-999-3500, 800-732-0911 [for emergencies]). Park facilities are generally open from March through late November; a schedule is online. In cases of inclement weather and at night in deer-hunting season (mid-November through early January), call the park to confirm whether Skyline Drive is open to vehicles. Overnight lodging in the park includes lodges, cabins, and campgrounds, including Loft Mountain Campground; for more information, visit nps.gov/shen/planyourvisit/lodging.htm or nps.gov/shen/planyourvisit/campgrounds.htm. Loft Mountain Wayside (milepost 79.5) sells groceries, camping and hiking supplies, and gifts. It is open daily from 9 A.M. to 6 P.M. between mid-April and early November; visit goshenandoah.com for additional concession information.

NEARBY

The towns of Harrisonburg and Crozet are good stopping points for hikers on their way into or out of Shenandoah. Loft Mountain—and its wayside—is a few miles north on Skyline Drive. You could also opt to see only Blackrock by a gentler route from the Blackrock Summit Parking Area at milepost 85 (Trip 31). The hikes in this section (Trips 27–32) are all within about 30 minutes of one another and within an hour's drive of the Central District hikes on Skyline Drive (Trips 14–26).

31

BLACKROCK

This short, gentle hike leads to one of the most compelling vistas in Virginia, an awe-inspiring 360-degree view of the South District of Shenandoah National Park.

DIRECTIONS

From the north: From I-66, Exit 43A, take US 29 South 54.5 miles to its junction with VA 33 in Ruckersville. Turn right (west) onto VA 33 and continue 14.4 miles to the park's Swift Run Gap entrance (fee). Enter the park and head left (south) on Skyline Drive to the Blackrock Summit Parking Area (between mileposts 84 and 85).

From the south: From I-64, take Exit 99 (US 250) and follow signs for Skyline Drive. Enter the park through the Rockfish Gap entrance (fee). Drive north on Skyline Drive, past the Blackrock Gap Parking Area (between mileposts 88 and 87), to the Blackrock Summit Parking Area (between mileposts 85 and 84). *GPS coordinates:* 38° 13.368′ N, 78° 43.997′ W.

TRAIL DESCRIPTION

Few trails, especially in this region, offer such reward for so little effort.

From the parking lot, look westward to find the big, broad spur trail leading to the Appalachian Trail (AT). The blue-blazed Trayfoot Mountain Trail climbs slightly as it leads about 800 feet to an intersection with the AT and its hallmark white blazes. Turn left and head south on the AT. (Trayfoot Mountain Trail continues to the summit of Blackrock by a slightly different route, on the left.)

The AT climbs about 150 feet in elevation, but the grade never approaches anything resembling steep. The mountain rises above you on the left, and with a keen eye you can spot the blue-blazed trail shadowing the AT through

LOCATION
South District, Shenandoah National Park, VA

RATING
Easy

DISTANCE
1.2 miles round-trip

ELEVATION GAIN
300 feet

ESTIMATED TIME
1–1.5 hours

MAPS
Map 11, Appalachian Trail and other trails in Shenandoah National Park, South District (PATC): www.patc.net/PATC/ Our_Store/PATC_Maps.aspx

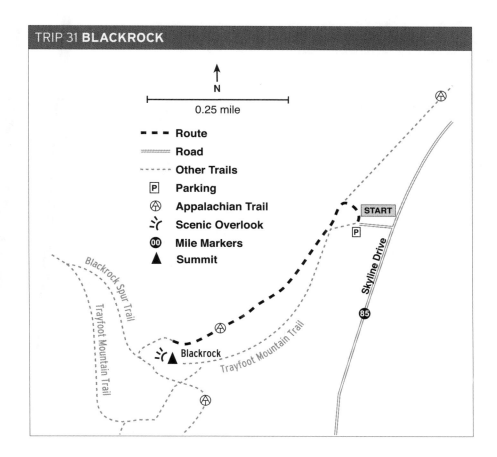

the forest. After about 0.5 mile, the AT crosses a rockfall and descends to the right. Be careful as you navigate this terrain because the footing is somewhat treacherous. Pause and look left for a view of the top of Blackrock Mountain, and start to gain an appreciation for this vantage point.

Just past the rockfall, the trail reaches a post marking an intersection with Trayfoot Mountain Trail. Leave the AT and scramble over the boulders to the left to reach the summit's garden of rocks. Take your time and be sure of your foot placement, but the scrambling isn't too difficult.

From the summit, the scene is spectacular, especially westward. To the right, a wide-ranging view takes in all of Big Run's drainage—the largest in the park— as well as Brown Mountain, Rockytop, Austin Mountain, and several other peaks. The formidable ridgeline of Trayfoot Mountain and Furnace Mountain (Trip 30) rises directly ahead. On your left lies the valley of Paine Run.

This vista makes for an especially good sunrise or sunset hike. The trail is not especially difficult to follow in the dark; just make sure to bring your headlamp

The view from Blackrock is one of the authors' favorites in the region. From this vantage, one can easily trace the route of several of the hikes described in this book, such as Big Run, Trayfoot, and Riprap Hollow.

or a flashlight. Once you're ready, retrace your route to return to your vehicle. Alternatively, you can return on the blue-blazed Trayfoot Mountain Trail and make a teardrop loop. Be careful, however, not to continue farther south, because you'll end up back at Skyline Drive, but on the wrong side.

DID YOU KNOW?

Blackrock is one of just five true 360-degree viewing points in the park. The others are Mary's Rock (Trip 15), Hawksbill (Trip 21), Old Rag (Trip 23), and Bearfence (Trip 26). Though there are many fine views in the Shenandoah region, its lush vegetation does tend to interfere with seeing sweeping panoramas from its summits.

MORE INFORMATION

Shenandoah National Park (nps.gov/shen, 540-999-3500, 800-732-0911 [for emergencies]). Park facilities are generally open March through late November; a schedule is online. In cases of inclement weather and at night in deer-hunting season (mid-November through early January), call the park to confirm whether Skyline Drive is open to vehicles. Overnight accommodations in the park include lodges, cabins, and campgrounds, such as Loft Mountain Campground; for more information, visit nps.gov/shen/planyourvisit/lodging.htm or nps.gov/shen/planyourvisit/campgrounds.htm.

NEARBY

If you're looking for further hiking nearby, you could opt to just see Blackrock as part of a more challenging route to tackle Trayfoot Mountain (Trip 30). The hikes in this section (Trips 27–32) are all within about 30 minutes of one another and within an hour's drive of the Central District hikes on Skyline Drive (Trips 14–26).

For post-hike refreshments, your best bets are along your route homeward, perhaps Waynesboro to the south or Warrenton to the north. Loft Mountain Wayside also makes a good spot for a break.

32

RIPRAP HOLLOW

With a swimming hole, sweeping views, and waterfalls, this valley offers some of the best hiking in Shenandoah National Park's South District.

DIRECTIONS

From the north: From I-66, Exit 43A, take US 29 South 54.5 miles to its junction with VA 33 in Ruckersville. Turn right (west) onto VA 33 and continue 14.4 miles to the park's Swift Run Gap entrance (fee). Enter the park and head left (south) on Skyline Drive to the Riprap Parking Area (just past milepost 90).

From the south: From I-64, Exit 99 (US 250), follow signs for Skyline Drive and enter the park through the Rockfish Gap entrance (fee). Drive north on Skyline Drive to the Riprap Parking Area (just past milepost 90). *GPS coordinates:* 38° 10.656′ N, 78° 45.914′ W.

TRAIL DESCRIPTION

Many describe Riprap as one of the better hikes in Shenandoah. After completing this trip, you will probably agree. While this is an excellent venture any time of year, summer allows visitors to take advantage of a cooling break in the swimming hole—just remember that the hike is all uphill from there.

From the parking lot, head along the blue-blazed trail. In just a few yards, arrive at an intersection with the Appalachian Trail (AT) and turn right. The white-blazed AT heads uphill for a bit and then arrives at another intersection in 0.5 mile, this time with blue-blazed Riprap Trail. Turn left onto Riprap Trail and follow as it dips and climbs, passing a rocky slope just before Calvary Rocks at 1.2 miles. Stop here and take some time to enjoy the first vista of the hike.

LOCATION
South District, Shenandoah National Park, VA

RATING
Strenuous

DISTANCE
9.5-mile loop

ELEVATION GAIN
2,365 feet

ESTIMATED TIME
5-6 hours

MAPS
Map 11, Appalachian Trail and other trails in Shenandoah National Park, South District (PATC): www.patc.net/PATC/Our_Store/PATC_Maps.aspx

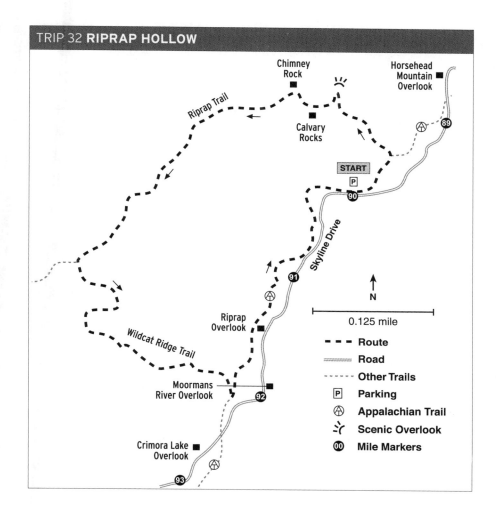

The second vantage point isn't too far away. Continue along the trail to Chimney Rock at 1.5 miles to more views of the surrounding area. From here, the trail starts to work its way downhill. It's a pleasant walk, with an occasional steep descent, that eventually flattens out for a bit as it starts to follow a streambed. At 3.2 miles, the stream that has been running to your side erupts into a cascade as it passes through a small gorge and transforms into a mini waterfall.

The path climbs uphill briefly. Look carefully at a confusing intersection where the trail seems to split; keep to your right here, following the blue-blazed trail. After climbing a bit more, the trail then dips back down to the stream, crosses it, and leads to the long-anticipated swimming hole at 3.6 miles. If the weather is good, plan for a long break here. Wade along the shallow parts, or, if you're feeling brave and the temperatures are right, plunge into the deep water and go for a quick swim.

It may be all uphill after this cascade leading to a swimming hole, 3.6 miles into the hike, but waterfalls like these make the climb back to Skyline Drive worth the trip.

From here, the hike continues alongside the stream. Arrive at an intersection with Wildcat Ridge Trail at 4.1 miles and turn left. The route crosses the stream twice before the real workout begins. For the next 2.5 miles, the trail climbs back up to the ridge—steeply at times—before arriving at the intersection with the AT at 6.5 miles. Turn left onto the AT and follow the white blazes over relatively flat terrain with occasional dips and rises. Continue on the AT back to the original spur trail and the parking lot.

DID YOU KNOW?

The rocks at Calvary Rocks are among the "youngest" in the park, evidence of the geological shifts that led to the creation of the Shenandoah Mountains. The plates that make up North America, Europe, and North Africa collided, closing the ocean and pushing up sediment from that ocean to become the Appalachian Mountains. Some of these sedimentary rocks can be seen in the park, more so in the South District, where they are exposed. Part of the Chilhowee Group, these white quartzite rocks are roughly 500 million years young and are part of the Erwin Formation.

MORE INFORMATION

Shenandoah National Park (nps.gov/shen, 540-999-3500, 800-732-0911 [for emergencies]). Park facilities are generally open from March through late November; a schedule is online. In cases of inclement weather and at night in deer-hunting season (mid-November through early January), call the park to confirm whether Skyline Drive is open to vehicles. Overnight accommodations in the park include lodges, cabins, and campgrounds, such as Loft Mountain Campground; for more information, visit nps.gov/shen/planyourvisit/lodging .htm or nps.gov/shen/planyourvisit/campgrounds.htm.

NEARBY

The towns of Harrisonburg and Crozet are good stopping points for visitors on their way into or out of Shenandoah. Loft Mountain—and its wayside—is a few miles north on Skyline Drive. The hikes in this section (Trips 27–32) are all within about 30 minutes of one another and within an hour's drive of the Central District hikes on Skyline Drive (Trips 14–26). The nearest hike to this trailhead is Trayfoot Mountain (Trip 30).

SECTION 5
MASSANUTTEN MOUNTAIN

West of Shenandoah National Park, the Shenandoah River's South Fork etches a path around the foot of three long, parallel ridges. The official name of these three collective ridges is Massanutten Mountain, but hikers more often refer to them as the Massanuttens.  With a peak elevation of 2,922 feet, these ridges stretch across 45 miles, bisecting the Shenandoah Valley.

Much of the land here is protected by the George Washington National Forest, which encompasses more than 1 million acres of land (95 percent of which is in Virginia; the rest is in West Virginia). Together, the administratively combined George Washington and Jefferson National Forests protect more than 1.8 million acres of land in Virginia, West Virginia, and Kentucky. On Massanutten Mountain's west face, 10,000 acres of forest have been identified as a sensitive viewshed, limiting the impact that development of roads and trails can have on the beauty of these wild ridges. Other projects to improve recreation resources, protect the forest against human impact, limit the effects of natural threats like the gypsy moth and woolly adelgid, and expand interpretive programs are underway.

This mountain and the valley it surrounds nearly served as the Continental Army's last refuge against the British Army during the American Revolution, but the siege of Yorktown swayed the course of history, and retreat to Fort Valley was unnecessary.

Facing page: Pictured here, the original CCC-constructed lookout point atop Kennedy Peak has been recently renovated into a newer, safer structure, which opened on July 17, 2014.

When you're visiting the area, stop by the Massanutten Visitor Center on VA 211 in New Market for more information about the natural and cultural history of this singular area. Or, stop for a walk on the 0.5-mile, accessible Storybook Trail (VA 211 to Forest Road [FR] 274, then 1.5 miles to Storybook Trail) for an outdoor, interpretative experience.

33

BUZZARD ROCK

The dramatic knife-edge ridge of Buzzard Rock offers a commanding view of Fort Valley and the South Fork of the Shenandoah River.

DIRECTIONS

From I-66, Exit 6, in Front Royal, turn left (south) onto US 340. After about 1.2 miles, turn right onto VA 55 and head west for about 5 miles. Turn left on Fort Valley Road/VA 678 and enter George Washington National Forest. Continue about 4 miles south along Fort Valley Road to the sign for the Elizabeth Furnace Recreation Area on the left. There are several turnoffs—choose the one for the family campground. Turn left and cross the bridge over Passage Creek to reach the parking lot. *GPS coordinates: 38° 55.668′ N, 78° 19.759′ W.*

TRAIL DESCRIPTION

From the parking lot, look east toward the ridge of Massanutten Mountain. You should be able to discern a gap along the ridgeline. This is Shawl Gap, and it will be your intermediary destination as you make your way from Elizabeth Furnace to Buzzard Rock.

When you're ready to get started, walk back along the road you drove in on until you reach the near side of the bridge. Look to the right and you should see orange and blue blazes along Passage Creek. This is the beginning point of the hike. For the first 2.4 miles, both colors mark Massanutten Trail (orange blazes) as it shares the path with the Tuscarora Trail (blue blazes). Follow the dual blazes along the bank of the creek, no doubt passing a number of anglers, who especially relish this area. Pass some signage for Pig Iron and Charcoal Interpretative Trail, which explains how iron was produced in the old stone furnaces. Keep track of the blue and orange blazes,

LOCATION
Massanutten Mountain, George Washington National Forest, VA

RATING
Strenuous

DISTANCE
9 miles round-trip

ELEVATION GAIN
3,433 feet

ESTIMATED TIME
4-6 hours

MAPS
Map G, trails in the Massanutten Mountain–North Half, Signal Knob to New Market Gap (PATC): www.patc.net/PATC/ Our_Store/PATC_Maps.aspx

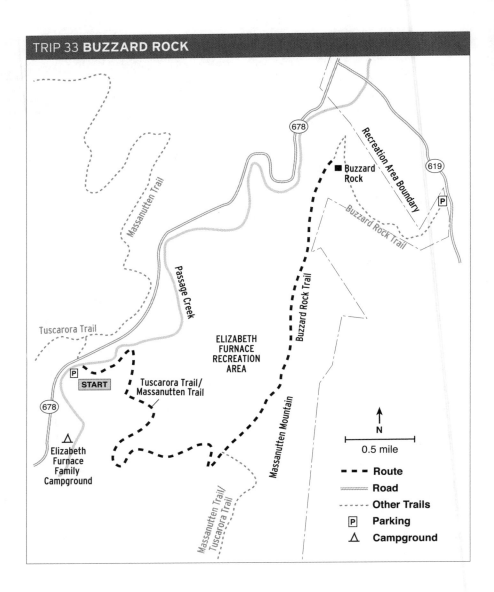

however, as it is possible to lose your way by straying onto one of the intersecting trails.

For the first 0.4 mile, the Massanutten/Tuscarora Trail is very mild-mannered and flat, but it quickly gets serious as it climbs toward Shawl Gap. Over the next 2.0 miles, the route gains about 1,200 feet as it switchbacks across the mountain. Throughout much of the climb, the path is well graded and makes for pleasant walking, but as you near the gap, it becomes especially steep and rocky. At 2.4 miles, once you've surmounted this climb, you arrive at a well-marked four-way intersection. The blue and orange blazes head south along the ridge; yellow

A hiker enjoys the sweeping valley views from the unusual rocky prow of Buzzard Rock on the north end of Massanutten Mountain.

blazes lead down the eastern face of the mountain; white blazes turn north along the ridgeline and eventually lead to Buzzard Rock.

Turn left to follow the white blazes of Buzzard Rock Trail and continue climbing about 0.8 mile and 466 feet more (nope, Shawl Gap is not the top). Watch for the numerous perches from which you can peer out over Fort Valley to the west or glimpse Shenandoah National Park to the east. Many of these offer impressive vistas. Eventually, the climb tops out at 4.5 miles, and you begin a descent to the cliffs of Buzzard Rock.

There's no mistaking the sheer rock faces that begin appearing on your left. Soon the route ambles along a knife's-edge ridge that is quite unusual for Virginia. Take time to explore the ridge; there are many excellent places to relax, have lunch, or get a terrific photo. Do be careful as you explore as the cliffs of Buzzard Rock are sheer enough to attract local climbers. Take care not to knock rocks down on them.

(If you're up for a short side trip, continue past the cliffs on the north side and walk down to a beautiful northward view of pastoral Virginia stretching toward Winchester. Of course, you'll have to walk back up again.)

Once you've enjoyed the break, return on the white blazes and then take the orange and blue blazes down to Elizabeth Furnace at 9.0 miles. Be careful on the descent, however, as there is an unmarked trail that crosses the marked route. If you do accidentally get on it, never fear, because all roads lead to Elizabeth Furnace. Still, it's better to stay on the blazes.

DID YOU KNOW?

Elizabeth Furnace takes its name from the blast furnace that, in the nineteenth century, produced pig iron. Operating from 1836 to 1888, the furnace used the water of Passage Creek for power; the pig iron was then transported to Harpers Ferry. Though the furnace lies in ruins, you can take a break from hiking to explore the remaining stone foundations. A series of placards explains the industrial process behind the mining and purification of the iron. If you do a lot of hiking in the area, you're sure to run into other furnaces of this type, such as Catherine Furnace in the South Massanutten.

MORE INFORMATION

George Washington and Jefferson National Forests, Lee Ranger District (fs.usda.gov/main/gwj, 540-984-4101). Check online for announcements concerning trail conditions, road closures, prescribed burns, and other events that may affect your hike.

NEARBY

If you want a shorter and much easier way to reach Buzzard Rock, there is another trailhead off VA 619 (38° 56.264′ N, 78° 17.313′ W). An out-and-back trip to the rocks from this trailhead will total about 4 miles with about 700 feet of gain and loss.

The nearest towns are Strasburg, Virginia (west along VA 55), and Front Royal (east along VA 55). Each offers all the businesses and services you would expect to find in a town along the interstate. There are number of big-box retail stores off I-66 at Exit 6.

34
KENNEDY PEAK

From this summit, enjoy one-of-a-kind views of Fort Valley, as well as the North and Central districts of Shenandoah National Park.

DIRECTIONS

From I-66, Exit 13, head west on VA 55 for 5.8 miles, through downtown Front Royal, to the junction with US 340. Turn left (south) onto US 340 and continue 23.2 miles, merging briefly with US 211 as you enter Luray. Turn left onto North Hawksbill Street, and in 0.3 mile, take a right onto Mechanic Street, which becomes Bixlers Ferry Road in 0.6 mile, and then VA 675 in 0.9 mile as it heads out of town. In 2.2 miles, after you cross the South Fork of the Shenandoah River, take a left, then a quick right. You are still on VA 675, now also VA 615. The road climbs into the mountains and in 2.8 miles tops out at Edith Gap, which is the trailhead for Kennedy Peak. The parking lot is on your left; a steeply sloping cut sometimes used for hang gliding is on your right; and the trail is just across the road. *GPS coordinates: 38° 43.523′ N, 78° 30.582′ W.*

TRAIL DESCRIPTION

The distinctively pyramidal shape of Kennedy Peak dominates the valley of the South Fork of the Shenandoah River. With the exception of the last few hundred yards beneath the summit, you stay on orange-blazed Massanutten Trail for the entire hike.

From the parking lot, look north across VA 675 and find the sign for Kennedy Peak and the orange blazes. Start hiking north along the big and broad Massanutten Trail. For the first 1.5 miles, the trail is rather flat. It does climb about 350 feet over this first stretch, but you'll hardly notice. Ahead of you, on the right, you should be able to

LOCATION
Massanutten Mountain, George Washington National Forest, VA

RATING
Moderate

DISTANCE
5.2 miles round-trip

ELEVATION GAIN
1,192 feet

ESTIMATED TIME
2–4 hours

MAPS
Map G, trails in the Massanutten Mountain–North Half, Signal Knob to New Market Gap (PATC): www.patc.net/PATC/Our_Store/PATC_Maps.aspx

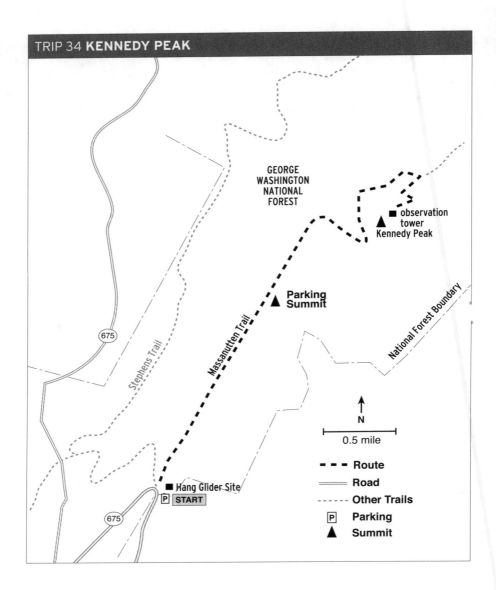

spot Kennedy Peak itself. At 1.5 miles, the trail dips down to a saddle at the mountain's shoulder and begins traversing right.

At this point the trail begins to climb. The path becomes narrower and rockier, then switchbacks to the left across the face of the mountain at 1.8 miles, gradually working its way around to the northeastern side of the peak. Look for an unblazed spur trail on the left at 2.3 miles that leads to westward views of Fort Valley.

Just beyond this unblazed spur, at 2.4 miles, a white-blazed spur trail intersects the Massanutten Trail, which continues north. Take the spur and begin a sharp

A hang glider takes off from Massanutten Mountain, high above Shenandoah Valley and near the beginning of the route to Kennedy Peak.

climb southwest to reach the top of the peak. Over the next 0.2 mile, the trail gains 185 feet to reach a shelter tower and big eastward vistas of the summit. Take your time and enjoy your resting spot.

When you're ready to return to your vehicle, you have only to retrace your steps, making sure to turn left onto the Massanutten Trail. Otherwise, the return to the trailhead is unproblematic.

DID YOU KNOW?

The observation tower atop Kennedy has stood there since it was built by the Civilian Conservation Corps (CCC) in the 1930s (see "Putting the Nation to Work," page 68). Though the CCC would build hundreds of such shelters throughout the nation, this was the first and was in close proximity to the first CCC camp, Camp Roosevelt, in Fort Valley. In the spring of 2014, the Potomac Appalachian Trail Club and the U.S. Forest Service began to renovate the tower, which had become dilapidated and dangerous. The new tower is quite an improvement.

MORE INFORMATION

George Washington and Jefferson National Forests, Lee Ranger District (fs.usda.gov/main/gwj, 540-984-4101). Check online for announcements concerning trail conditions, road closures, prescribed burns, and other events that may affect your hike.

NEARBY

If want a longer circuit hike that includes Kennedy Peak, consider walking farther north on the Massanutten Trail, descending via Stephens Trail to Camp Roosevelt, and then climbing back to Edith Gap on the Massanutten Trail. This more strenuous option will net you about 9 miles and 2,300 feet of elevation. Be sure to bring along the Potomac Appalachian Trail Club's Map G if you're planning to tackle this extended jaunt.

Luray, Virginia, is the nearest spot to grab supplies or have a quick bite to eat after the hike, though you also pass through Front Royal on your way to and from the hike. If you're looking for more hiking in the area, the other trips in this section (Trips 33–38) are all nearby. Elizabeth Furnace offers excellent vehicle camping facilities. Shenandoah National Park is just across the valley.

35

DUNCAN KNOB

Scramble to reach an impressive vista of the south side of Massanutten Mountain, the Blue Ridge Mountains, and the Shenandoah Valley.

DIRECTIONS

From I-81, Exit 264, take US 211 east. In the town of New Market, turn left and follow US 11 briefly before turning right to get back onto US 211, which soon climbs into the mountains. In 3.6 miles, at the top of the gap, turn left onto Crisman Hollow Road/Forest Development Road 274. Although the road turns to gravel, it is well maintained and suitable for cars. Pass signed trailheads for Massanutten Storybook Trail, the Massanutten Trail, and Scothorn Gap Trail before reaching the Gap Creek trailhead, on the right, in 4.5 miles. *GPS coordinates:* 38° 42.549′ N, 78° 33.582′ W.

(*Note:* Crisman Hollow Road is closed during winter. Be sure to check with the Forest Service before venturing out in the colder months. If you're determined to reach Duncan Knob even with the road closed, longer variants of the hike can be started at US 211 in the south or VA 675 in the north.)

TRAIL DESCRIPTION

The rocky top of Duncan Knob (2,803 feet) is one of the most dramatic perches in the region. To the south sits Massanutten Mountain; to the east, the ridges of Shenandoah National Park; to the west, the Alleghenies. In between lie the valleys created by the forks of the Shenandoah River. Add to these glorious views the excitement of the final scramble to the knob's summit, and you have an ideal short hike that introduces you to the area. (Be prepared to use your hands and be very cautious if the rocks are wet.)

At the trailhead at Crisman Hollow Road, look for the blue blazes headed southward, away from the road. These mark Gap Creek Trail and lead initially through a few

LOCATION
Massanutten Mountain,
George Washington National
Forest, VA

RATING
Moderate

DISTANCE
3.5 miles round-trip

ELEVATION GAIN
1,163 feet

ESTIMATED TIME
2-3 hours

MAPS
Map G, trails in the
Massanutten Mountain–
North Half, Signal Knob to
New Market Gap (PATC):
www.patc.net/PATC/
Our_Store/PATC_Maps.aspx

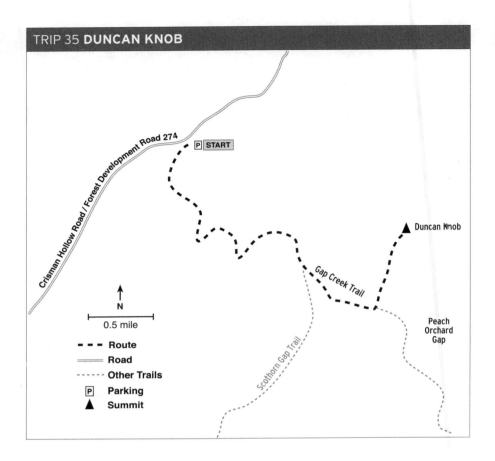

Crisman Hollow Road / Forest Development Road 274

P START

Duncan Knob ▲

Gap Creek Trail

Peach
Orchard
Gap

N

0.5 mile

Scothorn Gap Trail

- - - Route
═══ Road
----- Other Trails
P Parking
▲ Summit

impromptu campsites along Little Passage Creek. Cross the creek on a small bridge at 0.2 mile. The trail then gets down to business on its 1,171-foot climb to the top of the knob. Over the next mile, the route switchbacks four times on a moderate grade as it ascends through the forest.

At 1.25 miles, you arrive at a three-way intersection where yellow-blazed Scothorn Gap Trail traverses the forest to the southwest. Go straight and follow the blue blazes to the mountain's shoulder. The soil becomes rather sandy as you near the top.

In another 0.25 mile, at Peach Orchard Gap, the trail enters a saddle atop the mountain. A large fire ring and a campsite on the right mark the spot. Look to the left and you should see a white-blazed trail heading to the summit of Duncan Knob. Follow this trail, which climbs moderately and brings you at last to the foot of the knob at 1.75 miles. To reach the summit, you'll need to scramble up a challenging boulder field.

As you begin making your way up the rocks, remember to bear left. Keep your hands free, as you'll certainly need to use them to advance. Fortunately,

The scramble to the top of Duncan Knob is as rewarding as the views from its summit. Here, a hiker tackles one of the Class 3 moves near the top of the mountain. Photo by Andrew Lydon.

the rocks are fairly stable, but if they are wet, this scramble can be a bit treacherous. When scrambling, always remember to have good holds with three points before you move the fourth. Once you reach the summit, clamber out onto the rocky ledges, which make an ideal resting point to survey the route you've walked.

When you're ready, retrace your steps back to Peach Orchard Gap. Be especially careful descending the rocks, and take heed—you'll probably veer too far to the right on the descent. Many hikers find themselves at the treeline and at a bit of a loss concerning the location of the blazes. When you descend, look to the left to spot the white blazes. If you reach the foot of the scramble and don't see the blazes, skirt around to the left. A good-sized cairn marks the trail. If you become truly disoriented, take out your compass and walk a southwest bearing, staying on the shoulder of the mountain. Gap Creek Trail crosses your path in that direction, and you're sure to find it.

From Peach Orchard Gap, the walk to your vehicle is a straightforward descent following blue-blazed Gap Creek Trail to Crisman Hollow Road.

DID YOU KNOW?

The origin of the American Indian word Massanutten is shrouded in the mists of history. Some people claim that the word describes a basket, which American Indians believed the mountains, with their distinctive shape, resembled. Others have claimed that the word means "potato field" and that native inhabitants planted fields of sweet potatoes in the valleys. The Potomac Appalachian Trail Club (PATC) maintains an interesting archival note on the history of the Massanuttens range at patc.us/history/archive/massntn.html.

MORE INFORMATION

George Washington and Jefferson National Forests, Lee Ranger District (fs.usda .gov/main/gwj, 540-984-4101). Check online for announcements concerning trail conditions, road closures, prescribed burns, and other events that may affect your hike.

NEARBY

If, after returning to your car, you're ready for more, look across Crisman Hollow Road where the blue blazes continue past a forest gate. A 2.7-mile round-trip (with about 900 feet of gain) will take you to Jawbone Gap, where you can gaze back at Duncan Knob from another rock outcropping. To reach this point, follow the blue blazes, first on moderately graded old forest roads, then on a steeper footpath. Watch carefully for the sudden right-hand turn where the footpath leaves the road. At Jawbone Gap, you'll encounter a four-way intersection with the orange blazes of the Massanutten Trail leading away in two directions. Follow the *white* blazes (left) about 0.2 mile to the outcropping. After admiring the vista, retrace your steps for an easy descent back to your car.

If you're up for more than one hike in a weekend, consider combining the Duncan Knob trip with a visit to Strickler Knob (Trip 37) while setting up a base camp at Peach Orchard Gap or Duncan Hollow.

There are several restaurants where US 211 crosses Massanutten Mountain, and the town of New Market has a number of restaurants, shops, and gas stations.

GRANDER THAN THE HIMALAYA

Three million years ago, the Appalachian Mountains were in their prime, rivaling the Himalaya in size. Born from tectonic shifts in the earth and worn down by time, the Appalachians now offer hikers long ridgelines to explore and glimpses of ancient rock to discover—like the columnar jointing found on Compton Peak (Trip 7).

Shenandoah National Park is part of the Appalachian Range, which spans from Maine to Georgia. The range first formed during the Grenville orogeny, when tectonic plates collided 1 to 1.2 billion years ago, creating mountains that stretched from modern-day Texas to Quebec. Some of the rocks made by the heat and pressure of this collision are still visible in Shenandoah today. Mary's Rock (Trip 15), Old Rag (Trip 23), and Hogback Mountain have examples of these igneous and metamorphic rocks.

In Shenandoah, the Grenville orogeny's formations slowly succumbed to time, and tall peaks were worn down to smaller hills. About 500 million years ago, tectonic plates shifted again, this time moving apart. Rifts allowed lava to flow into valleys and eventually created an ocean. Some of these old lava flows are still visible in Shenandoah today—Big Meadows sits on one of them—and the layers of this rock look like staircases in some parts of the park. These lava flows can be seen along a number of hikes, including near Stony Man (Trip 16), Hightop (Trip 27), and Bearfence (Trip 26). The basalt rock was named greenstone because of its unusual green color.

When the plates that make up North America, Europe, and North Africa collided, ocean sediment vaulted skyward to become the Appalachian Mountains. Some of these sedimentary rocks can be seen in the park. Geologists divided the rocks, known together as the Chilhowee Group, into four formations to describe their sources more accurately. Three of these lie within the Shenandoah Valley: the Weverton Formation, with early river deposits; the Hampton Formation, with thick lagoon deposits; and the Erwin Formation, with quartzite cliffs and boulders. Of these, the Erwin Formation can be seen along some spots in the park's South District, including Blackrock (Trip 31).

All this shifting led to the creation of other mountains in the Shenandoah Valley. Massanutten Mountain, part of the Blue Ridge Range within the Appalachians, is a unique geologic feature—a doubly plunging synclinorium. Nongeologists would describe it as a mountain that has a downward fold with the youngest rock layers at the center. It also has two distinct sections divided by Market Gap: the northern part has three parallel ridges that form Fort Valley and Little Fort Valley, and the southern part consists of ridges separated by gorges.

Eventually, the plates shifted again, and time played its part with the mountains, transforming them into the ranges that we recognize today.

You'll feel much farther than only 90 minutes away from Washington, D.C., as you climb for stunning views from Signal Knob.

DIRECTIONS

From I-66, Exit 6, in Front Royal, turn left (south) onto US 340. After about 1.2 miles, turn right onto VA 55 and head west about 5 miles. Turn left onto Fort Valley Road/VA 678 and enter George Washington National Forest. Drive 3.5 miles and then turn right into the Signal Knob Parking Area. *GPS coordinates:* 38° 56.102′ N, 78° 19.174′ W.

TRAIL DESCRIPTION

Signal Knob is a perfect hike for those seeking to try longer-mileage days. With a few long, steady climbs, stretches of rock-hopping, and a viewing point perfect for lunch, this trail has something for everyone. Massanutten Trail, the 71-mile route running along much of the mountain's ridgeline, cuts through the Signal Knob parking lot. While most hikers hike Signal Knob counterclockwise, this description goes clockwise, saving the better views for the end. To walk this loop, start on Massanutten Trail, switch quickly to the Tuscarora Trail, and then rejoin Massanutten Trail for the final half.

In the parking lot, head south to find the start of this loop. After only 40 feet, the path arrives at an intersection with orange-blazed Massanutten Trail. Turn left here, and follow the orange blazes. While well marked, this first stretch of trail was slightly eroded when the authors most recently hiked it, so keep an eye on your footing. At 0.5 mile, the path arrives at a three-way intersection. Massanutten Trail turns left here, but your route is straight ahead on blue-blazed Tuscarora Trail. Start following the blue blazes, and watch for a tricky hard left turn at 0.75 mile.

LOCATION
Massanutten Mountain, George Washington National Forest, VA

RATING
Strenuous

DISTANCE
10-mile loop

ELEVATION GAIN
2,919 feet

ESTIMATED TIME
5-6 hours

MAPS
Map G, trails in the Massanutten Mountain–North Half, Signal Knob to New Market Gap (PATC): www.patc.net/PATC/Our_Store/PATC_Maps.aspx

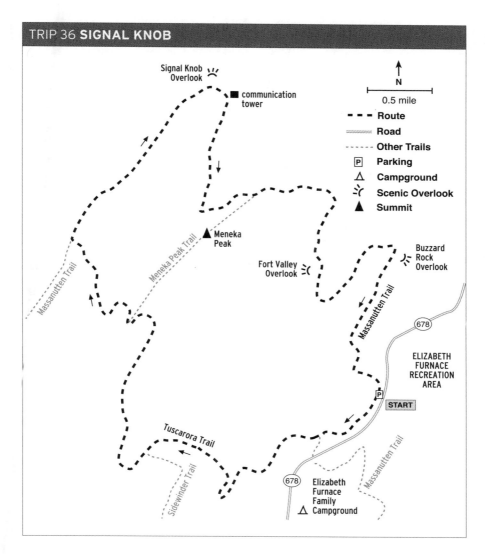

After you cross a stream, you arrive at another three-way intersection at 1.2 miles. A white-blazed connector trail for Elizabeth Furnace goes to your left. Continue straight, following the Tuscarora Trail.

As you climb, the surroundings begin to change—tall trees yield to mountain laurels as the trail eventually levels out for a bit. Arrive at another three-way intersection at 2.1 miles, this time with pink-blazed Sidewinder Trail. Continue to follow blue-blazed Tuscarora Trail as it takes a quick hairpin turn to the right, promptly switchbacks left again, and then starts to get progressively rockier.

After another switchback, this time to the right, views of the surrounding valley start to open up to your right at 2.6 miles. From here, you can clearly see just how far you've come.

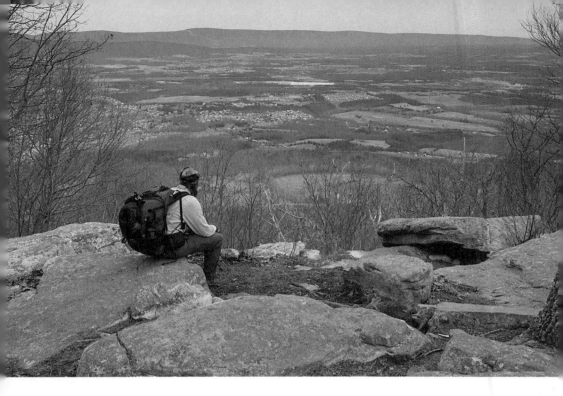

A hiker pauses to rest and enjoy the view from Signal Knob before tackling the long descent. At the very northern tip of Massanutten Mountain, Signal Knob offers a far-ranging view of Virginia's ridge and valley system.

But the climb isn't over yet. The trail continues its steady incline for another mile and then switchbacks to the left at 3.7 miles. The path gets rockier as it gets closer to the ridge, and at 3.9 miles you gain the top of the first climb at a three-way intersection with white-blazed Meneka Peak Trail. Continue to follow blue-blazed Tuscarora Trail; while not well marked at this point, your route is an obvious one as it starts to descend the mountain.

(Meneka Peak Trail is an option for those seeking either to shorten the hike or to cut out the second climb. This white-blazed trail climbs for a bit but mostly stays along the ridge. In 1.0 mile, you will arrive at an intersection with Massanutten Trail. To your left is Signal Knob, and to your right is your route back to the parking area. Taking this option and skipping Signal Knob shortens the hike by 2.0 miles.)

You lose some elevation on this steep, and at times rocky, section of the Tuscarora Trail, which drops 500 feet in just a little more than 0.5 mile. Cross Passage Creek on an easy rock-hop, and arrive at an intersection with a fire road at 4.7 miles. Here, depart the Tuscarora Trail and regain orange-blazed Massanutten Trail with a right turn. The orange-blazed fire road quickly starts recouping all the elevation you just lost. As you near the top of the fire road, around 5.6 miles, the path starts to get steeper. At 5.9 miles, the fire road continues straight up the hill while Massanutten Trail swings to the left to the Signal Knob Overlook. An arrow points the way to the impressive view at 5.9 miles; follow the path as it swings around a campsite before the knob. (If you happen to miss this turn, don't fret. The fire road ends where Massanutten Trail continues its loop past the overlook. If you arrive at this junction, look to the left to spy Signal Knob.)

From here, you can see the town of Strasburg, Virginia, and views of the northern Shenandoah Valley. It's a perfect spot to take a break and enjoy the scenery. You've arrived at the northern tip of Massanutten Trail, the counterpart of Strickler Knob (Trip 37) to the south.

Once you're ready to resume hiking, follow the orange blazes. The path quickly leads to a telecommunications tower at 6.0 miles, and then a plaque commemorating the hard work of the Massarock volunteer crew. The trail returns to the woods, becoming rocky at times and climbing for a bit longer. In 1.0 mile from the overlook, white-blazed Meneka Peak Trail comes in from the right. Go straight, following the orange blazes.

From here, the trail follows the ridge for a while and passes a number of campsites. At 7.75 miles, the path becomes steadily rockier, and you start to encounter stretches of rock fields to hop across.

You get a bit of a break from the rocks as you arrive at the Fort Valley Overlook, and then the trail swings slightly to the left at 8.2 miles. More rocky patches await as you continue your way down the mountain. At 8.8 miles, the route takes a hard right hairpin turn around a campsite surrounded by several boulders. Be sure to keep your eye on the orange blazes; many hikers have been known to miss this turn.

Once you have successfully navigated the turn, look for a glimpse of Buzzard Rock (Trip 33) to your left. If you have keen eyes, you may even see rock climbers tackling this popular climb.

From here, Massanutten Trail continues to descend. Watch your footing—the narrow path is eroded in places, so go slowly through those spots. Cross a small stream, and follow the trail as it swings to the left at 9.6 miles. Continue on the path as it steadily descends, and arrive back at the parking lot.

DID YOU KNOW?

Both the Union and Confederate armies used Signal Knob as a key vantage point for observing the movements of military units during the Civil War. The Confederates occupied it from 1862 to 1864, when the Union won control of the peak by defeating the 61st Georgia Volunteer Infantry.

MORE INFORMATION

George Washington and Jefferson National Forests, Lee Ranger District (fs.usda.gov/main/gwj, 540-984-4101). Check online for announcements concerning trail conditions, road closures, prescribed burns, and other events that may affect your hike.

NEARBY

With the 71-mile Massanutten Trail and 250-mile Tuscarora Trail intersecting in this area, you have multiple options for day hikes and longer treks. Buzzard Rock (Trip 33) sits directly across the valley from Signal Knob.

The town of Front Royal has multiple restaurants for hungry hikers, most of them along its quaint Main Street.

37

STRICKLER KNOB

Follow the rocky ridge of Middle Mountain to reach the dramatic prominence of Strickler Knob and its commanding view southward.

DIRECTIONS

From the junction of I-66 and I-81, head south on I-81 toward Roanoke. About 35 miles later, take Exit 264 for US 211, and turn left onto West Old Cross Street to pass under the interstate. You'll enter the town of New Market. Turn left onto North Congress Street, and then turn right onto US 211, which will head into the mountains. Reach the top of the pass approximately 2 miles west of New Market. As you descend the eastern side, look for a trailhead parking lot on the right, about 5.7 miles from New Market. *GPS coordinates:* 38° 38.457' N, 78° 35.389' W.

TRAIL DESCRIPTION

When you're ready to begin, look north across VA 211 from the trailhead parking lot. You should be able to spot a gate barring access to a grassy forest road and a white blaze in the shape of a lowercase *i*, almost like an information icon. You'll see this distinctive blaze along trails throughout the Massanuttens. It marks Massanutten Connector Trail as it heads north to rendezvous with orange-blazed Massanutten Trail.

At first, Massanutten Connector Trail follows a grassy old road, but after 1.1 miles, it leaves this road on the left and becomes more of a footpath. When there are few or no leaves on the trees, you should be able to make out the distinctive shape of Strickler Knob ahead on your right. To your left is the ridgeline of Waterfall Mountain. The route heads into the hollow between these ridges. A few quick switchbacks bring you down to the junction with orange-blazed Massanutten Trail at 1.8 miles. The Massanutten

LOCATION
Massanutten Mountain, George Washington National Forest, VA

RATING
Strenuous

DISTANCE
10 miles round-trip

ELEVATION GAIN
2,215 feet

ESTIMATED TIME
5-6 hours

MAPS
Map G, trails in the Massanutten Mountain–North Half, Signal Knob to New Market Gap (PATC): www.patc.net/PATC/Our_Store/PATC_Maps.aspx

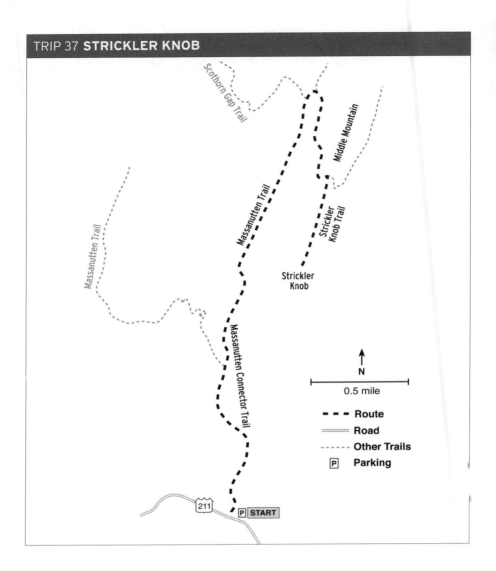

Scothorn Gap Trail

Middle Mountain

Massanutten Trail

Strickler Knob Trail

Massanutten Trail

Strickler Knob

Massanutten Connector Trail

N

0.5 mile

- - - Route
═══ Road
----- Other Trails
P   Parking

211

P START

Connector Trail ends here with the Massanutten Trail heading off to the west and the east.

Turning left would take you steeply up Waterfall Mountain. Your path, however, is straight ahead, on the eastward Massanutten Trail. Begin a gentle but sustained climb up the hollow between the mountains. The trail takes you down to Big Run for a quick, easy rock-hop crossing before ascending again for some time on the east bank of the creek. It then descends for a second crossing of Big Run at 2.4 miles and climbs more determinedly on the west bank. The terrain becomes rockier as you near the top of the hollow. When you reach a dilapidated sign telling you that Scothorn Gap is about 0.5 mile ahead, the grade levels off.

A turkey vulture guards the rocks signaling the end of the Strickler Knob hike.

At 3.6 miles, the trail reaches the four-way intersection in Scothorn Gap. Yellow blazes to the left head to Crisman Hollow Road; yellow blazes ahead lead to Duncan Knob (Trip 35). Your route turns right to follow the orange blazes of the Massanutten Trail. Climb along this gently graded old road for about 0.6 mile, until it reaches the crest of Middle Mountain at 4.25 miles. A large stone cairn marks the unnamed trail that heads southward on this ridgeline to reach Strickler Knob in another 0.75 mile.

This trail has a peculiar existence: it doesn't always appear on official maps of the area, and it is sometimes referred to as a bushwhack. When the authors last walked it for this book, however, it was blazed bright pink with fresh paint, and someone had obviously been working to maintain it. In fact, it was as well maintained as any trail in the area. If you find that the trail is in less than ideal condition, just remember that you have only to follow the ridgeline south to reach the knob. There is no ascending or descending to speak of.

The path, however, is rather rocky and rugged, so be prepared for fractured ground as you make your way to the knob. Once you near your destination, a few rock obstacles require you to use your hands to advance, but they should not test your resolve. (Do be cautious if the rocks are wet, however.) Summiting Strickler Knob at 5.0 miles requires some additional scrambling but rewards you with magnificent vistas of the southern Shenandoah National Park to the east, the southern Massanutten ridges straight ahead, and the mountains of West Virginia to the west.

When you've taken in this scene, return along the pink blazes to rejoin the Massanutten Trail. Descend to Scothorn Gap, then follow the Massanutten and Massanutten Connector trails back to US 211 and your vehicle.

DID YOU KNOW?
The orange blazes of the Massanutten Trail represent one of the major arteries of the region, tracing a 71-mile loop around this distinctive series of ridgelines. In the north, the Massanutten Trail shares space with the Tuscarora Trail, which allows you to join up with the Appalachian Trail in Shenandoah National Park. Opportunities for exploration abound.

MORE INFORMATION
George Washington and Jefferson National Forests, Lee Ranger District (fs.usda.gov/main/gwj, 540-984-4101). Check online for announcements concerning trail conditions, road closures, prescribed burns, and other events that may affect your hike.

NEARBY
If you're looking for a shorter hike to Strickler Knob, park at the Scothorn Gap trailhead on Crisman Hollow Road. Follow the yellow-blazed Scothorn Gap Trail about 1.4 miles through the forest to the four-way intersection described above. Go straight on orange-blazed Massanutten Trail to arrive at the cairn atop Middle Mountain. Your round-trip to Strickler Knob and back from this direction should be about 6 miles.

If you're up for more than one hike in a weekend, consider combining the described route with a visit to Duncan Knob (Trip 35). Set up a base camp at Peach Orchard Gap, at Duncan Hollow, or along Crisman Hollow Road.

For post-hike refreshments, look no farther than the restaurants along US 211 or the town of New Market. If you're heading back to Washington, D.C., make a stop in Front Royal.

38

EMERALD POND

Sweeping valley views and a glistening pond make choosing a lunch spot difficult. Plan on lingering to take in the impressive sights along this gem of a hike.

DIRECTIONS

From I-81, Exit 264, take US 211 east. In the town of New Market, turn left and follow US 11 briefly before turning right onto US 211, which soon climbs into the mountains. Drive 3.7 miles, and as the road starts to descend, look for the now-closed Massanutten Visitor Center to the right. The parking area is next to the visitor center. *GPS coordinates:* 38° 38.318′ N, 78° 36.369′ W.

TRAIL DESCRIPTION

Despite its length, the Emerald Pond hike is a fairly moderate one. A stiff climb at the beginning eases out once the route meets the ridge. A mild descent leads to the lovely Emerald Pond before a mild climb back to the ridge. This is a good choice for those interested in trying out longer miles.

Look toward the entrance of the parking lot to spot white-blazed Wildflower Trail. (A second trail, Nature Trail, starts near the back of the parking lot, and can cause confusion at the start.)

Make your way down Wildflower Trail, which has some interpretive signs along the path. At 0.3 mile, arrive at an intersection with orange-blazed Massanutten South Trail. Turn right here to begin following this trail, and get ready for your climb of the day.

The trail can be muddy and rocky at times, and the first part of the climb is the steepest. The path bends to the right as it works its way uphill and then swings to the left. (Watch for a potentially confusing stretch here, as the

LOCATION
Massanutten Mountain, George Washington National Forest, VA

RATING
Moderate

DISTANCE
8.8 miles round-trip

ELEVATION GAIN
1,562 feet

ESTIMATED TIME
4-5 hours

MAPS
Map H, trails in the Massanutten Mountain– South Half, New Market Gap to Massanutten Peak (PATC): www.patc.net/PATC/ Our_Store/PATC_Maps.aspx

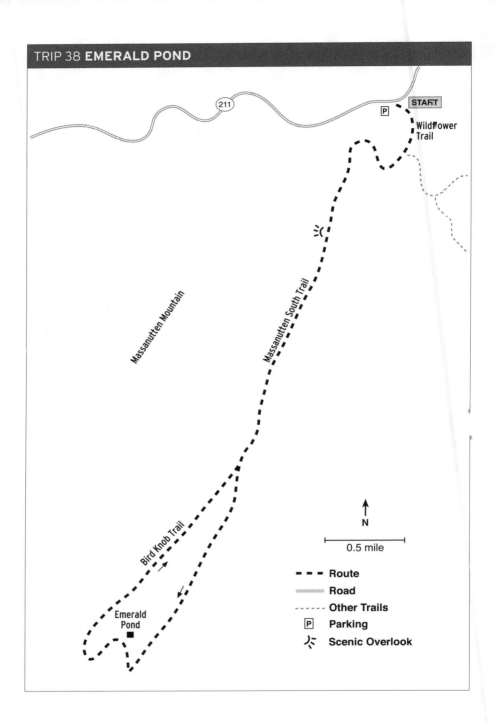

TRIP 38 **EMERALD POND**

211

START

P

Wildflower
Trail

Massanutten Mountain

Massanutten South Trail

Bird Knob Trail

N

0.5 mile

Emerald
Pond

- - - Route
Road
Other Trails
P Parking
Scenic Overlook

Hikers and dogs alike will enjoy the clear waters of Emerald Pond, which provides an almost oasis-like feeling in the southern Massanutten region.

route almost appears to go straight ahead.) Pass a large boulder at 0.8 mile, and then begin a short and rocky climb. At 1.4 miles, the ascent begins to ease out, and just a few tenths of a mile later, your reward for all that effort comes as you arrive at the first of two vistas that face to the west.

The trail begins to flatten out and then arrives at an intersection with white-blazed Bird Knob Trail at 2.2 miles. Stay to the right to follow Bird Knob Trail. The route starts a slight descent and then arrives at a large clearing at 4.0 miles. This can be a confusing section, but turn to the left to follow the edge of the clearing where the trail switches to a forest road. Follow this road to an intersection with the path to Emerald Pond at 4.2 miles.

A short walk is all that remains between you and Emerald Pond, which lives up to its name: the water has a bright greenish-blue hue that pops out of the landscape, especially on a sunny day. Follow a path around the spring-fed pond to find a good place to take a break and enjoy the clear waters—just note that this can be a very popular spot in summer.

Follow the path back to Bird Knob Trail and turn left onto it to resume the hike. Very quickly, you pass a gate and reach an intersection with Massanutten South Trail, which is now a forest road. Turn left here to start following the road, which is sporadically blazed orange and has a steady, relatively mild climb. At 5.2 miles, the forest road turns to the right, but Massanutten South Trail continues straight. Look for a gate here to help guide your path forward—be sure to go past that gate.

The trail enters the woods and flattens out before arriving again at the intersection with Bird Knob Trail at 6.5 miles. Turn to the right here and retrace your steps past the vistas and back down the mountain to Wildflower Trail. Turn left to return along this path and to your car.

DID YOU KNOW?

New Market Gap, at 1,804 feet, divides Massanutten almost evenly into its northern and southern sections. It is a wind gap, which is a gap where water once flowed but that now is dry.

MORE INFORMATION

George Washington and Jefferson National Forests, Lee Ranger District (fs.usda.gov/main/gwj, 540-984-4101). Check online for announcements concerning trail conditions, road closures, prescribed burns, and other events that may affect your hike.

NEARBY

Nearby hikes include Duncan Knob (Trip 35) and Strickler Knob (Trip 37). There are several restaurants along US 211 near the top of Massanutten Mountain, and the little town of New Market has a number of restaurants, shops, and gas stations.

SECTION 6
GREAT NORTH MOUNTAIN AND RAMSEYS DRAFT WILDERNESS

Beyond the foot of Massanut-ten Mountain, across the North Fork of the Shenan-doah River, and beyond the Virginia towns of Strasburg, Woodstock, and Edinburg, another ridge-and-valley sys-tem, typical of the Appala-chians, rises to the northwest. Great North Mountain is 50 miles long with a high point of 3,293 feet, but like many of its Appalachian cousins, it lacks a single, defined summit. In the south, part of the ridge forms the border between Virginia and West Virginia. In the north, VA/WV 55 crosses the ridge. Between and around these two points, much of the mountain itself is protected by the George Washington National Forest as part of the Lee Ranger District. The mountain's height and prominence over the valley give it views over the Shenandoah River, as well as west into the Allegheny Mountains of West Virginia. Three hikes described in this section are on Great North Mountain: Big Schloss (Trip 39), Tibbet Knob (Trip 40), and Halfmoon Mountain (Trip 41).

Also along Virginia's western state border, largely west of Shenandoah National Park's southernmost district, is the 6,518-acre Ramseys Draft Wilder-ness, one of 23 Wildernesses protected by the George Washington and Jefferson National Forests. Managed by means that preserve the true "untrammeled" spirit of the land, Wildernesses like this one make for more primitive experiences for those who recreate in them. Ramseys Draft Wilderness is traversed by the 26.2-mile Wild Oak National Recreation Trail, a popular backpacking loop in the area.

39

BIG SCHLOSS

On the border between Virginia and West Virginia, climb to a spectacular view of the Trout Run valley from the dramatic cliffs of Big Schloss.

DIRECTIONS

From I-81, Exit 283, follow VA 42 west 5.3 miles. Take a right onto VA 768/Union Church Road, which quickly becomes VA 623/Back Road. About 0.25 mile farther along, take a right onto VA 675/Wolf Gap Road and follow it for 6.3 miles to the Virginia–West Virginia state line. As the road crests the ridge on the border, turn right into the Wolf Gap Recreation Area, where there is a parking lot for day-hikers, as well as restrooms. *GPS coordinates: 38° 55.463' N, 78° 41.359' W.*

TRAIL DESCRIPTION

From the parking lot, walk through the Wolf Gap Recreation Area and locate orange-blazed Mill Mountain Trail on the north side of the campground. (If you cross VA 675 instead, you'll find the trail to Tibbet Knob [Trip 40].) The broad, well-worn path proceeds north along Great North Mountain, essentially following the border between Virginia and West Virginia. Over the next 0.8 mile, the trail gains about 650 feet, switchbacking periodically as it climbs the westward face of the mountain.

If the day is clear, you'll know when you've crested Great North Mountain: this high point commands impressive vistas of the Virginia Blue Ridge Mountains to the east and the Trout Run valley to the west. Your route continues north, however, descending gradually as the trail winds its way past several outlooks amid a number of rock formations. For a ridge in the Mid-Atlantic, this line is sharply defined and views will open out, often on both sides simultaneously, as you head toward Big Schloss.

LOCATION
Great North Mountain, George Washington National Forest, VA and WV

RATING
Moderate

DISTANCE
4.4 miles round-trip

ELEVATION GAIN
1,297 feet

ESTIMATED TIME
3-4 hours

MAPS
Map F, Great North Mountain–North Half of George Washington National Forest, Lee Ranger District–Virginia and West Virginia (PATC): www.patc.net/PATC/Our_Store/PATC_Maps.aspx

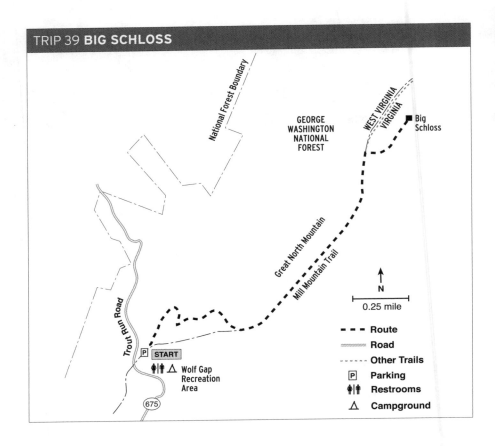

At 1.6 miles, Mill Mountain Trail reaches a broad ridgeback with a few improvised campsites just south of Big Schloss itself. From this point, the trail climbs gently and, at 1.9 miles, arrives at a white-blazed spur trail on the right, where your route leaves Mill Mountain Trail. The white-blazed spur leads toward the Schloss, at first climbing steeply and ruggedly, but soon leveling out as you approach the cliffs at 2.2 miles.

Cross a little wooden bridge over a particularly wide fissure to reach the best views. Take time to explore this striking feature, as viewing points open out on all sides. For an especially lovely vista, stand at the very head of the cliffs, where the Trout Run valley is displayed incomparably beneath you. You'll be glad you brought your camera!

After you've enjoyed soaking up the scenery, return the way you came to reach your vehicle at Wolf Gap.

DID YOU KNOW?

Until the Civil War, West Virginia and Virginia were united politically. When Virginia voted to secede from the Union on April 17, 1861, the delegates from the area that would become West Virginia voted 30 to 17 to remain a part of the

Hikers approach the craggy prow of Big Schloss from the north along the Mill Mountain Trail.

United States. In 1863, West Virginia joined the Union as a new state. Initially, delegates had planned to name the state Kanawha (after a river), but they decided instead to adopt the name of West Virginia.

MORE INFORMATION

George Washington and Jefferson National Forests, Lee Ranger District (fs.usda.gov/main/gwj; 540-984-4101). Check online for announcements concerning trail conditions, road closures, prescribed burns, and other events that may affect your hike.

NEARBY

The Trout Run valley offers hikers numerous opportunities to get out and explore. Big Schloss pairs nicely with the route to Tibbet Knob (Trip 40), which also leaves from the Wolf Gap Recreation Area. Nearby, Halfmoon Mountain (Trip 41) offers very fine views of the valley. The Wolf Gap and Trout Run recreation areas both offer vehicle camping, and for those seeking a backcountry challenge, *AMC's Best Backpacking in the Mid-Atlantic* describes a 27-mile loop that circumnavigates the valley and ties together all of these sights. Finally, the Tuscarora Trail passes through the area on its journey from Shenandoah National Park to the Appalachian Trail near Harrisburg, Pennsylvania.

The nearest towns are Wardensville, West Virginia, to the west (22 minutes), and Woodstock, Virginia, to the east (27 minutes).

THE TUSCARORA TRAIL

One of the great footpaths of the region, the Tuscarora Trail is often wilder than more frequently walked counterparts like the Appalachian Trail, offering hikers greater opportunities for solitude. The trail stretches 250 miles from Hogback Overlook in Shenandoah National Park to Blue Mountain, west of Harrisburg, Pennsylvania. As it traces this arc from the south to the north, it passes through four states—Virginia, West Virginia, Maryland, and Pennsylvania—and eventually joins up with the Appalachian Trail at the Tuscarora Trail's northern terminus.

This junction isn't happenstance: In the 1960s, members of the Potomac Appalachian Trail Club became concerned that developments and disputes over land rights in northern Virginia and near Harpers Ferry, West Virginia, would mean that the Appalachian Trail could be closed to future hikers. Club members began scouting and building an alternate route, which took hikers through wilder lands to the west. Old-timers know the southern section of the trail as "Big Blue," for its blue blazes. In 1995, the entire length of the Tuscarora Trail was opened after more than three decades of work.

The Tuscarora Trail takes its name from an American Indian tribe of Iroquois descent who lived in North Carolina. In the early eighteenth century, the Tuscarora clashed with European settlers, reportedly due to the settlers taking Tuscarora children as slaves. Beginning in 1714, the Tuscarora survivors of this conflict began migrating north to return to their ancestral lands in Pennsylvania and New York. This migration took 90 years, and the path these refugees followed was referred to as the "Tuscarora Path." Descendants of these Tuscarora still live near Niagara Falls, New York.

The modern trail doesn't follow the exact path of these displaced people, as the Tuscarora would have preferred to pass through valleys instead of following ridgelines; however, as you walk the trails of the Shenandoah Valley, don't be surprised to see the name "Tuscarora" attached to many places. The refugees lingered along their journey, and these place names are evidence of their passage.

You'll find yourself on the Tuscarora Trail if you walk Overall Run (Trip 10), the Buzzard Rock hike (Trip 33), the Signal Knob hike (Trip 36), or White Rock Cliff (Trip 42). To learn more about the Tuscarora Trail, see *The Tuscarora Trail: A Guide to the South Half in West Virginia and Virginia* (Potomac Appalachian Trail Club, sixth edition, 2016).

40

TIBBET KNOB

Climb to the summit of Tibbet Knob and enjoy a spectacular view of the Trout Run valley from this crag high above the Virginia–West Virginia border.

DIRECTIONS

From I-81, Exit 283, follow VA 42 west 5.3 miles. Take a right onto VA 768/Union Church Road, which quickly becomes VA 623/Back Road. About 0.25 mile farther along, take a right onto VA 675/Wolf Gap Road and follow it for 6.3 miles to the Virginia–West Virginia state line. As the road crests the ridge on the border, turn right into the Wolf Gap Recreation Area, where there is a parking lot for day-hikers, as well as restrooms. *GPS coordinates:* 38° 55.463′ N, 78° 41.359′ W.

TRAIL DESCRIPTION

From the parking lot, cross VA 675 and look for the sign for Tibbet Knob. (If you walk through the recreation area instead, you'll reach the trailhead for Big Schloss [Trip 39].) Orange-blazed Tibbet Knob Trail passes a primitive campsite on the right and then in about 0.2 mile begins a steady climb. Though it is not steep, this grade leads you up to your first sight of the Massanutten ridges and Blue Ridge Mountains eastward, on your left at 0.5 mile. At this point the route follows a fairly typical Virginia ridge. Looking ahead you can see a knob that the trail will round before climbing Tibbet Knob itself.

The path descends briefly and then evens out. The footing is rather rocky, so take care. As the route winds around the knob you saw, it passes through a more densely forested area. Eventually the trail begins to climb a bit, and you reach obscured views to the left and the right. After passing a switchback, the ascent to the ridgeline is more aggressive.

LOCATION
Great North Mountain, George Washington National Forest, VA and WV

RATING
Easy

DISTANCE
3.1 miles round-trip

ELEVATION GAIN
1,001 feet

ESTIMATED TIME
2–4 hours

MAPS
Map F, Great North Mountain–North Half of George Washington National Forest, Lee Ranger District–Virginia and West Virginia (PATC): www.patc.net/PATC/Our_Store/PATC_Maps.aspx

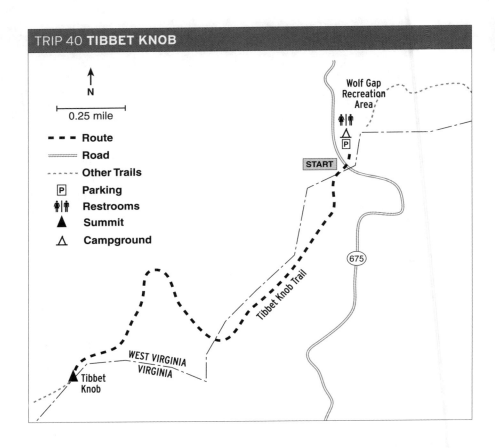

About 0.25 mile shy of the summit of Tibbet Knob, a quick turn in the trail leads to the first stretch of rocky terrain considered Class 3 in the Yosemite Decimal System, which means that you'll periodically need your hands to advance but ropes are not required. If you use trekking poles, affix them to your pack, because they are more encumbrances than aids when scrambling. Make sure that you always have three points in firm contact with rock before moving a fourth. The two stretches of Class 3 ground on this hike are not especially troublesome; just remember to be sure of your footing and balance before you advance.

The first scramble is about 50 or 60 feet long. After that, you cross relatively even ground. The second stretch of Class 3 terrain, and the steeper of the two, comes very near the summit at 1.5 miles.

Just beyond the second bit of scrambling, the route passes through some thick woods and then emerges on top of Tibbet Knob (2,930 feet). The rocky outcropping offers a beautiful 180-degree vista to the west, including Big Schloss in the north and Devil's Hole Mountain in the northwest.

Savor this amazing view and perhaps enjoy your lunch or a snack. When the time comes to return, merely retrace your steps to Wolf Gap and your vehicle.

For a short hike, Tibbet Knob offers an excellent view of the Trout Run valley. If you look directly north, as in this photo, you can see Big Schloss and Halfmoon Mountain.

DID YOU KNOW?

Standing atop Tibbet Knob, you're near the western boundary of the ridge-and-valley system that typifies Virginia and the Shenandoah Valley. Westward, the ridges you can see are more properly referred to as the Alleghenies.

MORE INFORMATION

George Washington and Jefferson National Forests, Lee Ranger District (fs.usda.gov/main/gwj; 540-984-4101). Check online for announcements concerning trail conditions, road closures, prescribed burns, and other events that may affect your hike.

NEARBY

The Trout Run valley offers hikers numerous opportunities to get out and explore. The route to Big Schloss (Trip 39) also leaves from Wolf Gap Recreation Area. Nearby, Halfmoon Mountain (Trip 41) has very fine views of the valley. The Wolf Gap and Trout Run recreation areas both offer vehicle camping, and for those seeking a backcountry challenge, *AMC's Best Backpacking in the Mid-Atlantic* offers a 27-mile loop that circumnavigates the valley and ties together all of these sights. Finally, the Tuscarora Trail passes through the area on its journey from the Shenandoah National Park to the Appalachian Trail near Harrisburg, Pennsylvania.

When it's time to return to civilization, head either to Wardensville, West Virginia (22 minutes to the north), or to Woodstock, Virginia (27 minutes to the east), for an array of local businesses.

41

HALFMOON MOUNTAIN

Climb high to enjoy an eagle's-eye view of the Trout Run valley from the north, taking in Big Schloss and Tibbet Knob.

DIRECTIONS

From I-81, Exit 296, near Strasburg, head west on US 48/ VA 55/WV 55 for about 19.9 miles over the mountains into Wardensville. In town, turn left onto Trout Run Valley Road, and follow it south for about 6 miles. The turnoff for Bucktail Trail is on the left. Bear right at the circle and look for the trail sign on the right. Parking is abundant. *GPS coordinates:* 39° 0.834' N, 78° 39.827' W.

TRAIL DESCRIPTION

The trickiest part of this hike is certainly the beginning. From the sign marking the start of Bucktail Trail, walk into the woods for a few yards on an orange-blazed forest road. The path broadens into a clearing, but continue to follow the orange blazes, which lead left. Keep your eyes peeled for a pink-blazed footpath on your right at 0.2 mile: this is Bucktail Cutoff Trail, which heads east along the foot of Halfmoon Mountain for about 2.5 miles.

Turn right onto Bucktail Cutoff Trail, which climbs gently (about 500 feet) to the knees of the mountain and then weaves its way along the undulations of the hollows, periodically dropping slightly to cross little creeks, all of which are easy to rock-hop. The trail makes its way east before entering some slightly more open country as it descends to Halfmoon Run. There is a bit of space between blazes here, but you should be able to scope out the route easily enough.

The trail follows an old forest road that reenters the woods and heads upstream along Halfmoon Run on the right. Hike along this idyllic little creek for a spell before Bucktail Cutoff Trail ends at yellow-blazed Halfmoon

LOCATION
Great North Mountain, George Washington National Forest, WV

RATING
Strenuous

DISTANCE
8.9 miles round-trip

ELEVATION GAIN
2,469 feet

ESTIMATED TIME
4-6 hours

MAPS
Map F, Great North Mountain–North Half of George Washington National Forest, Lee Ranger District–Virginia and West Virginia (PATC): www.patc.net/PATC/ Our_Store/PATC_Maps.aspx

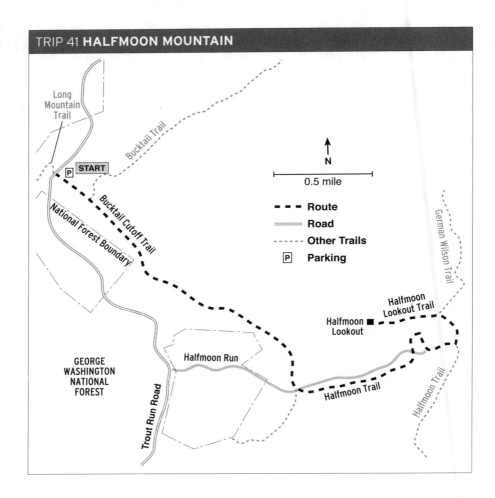

Long
Mountain
Trail

Bucktail Trail

P **START**

Bucktail Cutoff Trail

National Forest Boundary

N

0.5 mile

- - - **Route**
═══ **Road**
- - - **Other Trails**
P **Parking**

German Wilson Trail

Halfmoon
Lookout Trail

Halfmoon ■
Lookout

Halfmoon Run

GEORGE
WASHINGTON
NATIONAL
FOREST

Trout Run Road

Halfmoon Trail

Halfmoon Trail

Trail at 2.5 miles. The intersection of these two trails is marked by a good-sized backcountry campsite on the right.

Follow the yellow blazes to the left and begin climbing about 700 feet over the next mile. (If you follow the yellow blazes to the right, you arrive at another parking lot on Trout Run Valley Road.) Though this is definitely the most strenuous section of the trip, the trail is well graded and a pleasure to walk.

Once you arrive at the saddle between Halfmoon Mountain and Mill Mountain at 3.7 miles, pause to catch your breath at the intersection with white-blazed Halfmoon Lookout Trail. To the right, Halfmoon Trail leads to the Tuscarora Trail. Head left instead and follow the white blazes toward the summit of Halfmoon Mountain. The terrain here is very flat, but rocky. Pass pink-blazed German Wilson Trail on the right, and continue to follow the white blazes as they take you out on the promontory of the mountain.

The view south from Halfmoon Mountain. Located at the northern end of the Trout Run valley, from here you can look southward to Big Schloss and Tibbet Knob.

You've almost reached your objective when the trail bends sharply to the right at 4.4 miles, just shy of a well-placed campsite on the mountain's nose. This last stretch is quite steep and rocky, but mercifully short. At the summit, look for the ruins of an old fire tower and pause there to admire a fine vista, one of the best in the valley. To the south, on a clear day, you can spot Big Schloss and Tibbet Knob; still looking south, on the right, Long Mountain marches away to the south. Take your time and explore past the foundations, as there are other excellent views farther along the ridgeline.

When you're ready to leave, retrace your route carefully along Halfmoon Lookout Trail (white blazes), Halfmoon Trail (yellow blazes), Bucktail Cutoff Trail (pink blazes), and finally Bucktail Trail (orange blazes). Obviously, there are a number of turns here before you reach your vehicle.

DID YOU KNOW?

Fire towers like the one that once stood atop Halfmoon Mountain were staffed through the twentieth century to give rangers a heads-up concerning any forest fires. If you're in the mood to spend the night on the high and narrow ridge, go past the stone ruins of the tower's tumbled-down foundation and you'll find a number of small campsites.

MORE INFORMATION

George Washington and Jefferson National Forests, Lee Ranger District (fs.usda.gov/main/gwj, 540-984-4101). Check online for announcements concerning trail conditions, road closures, prescribed burns, and other events that may affect your hike.

NEARBY

The Trout Run valley offers hikers numerous opportunities to get out and explore. The routes to Big Schloss (Trip 39) and Tibbet Knob (Trip 40) both leave from Wolf Gap Recreation Area. Wolf Gap and Trout Run recreation areas both offer vehicle camping, and for those seeking a backcountry challenge, *AMC's Best Backpacking in the Mid-Atlantic* offers a 27-mile loop that circumnavigates the valley and ties together all of these sights. Finally, the Tuscarora Trail passes through the area on its journey from the Shenandoah Valley to the Appalachian Trail near Harrisburg, Pennsylvania.

The nearest towns are Wardensville, West Virginia, to the west, and Woodstock, Virginia, to the east.

THE APPALACHIAN TRAIL IN VIRGINIA

Of the 2,192 miles the Appalachian Trail (AT) covers on its route from Georgia to Maine, about one-quarter are in Virginia. The majority of those approximately 550 miles follow the state's ridge-and-valley topography through the Shenandoah Valley. As you study a map, you can trace the AT's line along the state's backbone, from Damascus, Virginia, to Harpers Ferry, West Virginia.

Within Virginia, the greatest American thru-hike can be divided into four sections. In southwest Virginia, the state's most remote section of the AT, the trail passes through some of the state's highlights, including the Grayson Highlands and Mount Rogers (the highest point in Virginia). In spring, when the rhododendron are blooming, few hiking destinations can rival the open balds of this area, where hikers can gaze south to the mountains of North Carolina and Tennessee. Damascus, Virginia, is perhaps the Platonic ideal of what a trail town should be. Though it is not, properly speaking, within the Shenandoah Valley, all hikers in the region should book the time to explore the trail in this distant and beautiful area.

Between the Grayson Highlands and Shenandoah National Park, the AT generally follows the Blue Ridge Parkway through the central portion of the state. Though the hiking is tougher in this section, with a number of big climbs, there are many superb vantage points, including Humpback Rocks (Trip 43).

For the next 104 or so miles, the AT stays up high in Shenandoah National Park, following Skyline Drive through this exceptionally beautiful mountain-scape. Some of the park's most memorable highlights are either on the AT itself, or a short hop, skip, and jump away, so day-hikers will often find themselves using the AT to make interesting loops. Trips in this book that follow portions of the AT in the park include Jeremy's Run (Trip 12), Mary's Rock (Trip 15), Doyles River and Jones Run Falls (Trip 28), Riprap Hollow (Trip 32), and many others.

After leaving Shenandoah National Park, the AT heads north through hilly piedmont terrain, eventually following the West Virginia border to Harpers Ferry and Loudoun Heights (Trips 2 and 3) before crossing the Potomac into Maryland. The stretch of trail near Raven Rocks (Trip 4), just south of Snickers Gap, is infamously nicknamed the Roller Coaster for its series of what a thru-hiker would call "pointless ups and downs," or PUDs.

42

WHITE ROCK CLIFF/OPA OVERLOOK

On a clear day, you can see for miles—across the Shenandoah Valley to Massanutten Mountain and even to Shenandoah National Park—from the overlook at White Rock Cliff.

DIRECTIONS

From I-81, take Exit 296 for US 48 West/VA 55 West toward Strasburg. Drive on US 48 West/VA 55 West for 19.0 miles, then turn left onto Furnace Road. After 0.6 mile, turn right onto North Mountain Road, then make a quick left onto Waites Run Road. Follow this road for 6.0 miles until it splits. To access the trailhead, bear left at the split and proceed 0.3 mile to the parking area. This final section of the drive can be eroded. If you don't have a car with high clearance or feel uncomfortable driving this last bit, there are pull-offs for parking along Waites Run Road. *GPS coordinates: 39° 00.352′ N, 78° 35.327′ W.*

TRAIL DESCRIPTION

From the parking area, proceed past the gate and follow the forest road. Rather quickly, the path splits—stay on the forest road, which bears to the right, and do not follow the trail that appears to lead into the woods. Soon after, the forest road reaches the intersection with pink-blazed Old Mail Path. Turn right here to start following Old Mail Path. An informational board with maps and some convenient benches lie just ahead.

Follow the pink blazes as the route crosses Cove Run and then steadily ascends to a large clearing. Go straight ahead to the clearing and arrive at a forest road, which marks the intersection of Old Mail Path with Racer Hollow Camp Trail at 1.3 miles. (The sign is to your right as you pass through the clearing.) Note this intersection because you'll return here near the end of the hike.

LOCATION
Great North Mountain, George Washington National Forest, VA and WV

RATING
Moderate

DISTANCE
9.3 miles round-trip

ELEVATION GAIN
1,460 feet

ESTIMATED TIME
4-5 hours

MAPS
Map F, Great North Mountain–North Half of George Washington National Forest, Lee Ranger District–Virginia and West Virginia (PATC): www.patc.net/PATC/Our_Store/PATC_Maps.aspx

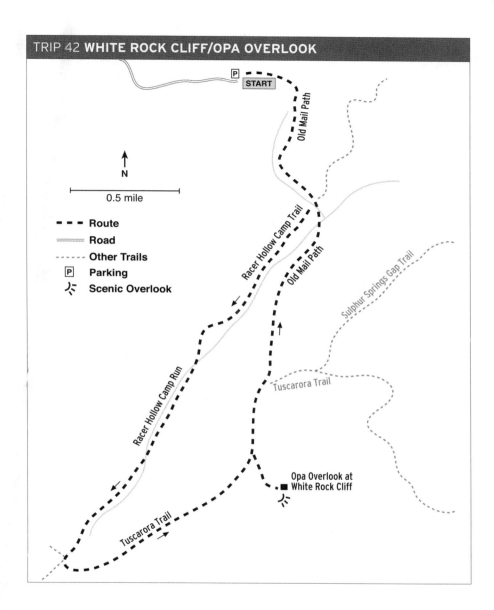

Begin to follow orange-blazed Racer Hollow Camp Trail, which continues as a wide forest road for a little bit before entering the woods. The trail remains level briefly before a slight dip down to Racer Hollow Camp Run. Cross the run carefully.

From here, you start to make a steady ascent up the mountain, crossing the run several times as you make your way forward. The path can be steep at times—and quite muddy after a storm—but the grade eases occasionally to give your legs a break. Watch out for an eroded section near the top of the climb that can be slippery in wet conditions.

Even dogs agree that the views from White Rock Cliff can't be beat. On a clear day, you can gaze across the valley to Shenandoah National Park itself.

Racer Hollow Camp Trail eventually peels away from the run as it nears the top of Little Sluice Mountain. After passing a large campsite, proceed a few more steps before reaching the intersection with the Tuscarora Trail at 4.4 miles. Turn left here, and follow the blue blazes.

There's a bit of mild climbing left to do, but the Tuscarora Trail eventually flattens out. Enjoy this nice, easy stretch of ridge walk.

When the ridge starts to descend, keep an eye out to your right for the side trail that leads to Opa Lookout at White Rock Cliff. A cairn marks the turn at 5.7 miles. (A rather large campsite to the left just past the intersection also helps pinpoint the location.)

Once you spot the trail, turn right to follow the white blazes of White Rock Lookout Trail—your goal is just 0.2 mile away. The trail descends before arriving at the base of the overlook. Scramble up—this is an easy one—to find the east-facing views. On a clear day, you can see all the way to Shenandoah National Park. There's no better place for a break, so sit back and enjoy the vista.

When you're ready to resume the hike, take the lookout trail back to the Tuscarora Trail, and turn right to follow the blue blazes. The trail starts to descend rather sharply and then arrives at an intersection with Old Mail Path at 6.8 miles. Turn left here to pick up Old Mail Path. Keep an eye on the pink blazes, which can be a bit sporadic at times, as you make your way downhill, sometimes rather steeply.

Arrive at the intersection with Racer Hollow Camp Trail at 8.0 miles, which you saw earlier in the day. Pass through this intersection and retrace your steps across the clearing and into the woods. Continue following Old Mail Path back to the forest road and to your car.

DID YOU KNOW?

Little Sluice Mountain is an excellent example of the Ridge-and-Valley Appalachians. These mountains extend from southeastern New York to Alabama and are known for their long, even ridges and equally long valleys. Before the advent of automobiles, these lengthy ridges made east–west travel difficult in general— and nearly impossible for trains.

MORE INFORMATION

George Washington and Jefferson National Forests, Lee Ranger District (fs.usda.gov/main/gwj, 540-984-4101). Check online for announcements concerning trail conditions, road closures, prescribed burns, and other events that may affect your hike.

NEARBY

This area offers numerous opportunities to get out and explore. Nearby hikes include Big Schloss (Trip 39) and Halfmoon Mountain (Trip 41), which both provide very fine views of the valley. The Tuscarora Trail passes through here on its journey from Shenandoah National Park to the Appalachian Trail near Harrisburg, Pennsylvania. When it's time to return to civilization, head to Wardensville, West Virginia, for an array of local businesses.

SECTION 7

JEFFERSON NATIONAL FOREST AND THE BLUE RIDGE MOUNTAINS

On its south side—beyond the reaches of the Shenandoah River—the Shenandoah Valley stretches geologically and culturally into the James and Roanoke river valleys. Like the rest of the Shenandoah area, the valley here is bounded to the east by the Blue Ridge Mountains and the northern Virginia highlands, and to the west by ridge-and-valley formations.

The Blue Ridge Parkway runs for 469 miles through the Great Smoky Mountains and connects Shenandoah National Park with this range. Humpback Rocks (Trip 43) sits near the top of the parkway, and the route offers easy access to a number of other hikes, including Spy Rock (Trip 44), Crabtree Falls (Trip 45), and Three Ridges (Trip 50).

Combined administratively with George Washington National Forest in 1995, Jefferson National Forest encompasses 709,596 acres, 690,106 of which are in Virginia. The four districts of Jefferson National Forest stretch mostly south of

Facing page: Humpback Rocks offers expansive views of Virginia's Blue Ridge, looking westwards, as well as a few rock outcroppings to scramble up.

the Shenandoah Valley and the George Washington National Forest districts: Glenwood–Pedlar Ranger District, south of I-64 and east of I-81 (comanaged with George Washington National Forest); Eastern Divide Ranger District, west of I-81 and stretching from near I-64 in the north southward across I-77; Mount Rogers National Recreation Area, which lies just southwest of there; and the Clinch Ranger District, along Virginia's westernmost border with Kentucky. Most of the hikes in this section fall within the Glenwood–Pedlar Ranger District (Trips 43–50).

43

HUMPBACK ROCKS

A sharp climb leads to an expansive view of the Blue Ridge Mountains from a dramatic rock formation.

DIRECTIONS

From the junction of I-66 and I-81, head south on I-81 toward Roanoke. After about 79 miles, take Exit 221 for I-64 East toward Richmond. Head east on I-64 for 12.0 miles, and then take Exit 99 for US 250 toward Afton/Waynesboro. Follow the signs to head south on the Blue Ridge Parkway. About 6 miles down the parkway, look for the Humpback Gap Overlook parking lot on the left, where parking spots are abundant. *GPS coordinates: 37° 58.115′ N, 78° 53.793′ W.*

TRAIL DESCRIPTION

This hike is a punchy ascent from the Blue Ridge Parkway to the striking formation of Humpback Rocks. The good news is that the hike is short—just a mile out and a mile back. The bad news is that it's a challenging uphill climb. New hikers will definitely feel this one the next day.

The blue-blazed trail starts just behind the informational placard at the south end of the parking lot. At first, the route is fairly sedate. The wide gravel pathway climbs gently but steadily away from the road. There's even an occasional bench where you can rest and catch your breath. After a few minutes of hiking, you come to a constructed wooden staircase that marks where the trail becomes much more serious about ascending the mountain. From this point forward, the climb becomes steep and rocky as the route switchbacks up the mountain. Don't hesitate to take frequent breaks.

Eventually, the rocky switchbacks ease off, and the path tops out just behind Humpback Rocks. At a signed intersection, bear left, still on blue blazes. (A right turn will

LOCATION
Glenwood–Pedlar Ranger District, George Washington and Jefferson National Forests, VA

RATING
Strenuous

DISTANCE
2 miles round-trip

ELEVATION GAIN
900 feet

ESTIMATED TIME
2 hours

MAPS
Trails Illustrated: Lexington/Blue Ridge Mountains, George Washington and Jefferson National Forests, Map 789 (National Geographic): natgeomaps.com/ti-789 -lexington-blue-ridge-mts -george-washington-and -jefferson-national-forests

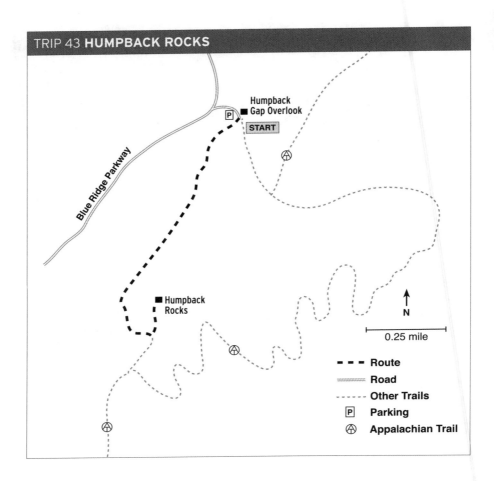

take you to the Appalachian Trail in 0.25 mile.) Pass a big pile of rocks and emerge onto the Humpback formation, where you'll see a sweeping western vista of the Appalachians marching out to West Virginia.

Take time to enjoy the view, and feel free to scramble about the rocks, exploring different outlooks. Do take care, however, to respect the various barriers meant to promote revegetation on this highly visited site.

When you've had your fill of the spectacular scenery, retrace your steps and carefully descend the steep sections back to the parking lot. Going down will be a lot easier than going up.

DID YOU KNOW?

Nearby Humpback Gap was a popular camping spot for nineteenth-century travelers, many of whom hauled goods over the Blue Ridge Mountains and into the Shenandoah Valley. This route fell into disuse after the advent of the railroads. Stop by the Humpback Rocks Visitor Center to see an outdoor farm

An extremely popular hike, many visitors to the Blue Ridge Parkway tough out this steep climb for amazing views of the Appalachians.

museum that describes how early settlers farmed, gardened, wove baskets, and generally made a living in the area.

MORE INFORMATION

George Washington and Jefferson National Forests, Glenwood–Pedlar Ranger District (fs.usda.gov/main/gwj, 540-291-2188). Check online for announcements concerning trail conditions, road closures, prescribed burns, and other events that may affect your hike.

NEARBY

The Appalachian Trail (AT) passes nearby, running along the backbone of the Blue Ridge Mountains for many miles to the south and north. If you'd like to hike a slightly longer route (about 4 miles), when you come off the rocks, instead of veering to the right to retrace your steps, follow the blue-blazed trail uphill about 0.25 mile to reach an intersection with the Appalachian Trail. Turn left to follow the AT downhill to the Humpback Gap Overlook parking lot, where your car is.

For a lengthier trek (about 10 miles), drive past the Humpback Gap Overlook parking lot and continue south on the Blue Ridge Parkway to just past mile marker 9. Park in the bay on the left for Dripping Rock (37° 56.475′ N, 78° 56.191′ W). The AT crosses here, and by heading north you reach Humpback Rocks after a much longer approach. The main advantage of this hike is that you not only pass the wooded summit of Humpback Mountain but also pass another rocky outlook that features views similar to those at Humpback Rocks but is much less frequented.

There are many other excellent hikes nearby. Spy Rock (Trip 44) also features impressive views; Crabtree Falls (Trip 45) and Apple Orchard Falls (Trip 46) are some of the best waterfall hikes in the region. Cold Mountain (Trip 47) includes some attractive and unusual balds—those shrubby or grassy fields where you would expect to find forest, which are common to the area—and Mount Pleasant (Trip 48) is a beautiful hike with wonderful scenery. Additionally, the Devil's Marbleyard (Trip 49) is a unique route that every hiker should do at least once. Farther north, the trails of the South District of Shenandoah National Park beckon. And simply driving the Blue Ridge Parkway is a pleasant experience with many attractive sights.

If you're in need of post-hike refreshment, consider the town of Roseland. The largest nearby town is, of course, Charlottesville.

44

SPY ROCK

A walk along an unassuming fire road leads you to one of the better views in the area. Time this hike for spring, when the rhododendrons are blooming.

DIRECTIONS

From I-81/I-64, Exit 205, take VA 606 east toward Raphine for 1.5 miles. Turn left onto US 11 North/North Lee Highway, and then make a quick right onto VA 56 East/Tye River Turnpike. Follow VA 56 East for 8.8 miles, and turn right onto Fish Hatchery Road/VA 690. Pass the hatchery, and follow the signs for hiker parking (0.5 mile). *GPS coordinates:* 37° 50.515′ N, 79° 7.876′ W.

TRAIL DESCRIPTION

This long, steady climb along a fire road eventually brings you to the Appalachian Trail (AT) and then to Spy Rock itself. The bonus after enjoying the great scenery: the return trip is all downhill.

From the parking lot, cross the dirt road and aim for a yellow gate that marks entry to a fire road. (When the authors hiked this route, the path was helpfully labeled with a green street sign for Spy Rock Road.) Head up the fire road, which is marked sporadically with blue blazes. The road starts out rather open but eventually gets more tree cover, lending some welcome shade on sunny days. Overall, the route is easy to follow, with the exception of one tricky left-hand turn. To make sure you take it, just stay to the left and keep an eye out for blue blazes.

The trail passes a red gate and then intersects the AT at 1.0 mile. Turn left onto the AT and keep climbing up the trail, passing a wooden gate. The ascent culminates with a sign that points the way to Spy Rock at 1.4 miles. Turn

LOCATION
Glenwood-Pedlar Ranger District, George Washington and Jefferson National Forests, VA

RATING
Moderate

DISTANCE
3.2 miles round-trip

ELEVATION GAIN
1,223 feet

ESTIMATED TIME
1-2 hours

MAPS
Trails Illustrated: Lexington/Blue Ridge Mountains, George Washington and Jefferson National Forests, Map 789 (National Geographic): natgeomaps.com/ti-789 -lexington-blue-ridge-mts -george-washington-and -jefferson-national-forests

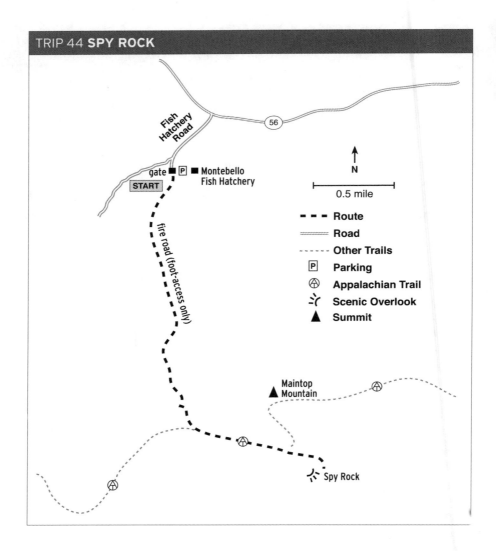

right onto this spur trail from the AT, and walk through a large camping area before arriving at the base of Spy Rock.

Follow the blue-blazed trail to the left, which wraps around Spy Rock and brings you to the top. At 3,877 feet, Spy Rock has a 360-degree vista of the area, giving you a good look at the famous Religious Range, which includes the Priest, Little Priest, the Friar, the Little Friar, and the Cardinal.

After enjoying the sights, retrace your steps back down the AT and the fire road to your vehicle.

Build in time to enjoy Spy Rock's 360-degree views, as you'll want to linger to take in views of the surrounding mountains. Photo by Anna Creech, Creative Commons on Flickr.

DID YOU KNOW?

The panoramic views may have contributed to Spy Rock's name. It's rumored that Confederate soldiers used Spy Rock as a base to monitor Union troop movements in the valley below.

MORE INFORMATION

George Washington and Jefferson National Forests, Glenwood–Pedlar Ranger District (fs.usda.gov/main/gwj, 540-291-2188). Check online for announcements concerning trail conditions, road closures, prescribed burns, and other events that may affect your hike.

NEARBY

This hike serves as an excellent base to explore the area. Hikers up for a challenge can tackle nearby Three Ridges (Trip 50) or check out the famous Crabtree Falls (Trip 45).

If you're looking for a meal in the Blue Ridge area, stop in the town of Roseland.

45

CRABTREE FALLS

A steep climb rewards you with near-constant views of one of Virginia's prettiest waterfalls.

DIRECTIONS

From I-81/I-64, Exit 205, take VA 606 East toward Raphine for 1.5 miles. Turn left onto US 11 North/North Lee Highway, and then make a quick right onto VA 56 East/Tye River Turnpike. Follow VA 56 East for 11.8 miles and look for the Crabtree Falls parking lot on your right. Day-use fees apply. *GPS coordinates:* 37° 51.122′ N, 79° 4.655′ W.

TRAIL DESCRIPTION

Crabtree Falls is often listed as a "must-see" hike for anyone traveling the Blue Ridge Parkway. It invites lingering with its multiple overlooks and great views. With five major cascades falling a total distance of 1,200 feet, Crabtree is the highest vertical-drop cascading waterfall east of the Mississippi River. It is well worth the short hike.

Despite its elevation gain, the well-maintained, well-marked trail is easy to follow—guardrails and stairs help along the steeper portions. You could idle away the day here wandering up and down the trail, enjoying the sights of the falls and the surrounding valley.

Crabtree Falls Trail starts off paved and brings you quickly to the bottom of the lower falls at just 0.1 mile. It's a short distance for a great payoff, but even better views await you at the top. Keep following the trail, which now turns to dirt, swings to the right, and starts to switchback up the mountain. Numerous overlooks dot the trail and extend into the falls, giving you multiple opportunities to pause for pictures.

About 0.5 mile into the hike, pass a rock formation that may tempt you to scramble up the cave and navigate the chimney. It's another good spot to take a short break and enjoy the scenery below.

LOCATION
Glenwood-Pedlar Ranger District, George Washington and Jefferson National Forests, VA

RATING
Strenuous

DISTANCE
2.8 miles round-trip

ELEVATION GAIN
1,642 feet

ESTIMATED TIME
1-2 hours

MAPS
Trails Illustrated: Lexington/Blue Ridge Mountains, George Washington and Jefferson National Forests, Map 789 (National Geographic): natgeomaps.com/ti-789 -lexington-blue-ridge-mts -george-washington-and -jefferson-national-forests

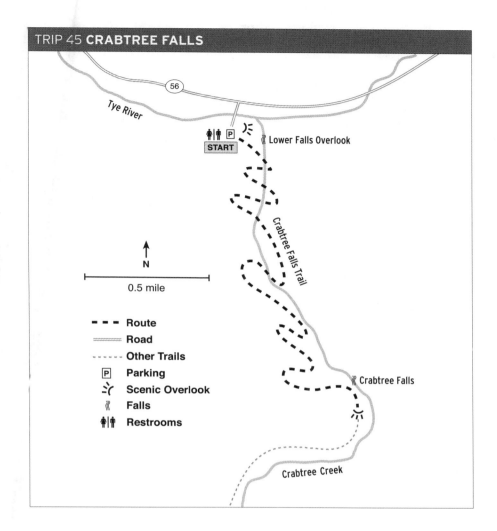

At about 1.4 miles, arrive at the top of the falls. Cross a small wooden bridge to an overlook that provides a vista of the valley and the Blue Ridge Mountains.

(*Caution:* Do not climb onto the rocks, which are slippery here. More than twenty people have fallen to their deaths while attempting to do so.)

When you're ready, turn around, cross back over the footbridge, and follow the trail to return to your vehicle.

DID YOU KNOW?

Crabtree Falls has had its fifteen minutes of fame. *The Waltons*—a popular 1970s television show set in rural Virginia—often referred to the falls as a Sunday outing for the Walton family. But its fame is in name only; the falls never appeared on the program during its nine-year run.

These lower falls give hikers a sense of the grandeur that's to come.

MORE INFORMATION

George Washington and Jefferson National Forests, Glenwood–Pedlar Ranger District (fs.usda.gov/main/gwj, 540-291-2188). Check online for announcements concerning trail conditions, road closures, prescribed burns, and other events that may affect your hike.

NEARBY

For a longer trip, turn left after the footbridge at the top of the falls and follow a trail that takes you along Crabtree Stream. This route flattens out and eventually leads you to the upper parking area about a mile from the overlook. To return to your vehicle from this point, simply turn around and retrace your steps. This hike is about 4.8 miles.

Crabtree Falls serves as an excellent base to explore the area. Spy Rock (Trip 44) is a good counterpart to Crabtree Falls, with a short distance but impressive views; if you are up for a challenge, hike nearby Three Ridges (Trip 50).

If you're looking for a meal in the Blue Ridge area, stop in Roseland (about 18 minutes away).

INVASIVE SPECIES IN VIRGINIA

Invasive species—nonnative plants, animals, and diseases that harm both the environment and the economy—are a serious problem in Virginia and the rest of the United States. Virginia's Department of Conservation and Recreation estimates that invasive species cost the state $1 billion and the nation upward of $120 billion annually. These species often spread quickly and aggressively, destroying native species, disrupting fragile ecosystems, harming crops, and spreading disease.

Hikers and other outdoorspeople have a deep and abiding interest in doing their part to prevent invasive species from attacking the environment we love and enjoy. Not only can invasive plants take over forests and trails, destroying cherished native species, some can cause direct harm to hikers. Anyone who has ever visited the South and been bitten by a fire ant or seen the damage caused by wild hogs can understand why hikers should be committed to keeping these troublesome pests from the Shenandoah Valley. A number of species are of immediate concern:

- **Emerald Ash Borer:** This wood-boring beetle was accidentally imported from Asia and has caused the deaths of more than 40 million ash trees.
- **Hemlock Woolly Adelgid:** The small, aphid-like insect first established itself near Richmond, Virginia, and has spread from Maine to Georgia. These insects have decimated one of the few remaining stands of old-growth hemlocks in the Shenandoah Valley near Ramseys Draft.
- **Kudzu:** Introduced from Japan and China in the early twentieth century, this climbing, semi-woody vine is common throughout the eastern half of the United States. When left to its own devices, kudzu can overwhelm native species, choking them under its leaves and vines.
- **Gypsy Moth:** From Virginia northward, the gypsy moth has exacted a terrible toll on hardwood forests, defoliating millions of acres since it was introduced in the late nineteenth century.
- **Fire Ant:** Fortunately, these biting pests are confined to the area around Tidewater, Virginia; a quarantine is in place to keep them from spreading through the state.

Although controlling infestations of invasive species is a monumental undertaking, you can do a great deal to help prevent the spread of these pests so that the places we love can remain natural and unaffected.

- Know what troublesome invasive plant species look like and avoid traveling through them.
- If you do travel through an infestation, try to remove all seeds from your clothes and person before you continue.
- Clean equipment—such as boots, tents, and clothing—between trips and when you leave one area for another.
- Do not transport firewood. Instead, gather or buy locally.

46

APPLE ORCHARD FALLS

This hike past the 200-foot cascade of Apple Orchard Falls is justifiably one of the most popular in Jefferson National Forest.

DIRECTIONS

From I-81, Exit 168, take VA 614 east, following the signs for Arcadia. After about 3.3 miles, take a left onto North Creek Road. At first the road is paved, but as you pass the established campsite on the left at about 2.8 miles, it becomes a single gravel lane. Keep going straight on this lane, which is not too rough and is suitable for cars. A few miles later, you'll arrive at a circular parking lot, which is the trailhead for both Apple Orchard Falls and Cornelius Creek trails. *GPS coordinates: 37° 31.780′ N, 79° 33.189′ W.*

TRAIL DESCRIPTION

On a warm summer day, catch the very striking Apple Orchard Falls and then stroll down the beautiful and verdant Cornelius Creek, which offers a couple of especially inviting swimming holes.

At the trailhead, orient yourself by looking toward the trails and away from the road. The trail to the left is Apple Orchard Falls Trail, and the one to the right, coming more directly down the mountain, is Cornelius Creek Trail. Both are blazed blue. Enter the forest on Apple Orchard Falls Trail and soon come upon a fork in the route. Follow the sign and bear right as the trail climbs gently, at times riding up high to the right of the creek. Eventually, at 1.7 miles, you'll arrive at two bridges over the creek. The lower one leads to another trailhead, so cross the creek at the higher bridge, then continue to follow the blue blazes as the path climbs more steeply and winds its way between boulders.

At 1.9 miles, the route reaches a boardwalk that takes you directly beneath the falls. Like many visitors, you will

LOCATION

Glenwood-Pedler Ranger District, George Washington and Jefferson National Forests, VA

RATING

Moderate

DISTANCE

6.7 miles round-trip

ELEVATION GAIN

2,438 feet

ESTIMATED TIME

3-5 hours

MAPS

Trails Illustrated: Lexington/Blue Ridge Mountains, George Washington and Jefferson National Forests, Map 789 (National Geographic): natgeomaps.com/ti-789 -lexington-blue-ridge-mts -george-washington-and -jefferson-national-forests

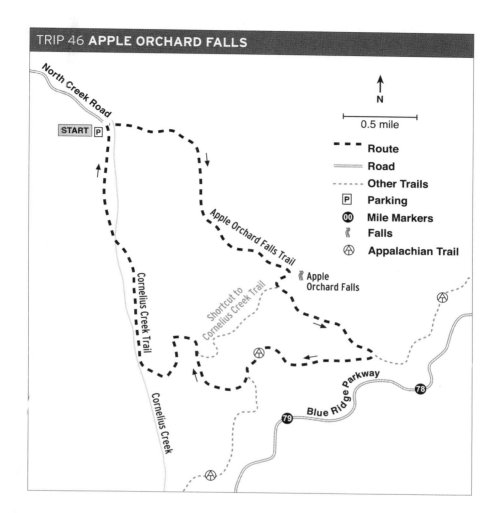

probably gasp in surprise at their beauty, especially on a spring day, when they are full of water. They seem to come from nowhere.

Beyond the falls, the trail continues to climb via wooden stairs and the occasional switchback. Stay alert; it's easy to miss one of the sharp left-hand turns, though you won't stray very far. The route passes an idyllic spot just above the falls where the creek tumbles over a boulder. It climbs more sedately along the left of the water and then crosses a grassy old forest road at 2.3 miles.

The trail then switchbacks slowly and steadily for about 0.5 mile, gaining about 500 vertical feet before it intersects with the Appalachian Trail (AT). Turn right onto the white-blazed AT, which through this stretch follows fairly gentle rolling terrain along the shoulder of the Blue Ridge Mountains.

(If you want a shortcut, at 2.3 miles consider following the road grade to the right. This will bring you to directly to Cornelius Creek Trail.)

A hiker admires the striking Apple Orchard Falls. This route takes hikers along an especially scenic circuit of falls linked together by a short stretch of the Appalachian Trail.

At 3.8 miles, turn right onto the blue-blazed Cornelius Creek Trail and begin your descent toward the trailhead, at first on a forest footpath. After you cross the old forest road, which you also crossed on your ascent, bear left and walk down the road grade. At 5.0 miles, you reach Cornelius Creek itself. The trail bears to the right on a lovely creekside stretch. Keep your eye out for attractive places to pause for a rest and soak your feet—there's at least one pool suitable for swimming, where the creek cascades over an 8-to-10-foot rock wall.

In the lower reaches of the creek, the trail leaps over the water a few times, both by bridge and by crossings, which are easy to rock-hop. Before long, Cornelius Creek's valley widens out and brings you back to the trailhead and your vehicle.

DID YOU KNOW?

Apple Orchard Falls takes its name from the mountain it drains. At an elevation of 4,244 feet, Apple Orchard Mountain is one of the most prominent peaks in Virginia. A radar post atop the bald summit makes the mountain. To reach the summit, follow the route as described to the intersection of Apple Orchard Falls

Trail and the AT. Instead of turning right (south) onto the AT, turn left (north). The peak is about 1.5 miles from the junction.

MORE INFORMATION

George Washington and Jefferson National Forests, Glenwood–Pedlar Ranger District (fs.usda.gov/main/gwj; 540-291-2188). Check online for announcements concerning trail conditions, road closures, prescribed burns, and other events that may affect your hike.

NEARBY

Of course, where the AT runs, there is always more hiking to be had. The Devil's Marbleyard (Trip 49) is the closest hike described in this book. Farther north, Cold Mountain (Trip 47) and Mount Pleasant (Trip 48) are well worth a visit.

Natural Bridge, Virginia, is a popular destination for tourists seeking to visit the caverns there, so you're likely to find an array of shops and services there (about 30 minutes). Looking for a bigger town? Lexington, Virginia, is your best bet. It's about 45 minutes by car.

47

COLD MOUNTAIN

Cold Mountain's alpine meadows and balds—grassy fields where you would normally expect heavy forest—are not especially large, but they are an interesting change of pace from the Mid-Atlantic's more expected ridgelines and forests.

DIRECTIONS

From I-81, Exit 188A, drive east on US 60 through the mountains past the Blue Ridge Parkway. At 12.5 miles from the interstate, take a left onto VA 634 and drive about 1.6 miles before turning right onto Wiggins Spring Road/VA 755. This route soon becomes a rather rough gravel road that, while accessible to cars, requires you to drive slowly and carefully. When you see the Appalachian Trail, you've reached Hog Camp Gap. Park here in the gravel lot. There are also more spots a few hundred yards up the road. *GPS coordinates: 37° 45.578' N, 79° 11.680' W.*

A 0.3-mile road walk (described below) connects the terminus of the trail to this parking lot.

TRAIL DESCRIPTION

As you wander across the bald fields of Cold Mountain (4,020 feet), sometimes referred to as Cole Mountain, you might imagine yourself strolling through the alpine meadows of New Hampshire, Colorado, Alaska, or Switzerland, which they resemble. Take special care to stay on the path in these areas; alpine vegetation is particularly fragile. There is a climb to get to these meadows, but it's not especially steep, and the unusual ecosystem and view at the top make for a singular Mid-Atlantic hike.

From Wiggins Spring Road and the parking lot, head south on the Appalachian Trail (AT) and begin a moderate switchback climb of about 500 feet over the next 0.9

LOCATION
Glenwood-Pedlar Ranger District, George Washington and Jefferson National Forests, VA

RATING
Moderate

DISTANCE
6.1 miles round-trip

ELEVATION GAIN
1,586 feet

ESTIMATED TIME
5-6 hours

MAPS
Trails Illustrated: Lexington/Blue Ridge Mountains, George Washington and Jefferson National Forests, Map 789 (National Geographic): natgeomaps.com/ti-789 -lexington-blue-ridge-mts -george-washington-and -jefferson-national-forests

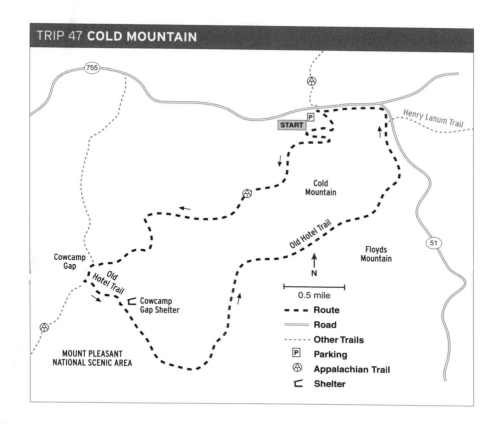

Cold Mountain

Floyds Mountain

Old Hotel Trail

Henry Lanum Trail

START

Cowcamp Gap

Old Hotel Trail

Cowcamp Gap Shelter

MOUNT PLEASANT NATIONAL SCENIC AREA

N

0.5 mile

- - - Route

===== Road

----- Other Trails

P Parking

Ⓐ Appalachian Trail

⊏ Shelter

mile to reach the top of Cold Mountain. As the trail opens out, note the signs warning against camping. In spring, wildflowers bloom in these open balds. Any time of the year, expect to see expansive views to the east, west, and south as you traverse the gently rolling meadows for the next 0.25 mile. The white blazes of the AT are marked on posts.

If you want a very short trip, simply walk back to your vehicle from here, but the remainder of the trail takes you past some attractive, if more typically Mid-Atlantic, scenery.

The forest closes about you as you descend the AT about 600 feet over 1.25 miles to Cowcamp Gap, where the white blazes meet the blue blazes of Old Hotel Trail. A short path to the right leads to an obscured view. Pause for a break here, then turn left to follow Old Hotel Trail as it rounds the eastern face of Cold Mountain. Once you arrive at a creek, a spur trail on the left takes you quickly to the AT's Cowcamp Gap Shelter. If you happen to be low on water, this is a good place to stop and fill up.

Continue to follow blue-blazed Old Hotel Trail on its descent. It bottoms out eventually, but then over the next mile or so covers some rolling terrain that ultimately gains another 550 feet. The grade evens out, and at 4.5 miles, you

Hikers (and a canine friend) enjoy the open balds of Cold Mountain. These unusual features offer an expansive view of southern Virginia.

arrive at some open meadows where camping is allowed. This popular site, with its wide-open fields, also makes a great spot for a picnic or a breather.

When you're ready, continue along Old Hotel Trail as it traverses the meadows and enters the woods. The remainder of the loop is gentle as the route draws near a streambed on the right, follows a sandy jeep trail, and passes through a copse of dead trees. At last, the trail bears to the right and arrives at the Mount Pleasant trailhead at 5.8 miles. To return to your vehicle, take a left onto the road and walk about 0.3 mile to reach the trailhead from which you started.

DID YOU KNOW?

The origin of balds, such as those on Cold Mountain, is a bit of a topographic mystery. While alpine peaks in the North—such as Mount Washington or the high peaks of the Adirondacks—are devoid of vegetation due to the combined effect of latitude and elevation, peaks in the South are not technically alpine because of the warmer climate. In some cases, such as with Cold Mountain, one peak develops a bald while another peak of similar elevation does not (for example, Mount Pleasant, though nearby to Cold Mountain, does not have balds). Most experts tend to believe that balds of this sort develop due to the habits of grazing animals. In some cases, the National Park Service and the U.S. Forest Service have continued to allow animals to graze these areas to maintain their open characteristics.

MORE INFORMATION

George Washington and Jefferson National Forests, Glenwood–Pedlar Ranger District (fs.usda.gov/main/gwj, 540-291-2188). Check online for announcements concerning trail conditions, road closures, prescribed burns, and other events that may affect your hike.

If you enjoy Cold Mountain, plan a trip to the Grayson Highlands, farther south in Virginia. See *AMC's Best Backpacking in the Mid-Atlantic* for a description of this beautiful region.

NEARBY

The Mount Pleasant loop (Trip 48) is a natural companion to Cold Mountain. If you want more miles, consider visiting Apple Orchard Falls (Trip 46) or the unique boulder field of the Devil's Marbleyard (Trip 49), both of which are in the vicinity.

Visitors to the area can find food, lodging, shopping, and more in Lexington. Nearby Natural Bridge is a popular destination for tourists seeking to visit the caverns. To learn more about visiting this attraction, visit naturalbridgeva.com/caverns.html.

48

MOUNT PLEASANT

Treasure the expansive vista of the Blue Ridge Mountains from the westward side of Mount Pleasant.

DIRECTIONS

From I-81, Exit 188A, drive east on US 60 over the mountains and pass the Blue Ridge Parkway. At 12.5 miles from the interstate, take a left onto VA 634 and drive about 1.6 miles before turning right onto Wiggins Spring Road/VA 755. This route soon becomes a rough gravel road that, while accessible to cars, requires you to drive slowly and carefully. When you see the Appalachian Trail, you've reached Hog Camp Gap. Park here. There are also more spots a few hundred yards up the road. *GPS coordinates:* 37° 45.578′ N, 79° 11.680′ W.

TRAIL DESCRIPTION

Given the stunning views from Mount Pleasant and the relative ease of reaching its summit, this hike may well offer one of the best payoffs in the Shenandoah Valley. From the parking lot, where the Appalachian Trail crosses Wiggins Spring Road, walk east along the road. It bears to the right at a sign for Mount Pleasant. On your right, pass the trailhead for Old Hotel Trail (the Cold Mountain loop, Trip 47, also travels through this point). Just ahead are dual trailheads for Henry Lanum Trail. Bear right. The left trail is your return route.

For the next 1.2 miles, Henry Lanum Trail descends very gently along a nearly flat road grade. It begins to wind through a few hollows and crosses a few creeks. (*Note:* The second creek is your only easy-to-reach, reliable water source on the route, so make sure you bring plenty of water.)

Just after the second creek crossing at 1.6 miles, the trail begins ascending to the gap between Mount

LOCATION
Glenwood-Pedlar Ranger District, George Washington and Jefferson National Forests, VA

RATING
Moderate

DISTANCE
6.5 miles round-trip

ELEVATION GAIN
1,781 feet

ESTIMATED TIME
3–5 hours

MAPS
Trails Illustrated: Lexington/Blue Ridge Mountains, George Washington and Jefferson National Forests, Map 789 (National Geographic): natgeomaps.com/ti-789 -lexington-blue-ridge-mts -george-washington-and -jefferson-national-forests

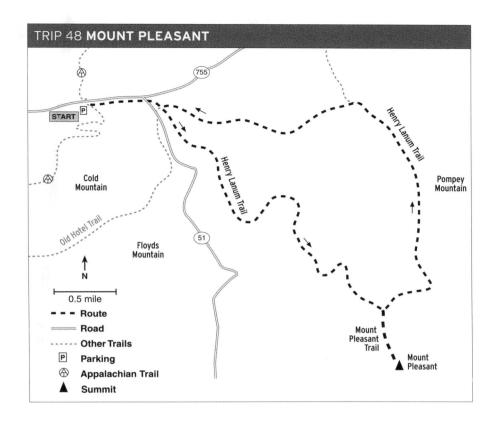

START

755

P

Cold
Mountain

Old Hotel Trail

Henry Lanum Trail

Henry Lanum Trail

Pompey
Mountain

Floyds
Mountain

51

N

0.5 mile

- - - Route

===== Road

----- Other Trails

P Parking

Ⓐ Appalachian Trail

▲ Summit

Mount
Pleasant
Trail

▲ Mount
Pleasant

Pleasant and Pompey Mountain, gaining approximately 500 feet of elevation over 0.9 mile. The climb is steady but not especially steep. The trail reaches a T intersection in the gap. To the left, the trail departs toward Pompey Mountain and the end of the route. For now, turn right and continue to the summit of Mount Pleasant.

As you begin the last 300 vertical feet of climbing, a sign on the left indicates another water source; but reaching it requires a bit of a descent down into the east-facing hollow. The remaining climb is a bit rougher than earlier sections of the trail, featuring a few rocky stretches, but you'll soon come to a second T intersection at 3.0 miles. On the left is an eastward vista; on the right, ahead, is a more dramatic westward view. Visit the latter first.

To reach the westward vista, make your way for about 0.1 mile along the ridge-line until you reach a campsite just beneath a rocky outcropping. A simple scramble brings you to the top of the outcropping, where you'll be able to drink in the westward vista of the Blue Ridge Mountains and Cold Mountain, and even look back at the route you just walked. (*Caution:* As you explore these exposed rocks, be careful. Rattlesnakes in the area are fond of sunning them-selves on the warm slabs.)

Sunset on Mount Pleasant. Located near Cold Mountain, hikers should consider combining the two trips, as the view from Mount Pleasant is not to be missed.

Return to the second T intersection, and follow the trail ahead to take in the eastward view over the piedmont—also very pretty but less dramatic. Return to that same T intersection, and turn right to head back to the gap between the mountains. From the gap and the first T intersection you encountered, continue straight. The trail climbs about 300 feet, fairly moderately, to the broad back of Pompey Mountain at 4.6 miles. Keep an eye out for this otherwise unremarkable summit. A small, unmarked track leads to the right to a rocky outcropping that offers a view of the eastern piedmont.

Back on the Henry Lanum Trail, the route descends about 400 feet, then climbs about 200 feet more—all in 0.8 mile—before beginning its final descent toward the trailhead. The walking, however, is gentle and pleasant, and the forest is beautiful and lush.

When you arrive at the Mount Pleasant trailhead, walk up the road to your vehicle.

DID YOU KNOW?

The Henry Lanum Loop was formerly known as Mount Pleasant/Pompey Mountain Trail, but it was renamed to honor Henry Lanum, an especially dedicated member of the local Appalachian Trail Club.

MORE INFORMATION

George Washington and Jefferson National Forests, Glenwood–Pedlar Ranger District (fs.usda.gov/main/gwj, 540-291-2188). Check online for announcements concerning trail conditions, road closures, prescribed burns, and other events that may affect your hike.

NEARBY

A short road walk connects the Hog Camp Gap parking lot and the Wiggins Spring trailhead, from which the route to Cold Mountain (Trip 47) departs.

Apple Orchard Falls (Trip 46) and the Devil's Marbleyard (Trip 49) are in the vicinity. Spy Rock (Trip 44) and Three Ridges (Trip 50) are also not far away.

If you're looking for post-hike refreshments, nearby Lexington has a wide range of restaurants and businesses.

49

DEVIL'S MARBLEYARD

The giant marble boulders here, very atypical for Virginia, look like they've been imported from the Andes or the Himalaya.

DIRECTIONS

From I-81, Exit 180A, take US 11 south for 2.3 miles. In Natural Bridge, Virginia, take a left (east) onto VA 689. In just over 1.0 mile, turn right onto VA 608 and then take an immediate left onto VA 130. In 2.0 miles, turn right onto VA 759. Cross the James River. On the south bank, pass the signs for Gunter Ridge and other Jefferson National Forest attractions. After 3.1 miles, take a left onto VA 781/ Petites Gap Road. You'll reach the parking lot for Belfast Trail in about 1.2 miles (on the left). The parking lot is rather small, and there are a few pull-out spots nearby, but be sure to get your vehicle's tires off the road, as there have been reports of poorly parked vehicles being towed. *GPS coordinates: 37° 34.270' N, 79° 29.501' W.*

TRAIL DESCRIPTION

You'll hardly believe your eyes as you emerge from the forest to scramble up a gigantic boulder field, filled with marble rocks sometimes as large as cars or buses.

From the parking lot, cross a bridge over Belfast Creek to begin hiking on blue-blazed Belfast Trail. Initially, the trail is wide, flat, and sandy. Pass the stone foundations and ruins of an old summer camp, cross Glenwood Horse Trail at an intersection, cross a creek or two, likely rock-hopping depending on the water level, and arrive at another intersection with the horse trail at 0.2 mile.

Here, Belfast Trail turns right and begins climbing more steeply and ruggedly as it follows the creek up the valley, giving you occasion to rock-hop across the creek a few more times. The trail bends right and begins a longer, steeper

LOCATION
Glenwood–Pedlar Ranger District, George Washington and Jefferson National Forests, VA

RATING
Moderate

DISTANCE
3.2 miles round-trip

ELEVATION GAIN
1,073 feet

ESTIMATED TIME
2–3 hours

MAPS
Trails Illustrated: Lexington/Blue Ridge Mountains, George Washington and Jefferson National Forests, Map 789 (National Geographic): natgeomaps.com/ti-789 -lexington-blue-ridge-mts -george-washington-and -jefferson-national-forests

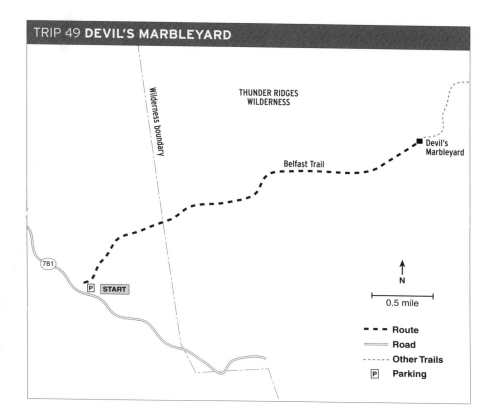

grade. At about 1.4 miles, between the trees, you should be able to glimpse the boulder field. The route runs along the right edge of the field, climbing steeply (and sometimes wetly) on rugged terrain. There are many access points from which you can reach the boulder field all along its length, so scramble to your heart's content, but be careful: as you will no doubt quickly realize, the "marbleyard" is a place where injuries can easily occur. Be sure of your footing and take your time.

Plan to visit the marbleyard at sunset, if possible. It can be a spectacular sight: the boulder field has plenty of western exposure, and the marble takes on a brilliant glow in the setting sun.

Once you've had your fill of scrambling, descend the way you came, via Belfast Trail, to your vehicle.

DID YOU KNOW?

The Devil's Marbleyard is a striking feature that is perfectly visible in satellite images. How did it form? Long ago—hundreds of millions of years—the area was a white-sand beach infested with worms that burrowed through the sand. If you look closely, you can still see striations in the rock that are the remnants of these tracks. Over time, the sand was buried and compressed into rock, which

The boulder field of the Devil's Marbleyard is a striking and unusual feature in Virginia. If you catch the sunset right, the rocks seem to take on a golden glow.

lay hidden for millennia. When the rock was finally exposed, ice did the work of breaking the surface into the boulder field we see today.

MORE INFORMATION

George Washington and Jefferson National Forests, Glenwood–Pedlar Ranger District (fs.usda.gov/main/gwj, 540-291-2188). Check online for announcements concerning trail conditions, road closures, prescribed burns, and other events that may affect your hike.

NEARBY

If you want a longer and more ambitious hike centered on the Devil's Marbleyard, consider climbing past the marbleyard. Just shy of the Appalachian Trail, Belfast Trail comes to a three-way intersection. By turning left, you can descend via Gunter Ridge Trail and return to your vehicle by Glenwood Horse Trail. Definitely bring your map along and do consider this variation a challenging one, as the loop will total between 10 and 11 miles.

After you've thoroughly explored the Devil's Marbleyard, consider driving a little farther south to hike Apple Orchard Falls (Trip 46). Cold Mountain (Trip 47) and Mount Pleasant (Trip 48) are also nearby.

To the north, Lexington offers the best nearby choice of local businesses (about 30 minutes); to the south, Roanoke is your best bet (approximately one hour).

50

THREE RIDGES

Climb—and then climb some more—for this epic hike filled with great views and even some waterfalls.

DIRECTIONS

From I-81/I-64, Exit 205, take VA 606 east toward Raphine for 1.5 miles. Turn left onto US 11 North/North Lee Highway, and then make a quick right onto VA 56 East/Tye River Turnpike. Follow VA 56 East for 16.6 miles and look for the parking lot on the right. *GPS coordinates: 37° 50.297′ N, 79° 1.392′ W.*

TRAIL DESCRIPTION

Make no mistake. This hike is one of the more strenuous in the area, starting off with a 5.3-mile ascent. However, it rewards those who persevere with vista after vista. It is a challenge well worth undertaking.

Starting from the parking lot, cross VA 56 and look for the white blaze that marks the Appalachian Trail (AT). For most of the day, you will be following white blazes. Walk over a suspension bridge that spans the River Tye. Then get ready to start climbing.

The trail meanders up through the trees and eventually leads to an intersection with Mau-Har Trail at 1.9 miles (your return route). Continue straight through the intersection to follow the AT. The trail will even out a bit, providing a welcome, if short, respite as it dips down and around the mountain. Cross a small stream, keeping an eye on the white blazes. Through the trees, the Harpers Creek Shelter appears, and side trails lead off to various campsites. This can be a confusing stretch, but keep following the white blazes to stay on the AT. Eventually, you arrive at an intersection with a spur trail to the shelter. Turn right to continue on the AT.

LOCATION
Glenwood-Pedlar Ranger District, George Washington and Jefferson National Forests, WV and VA

RATING
Strenuous

DISTANCE
13.2 miles

ELEVATION GAIN
4,914 feet

ESTIMATED TIME
6–7 hours

MAPS
Trails Illustrated: Lexington/Blue Ridge Mountains, George Washington and Jefferson National Forests, Map 789 (National Geographic): natgeomaps.com/ti-789 -lexington-blue-ridge-mts -george-washington-and -jefferson-national-forests

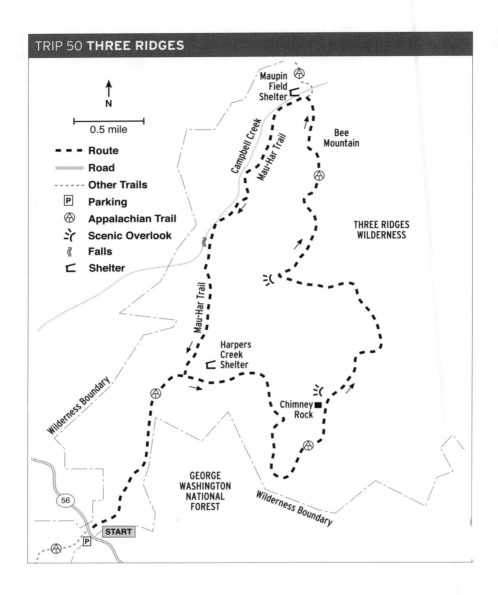

TRIP 50 THREE RIDGES

Legend:
- ▪ ▪ ▪ **Route**
- ═══ **Road**
- ----- **Other Trails**
- P **Parking**
- ⊕ **Appalachian Trail**
- ⅀ **Scenic Overlook**
- ≀ **Falls**
- ⊏ **Shelter**

Maupin Field Shelter

Bee Mountain

Campbell Creek

Mau-Har Trail

THREE RIDGES WILDERNESS

Mau-Har Trail

Harpers Creek Shelter

Chimney Rock

Wilderness Boundary

GEORGE WASHINGTON NATIONAL FOREST

Wilderness Boundary

56

START

As you ascend the mountain, the trail will get steep at times. Overall, the path is well marked and obvious, but some turns in switchbacks are tight, and a few may give you cause for a pause before moving forward. Just watch for the white blazes and continue up the trail. Roughly 3.5 miles into the hike, views of the valley start to come into sight, giving welcome spots for breaks. As the route progresses higher, more vistas of the surrounding valley and mountains in the distance emerge, and at 4.2 miles Chimney Rock tempts with a quick rock scramble to spy some of the best scenery of the trip.

Views like this make Three Ridges a challenge worth accepting. Photo by Miles Barger.

But the trail climbs still farther, finally reaching its peak—and the accompanying view—5.3 miles into the hike. The next 3.3 miles offer gentler hiking compared with the previous miles, passing another great outlook at 6.2 miles and making a mild climb over Bee Mountain. At 8.6 miles, you arrive at the Maupin Field Shelter; look for an information board and wooden post marking a left turn off the AT to the shelter itself. Depart the AT here, and follow the path to the shelter, passing several side trails that lead to nearby campsites. To the left of the shelter is a sign marking blue-blazed Mau-Har Trail, which is the next stage in your journey.

At first, Mau-Har Trail leads with a gentle descent through the trees. A few stream crossings require some quick rock-hopping—nothing too serious—before the trail becomes rocky and starts to descend more steeply as it makes its way down the mountain. The route follows the left bank of Campbell Creek; when flowing well, the creek has some enjoyable, but small, waterfalls to admire. The trail gets rockier as it continues to descend, with some large boulders to navigate. Keep an eye out for a tricky turn; the route seems to go right at one point but actually continues over the rocks. A partially hidden blue blaze to the left signals that you are on the correct path.

All the descending and rock-hopping leads to another treat: At 9.6 miles, a short spur trail to the right (sign: "Waterfalls") leads to a small campsite, a swimming hole, and some cascades—a good place to take a break, especially on a warm day.

After the waterfalls, the Mau-Har Trail becomes less rocky but leads to one last ascent for the day. It rises steadily, but not too steeply, and levels out after reaching the top of the climb. The trail then begins a gentle descent before arriving at another intersection with the AT at 11.3 miles; you passed this point earlier in the day. Turn right onto the AT and retrace your steps back downhill to your car.

DID YOU KNOW?

"Blue blazing" is the term that AT thru-hikers use for opting to take some of the side trails (typically marked with blue blazes, like Mau-Har Trail), rather than staying on the white-blazed route for the entire journey.

MORE INFORMATION

George Washington and Jefferson National Forests, Glenwood–Pedlar Ranger District (fs.usda.gov/main/gwj; 540-291-2188). Check online for announcements concerning trail conditions, road closures, prescribed burns, and other events that may affect your hike.

NEARBY

This hike serves as an excellent base to explore the area. If you want an easier journey, head to Spy Rock (Trip 44) or check out famous Crabtree Falls (Trip 45).

The town of Roseland has restaurants if you're looking for a meal nearby, and various breweries and cideries cater to those ready to sample local libations.

APPENDIX: INFORMATION AND RESOURCES

HARPERS FERRY NATIONAL HISTORICAL PARK
171 Shoreline Drive
P.O. Box 65
Harpers Ferry, WV 25425
304-535-6029
nps.gov/hafe

GEORGE WASHINGTON AND JEFFERSON NATIONAL FORESTS
5162 Valleypointe Parkway
Roanoke, VA 24019
888-265-0019 (toll free); 540-265-5100
fs.usda.gov/gwj

GLENWOOD-PEDLAR RANGER DISTRICT
Counties: Amherst, Augusta, Bedford, Botetourt, Nelson, and Rockbridge
27 Ranger Lane
Natural Bridge Station, VA 24579
540-291-2188

LEE RANGER DISTRICT
Counties: Frederick, Hampshire (WV), Hardy (WV), Page, Rockingham,
    Shenandoah, and Warren
95 Railroad Avenue
Edinburg, VA 22824
540-984-4101

NORTH RIVER RANGER DISTRICT
Counties: Augusta, Highland, Pendleton (WV), and Rockingham
401 Oakwood Drive
Harrisonburg, VA 22801
866-904-0240 (toll free); 540-432-0187 (local)

SHENANDOAH NATIONAL PARK
3655 Highway 211 East
Luray, VA 22835
540-999-3500 (information); 800-732-0911 (emergency);
    877-444-6777 (campground reservations)
nps.gov/shen; recreation.gov (campground reservations)

SHENANDOAH RIVER STATE PARK
350 Daughter of Stars Drive
Bentonville, VA 22610
540-622-6840; 800-933-7275 (reservations)
shenandoahriver@dcr.virginia.gov
dcr.virginia.gov/state-parks/shenandoah-river.shtml;
    reserveamerica.com (reservations)

SKY MEADOWS STATE PARK
11012 Edmonds Lane
Delaplane, VA 20144
540-592-3556; 800-933-7275 (reservations)
skymeadows@dcr.virginia.gov
www.dcr.virginia.gov/state-parks/sky-meadows.shtml;
    reserveamerica.com (reservations)

OTHER RESOURCES

AMC'S POTOMAC CHAPTER
chair@amcpotomac.org;
    outdoors.org/chapters/potomac

APPALACHIAN TRAIL CONSERVANCY, MID-ATLANTIC REGIONAL OFFICE
4 East First Street
Boiling Springs, PA 17007
717-258-5771; 888-287-8673 (store)
atc-maro@appalachiantrail.org;
    incident@appalachiantrail.org (incident report)
appalachiantrail.org; atctrailstore.org

POTOMAC APPALACHIAN TRAIL CLUB
118 Park Street, S.E.
Vienna, VA 22180-4609
703-242-0315
patc.net

INDEX

ABOUT THE AUTHORS

Jennifer Adach went on her first camping trip in 2004, and she was quickly bitten by the bug to get outdoors and to hike as much and as far as she could. Over the years, she has become an accomplished hiker and backpacker. She is now one of the organizers of the DC UL (Ultralight) Backpacking group and regularly leads backpacking trips for the group. Jennifer has thru-hiked Sweden's Kungsleden trail and California's John Muir Trail, section-hiked the Tuscarora Trail and Pennsylvania's Mid State Trail, and has logged several thousand miles on trails throughout the Mid-Atlantic area. At home, she's addicted to testing out new recipes and reading the latest in nonfiction. Jennifer grew up on Long Island and now resides in Old Town Alexandria, Virginia.

Michael R. Martin is a lifelong backpacker and outdoorsman. He grew up on the trails in Texas, Arkansas, New Mexico, Colorado, and points farther west; more recently, he has piled on several thousand miles (and a few hundred nights) in the Mid-Atlantic. His more exotic trips have taken him to Sweden, France, Nepal, Peru, and Iceland, where he completed a north–south crossing of the island—his most ambitious trip to date. Author of *AMC's Best Backpacking in the Mid-Atlantic*, he also leads, organizes, and teaches for the DC UL (Ultralight) Backpacking group. When he's not on the trail, or plotting new ways to sneak away and get on the trail, he's often writing, learning how to make his camera work, or trying to limber up his rusty video-gaming skills. His more permanent dwelling is Old Town Alexandria, Virginia.

ABOUT AMC IN THE MID-ATLANTIC

Each year, the Appalachian Mountain Club's Potomac, Delaware Valley, New York–North Jersey, and Mohawk Hudson chapters offer thousands of outdoor activities, including hiking, backpacking, bicycling, paddling, and climbing trips, as well as social, family, and young member programs. Members also maintain local trails, lead outdoor skills workshops, and promote stewardship of the region's natural resources. AMC manages Mohican Outdoor Center in the Delaware Water Gap National Recreation Area, a four-season, self-service destination for hiking, paddling, skiing, snowshoeing, and camping, a short distance from the Appalachian Trail in New Jersey.

AMC is a leader of the Highlands Coalition, which works to secure funding for land conservation funding in the four-state Highlands region of Connecticut, New York, New Jersey, and Pennsylvania. AMC also monitors energy development proposals across the region that impact public lands. It has been instrumental in developing the nearly 300-mile Pennsylvania Highlands Trail Network. AMC staff and volunteers maintain 1,800 miles of trails throughout the Northeastern and Mid-Atlantic states, including portions of the Appalachian Trail in Pennsylvania, Connecticut, Massachusetts, New Hampshire, and Maine.

To learn more about AMC's work in the Mid-Atlantic, visit outdoors.org.

AMC BOOK UPDATES

AMC Books strives to keep our guidebooks as up-to-date as possible to help you plan safe and enjoyable adventures. If we learn after publishing a book that relevant trails have been relocated or route or contact information has changed, we will post the updated information online. Before you hit the trail visit outdoors.org/books-maps and click the "Book Updates" tab.

While hiking, if you notice discrepancies with the trip descriptions or maps, or if you find any other errors in the book, please let us know by submitting them to amcbookupdates@outdoors.org or to Books Editor, c/o AMC, 10 City Square, Boston, MA 02129. We will verify all submissions and post key updates each month. AMC Books is dedicated to being a recognized leader in outdoor publishing. Thank you for your participation.

BE OUTDOORS™

Since 1876, the Appalachian Mountain Club has channeled your enthusiasm for the outdoors into everything we do and everywhere we work to protect. We're inspired by people exploring the natural world and deepening their appreciation of it.

With AMC chapters from Maine to Washington, D.C., including groups in Boston, New York City, and Philadelphia, you can enjoy activities like hiking, paddling, cycling, and skiing, and learn new outdoor skills. We offer advice, guidebooks, maps, and unique eco-lodges and huts to inspire your next outing.

Your visits, purchases, and donations also support conservation advocacy and research, youth programming, and caring for more than 1,800 miles of trails.

Join us!
outdoors.org/join

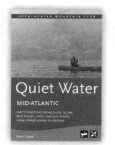